Technology Diffusion, Productivity Employment, and Phase Shifts in Developing Economies

Technology Diffusion, Productivity Employment, and Phase Shifts in Developing Economies

Kazushi Ohkawa and Katsuo Otsuka

UNIVERSITY OF TOKYO PRESS

HC
59.7
036
1994

Publication of this volume was supported in part by a grant from the International Development Center of Japan (IDCJ), Tokyo

ISBN 0-86008-506-6
ISBN 4-13-047062-0

Printed in Japan

Contents

Preface

This volume is the last in a series of three that sum up several decades of research on economic development—specifically, comparative research on the history of development in Japan and the developing countries.

It is also—and this must be reported with great sadness—the last work of Kazushi Ohkawa's research life. Professor Ohkawa died on November 13, 1993, just as the book went to press. He was 84 years old. I should like to pay tribute here to him, an example and teacher to many of us in economic development studies.

Kazushi Ohkawa was born in Numazu City, Shizuoka Prefecture, in 1908. He graduated from Tokyo Imperial University (present-day University of Tokyo) in 1933, and received the Ph.D in Agriculture from the University of Tokyo in 1952. He taught at Tokyo Imperial University, Utsunomiya Agricultural College (present-day Utsunomiya University), Hitotsubashi University, and the International Development Center of Japan. He was actively associated with the latter until shortly before his death.

His original research interest as a young scholar was agricultural economics, and he eventually concentrated on the study of Japan's long-term economic development. At the Economic Research Institute of Hitotsubashi University, he coordinated the giant task of collecting long-term economic statistics for Japan from 1868 onward; these were published in multi-volume form in Japanese and in a summary English-language volume. At the International Development Center of Japan, he shifted his focus to a comparison of Japan's development over time with the contemporary developing economies. In 1987 he was named a Person of Cultural Merit by the government of Japan for his contributions to empirical research on Japan's economy.

I met Professor Ohkawa for the first time at Hitotsubashi University in 1969, as a student, and was privileged to have him supervise my own early research. We collaborated in writing *Growth Mechanism of Developing Economies*, the second volume in the series of which the present book is the third and last. We began work on the present volume in 1991, and Professor Ohkawa completed the final revisions in the summer of 1993, in spite of his weakened physical condition. In August, I was able to inform him over the telephone that publication by the University of Tokyo Press had been contracted, and he repeated happily several times that this was very good news indeed. It was our last talk. I should like to dedicate this book to his memory.

The cooperation of many has contributed to the publication of this volume. The International Development Center of Japan, which was Professor Ohkawa's research home for his last years, provided not only logistic and moral support, but financial support as well for the publication. I am particularly grateful to Saburo Kawai, Chairman and President of IDCJ, for his advice and support. Tamiko Sakatani, Professor Ohkawa's longtime secretary, produced many drafts of the manuscript and helped in other ways too numerous to mention. Financial arrangements were facilitated by Yasunobu Kawato.

Professor Ohkawa's wife Sachiko was a source of help and encouragement not only to him but also his colleagues and coworkers.

I am also grateful to the editorial and production staff of the University of Tokyo Press for the speed and competence with which this volume was produced. I hope that it will be a useful tool for economists and practitioners in developing countries, and a fitting tribute to my co-author, who will be sorely missed.

Tokyo, January 1994   KATSUO OTSUKA

Introduction

The International Development Center of Japan (IDCJ) has been conducting studies on developing countries for over a decade. This volume is a product of those group research activities, although the authors alone are responsible for its contents. It aims at analyzing empirically the contemporary problems of economic development, focusing on technology diffusion, productivity growth, changes in the employment situation, and finally phase demarcation of the development path.

Based on the results of IDCJ group studies, two volumes have been published previously. First, *Lectures on Developing Economies* (cited as *OK* in this volume)[1] and second, *Growth Mechanism of Developing Economies* (cited as *DE* in this volume).[2] The themes of this third volume were selected to be complementary with those of *OK* and *DE*, as well as to amplify and expand the analysis in the earlier volumes.

The approach common to these three volumes is essentially empirical rather than theoretical. The activities of the IDCJ include training and project surveys as well as research, and this institutional requirement characterizes the style of study. In addition, Japan's historical experience of development is given special attention, not only to identify its possible relevance (or irrelevance) to contemporary development but, more basically, to illuminate the growth mechanism of development in general. *OK* in particular stressed the

---

[1] Kazushi Ohkawa and Hirohisa Kohama, *Lectures on Developing Economies: Japan's Experience and Its Relevance* (Tokyo: University of Tokyo Press, 1989).

[2] Kazushi Ohkawa, in collaboration with Katsuo Otsuka and Bernard Key, *Growth Mechanism of Developing Economies: Investment, Productivity and Employment* (Tokyo: International Development Center of Japan/International Center for Economic Growth, 1993).

ix

Japanese model, while *DE* and the present volume focus more on contemporary developing economies.

The conceptual framework and organizational approach in this volume are essentially the same as in the previous two volumes to fit the empirical requirements. With regard to the methodology dealing with technology diffusion, a "simplified" formula is proposed, extending that used in *OK*. Hypotheses are limited to those testable empirically. Quantitative measurements are thus aimed as far as possible at deriving operational factual analyses and policy implications. As a result, the present approach deviates from the conventional, neoclassical approach, stemming from the recognition of real problems encountered along the development path. It is the view of the authors that the disequilibrium process is of primary importance in assessing actual development, although market forces, which tend to operate to a state of equilibrium, are not ignored.

Another feature of the present approach pertains to the time dimension. The pattern of development is elucidated in long-term perspective, rather than in the shorter-term process of adjustment. The importance of the latter dimension is undeniable, but previous studies have lacked the former dimension of analysis. Phase demarcation of the development path is thus indispensable. Shifts in phase are achieved through the cumulative operation of historical elements as well as functional aspects. Substitution activity in response to changes in factor prices, for example, is analyzed in the present simplified formula as dependent solely on the input-output ratio. Although this is one disadvantage of the approach, it is necessary in examining the development process from a long-term perspective.

Finally, a model for developing economies is formulated based on a dualistic structure, instead of on a homogenous traditional-versus-modern structure. The process of change in this structure is an important aspect of development in terms of technology diffusion and factor prices. This is not a new viewpoint in development analysis, but two points are noteworthy. First, the model is quantified to allow it to be incorporated in the relevant analysis. Second, it is treated in association with another important dimension: domestic (or internal) versus international (or external) elements.

This volume is divided into seven chapters, but the contents are organized into three parts. The first and lengthiest part is composed of chapters 1, 2, 3, and 4, which examine the processes and patterns of technology diffusion conceptually and empirically. The second part, containing chapters 5 and 6, analyzes productivity growth and its relation to changes in employment income opportunities. The final part is chapter 7, which discusses the phases of development in a "generalized framework," followed by concluding remarks. The main conclusions can be summarized as follows.

Chapter 1 proposes a simplified formula deduced empirically from the cross-sectional data on contemporary developing countries, 1960–1985, compiled in *DE*. The formula and subsequent analysis are based on the input-output ratio (IOR) approach. Section II of this chapter reviews relevant theories and approaches, including those proposed in *DE*, on technological progress and technology diffusion. Chapters 2 and 3 apply the simplified formula and test it empirically. The results indicate that the formula is useful in elucidating the patterns and processes of technology diffusion both in Japan's historical experience and in contemporary developing economies. Three main points emerge: 1) the formula can distinguish between "smooth" and "unsmooth" processes of economic development. 2) Although external and internal dimensions are interrelated they should be analyzed separately. 3) The pattern of internal diffusion varies widely among nations, especially in the traditional sector, and thus development potential must be evaluated in appropriate terms.

Chapter 4 focuses on the role played by producer durables in technology diffusion. The usual emphasis on high factor prices for capital and low prices for labor often leads to recommendations of labor-intensive technology for developing economies. This is simplistic and sometimes unwarranted in light of the finding in preceding chapters that the degree of realization of potential differs widely even among nations with similar levels of per worker product (Y/L). This difference is significant in responses to high capital goods prices. The appropriate combination of capital-intensive and labor-intensive technology is made possible by the upgrading of long-term potential.

In chapter 5, productivity growth and residual growth (amplified from *DE*) are compared and integrated. Attention is drawn to the fact that differences in macro productivity growth rates do not necessarily stem from differences in productivity growth rates of industry, representing the modern sector, but from productivity differences in agriculture and services, representing the traditional sector. This suggests important policy implications concerning technology diffusion and sectoral allocation of resources.

The relation between productivity growth and labor employment is examined in chapter 6. A "trade-off" relation between the two has often been described in the industrial sector, although the phenomenon is not always witnessed. Instead, a higher rate of productivity growth tends to accompany a higher labor employment increase rate. In addition, sectoral inequality of per worker product is smaller with higher productivity growth. These factors are due to differences in residual growth between economies. The usual view can be misleading and unrealistic if the important contribution of residual growth to productivity growth is ignored. This positive aspect, however, is not the entire story. Due to the extremely low level of productivity of traditional agriculture in the initial stage of inaugurating modern economic growth, the lowest income levels are still in rural districts, and the problem of "poverty" continues even after notable agricultural development is achieved in subsequent years. This characterizes contemporary developing economies despite the trend of "convergence" in sectorwise inequality.

This leads to the important problem of wide differentials among developing countries with regard to achieving technology organization advances and hence macro productivity growth. *DE* emphasized the crucial role played by the differentials of social capability (SC) in dealing with production capacity (PC), which shows less variance between nations. In chapter 7, this conceptual interpretation is extended to elucidate empirically postwar productivity growth in historical phases.

Phase demarcation has previously been made in terms of trade patterns, labor markets, and capital investment performance. The trade pattern approach has most commonly been used (primary export substitution, secondary import substitution, etc.). Demarcation of phases is not only an analytical concern but also has important policy implications in long-term planning.

A new demarcation system is proposed which pertains to domestic productivity growth. Cross-sectional subgrouping is used to deal with the above-mentioned differentials as proxies of historical series to identify phases, including turning points, in sectorwise dimensions. For economies with favorable growth performance, phase shifts can be distinctly identified, whereas this is impossible for those with unfavorable growth. A concept of a "normal" path of development is thus induced from the experience of the former. It is hypothesized that following the normal path can lead to a growth pattern of "trend acceleration (TA)" if not interrupted by internal or external forces. In other words, TA is achieved as the result of operation of endogenous forces, while unfavorable growth patterns may be the result of interrupting forces, and not due to lack of endogenous potential. The perceived widening gap between developed and developing nations in terms of income or productivity level may be valid for the latter group of nations, but misleading for the former. On the contrary, what is illustrated by the performance of the former group is a catching-up process that has tended to narrow such gaps.

The basis for the normal path of development is essentially provided by the sustained operating of market mechanisms, as empirically deduced from contemporary development records. This implies that the pattern of operation of market mechanisms, including government function, tends to change from phase to phase. Recognition of such changes is important, although their empirical clarification is beyond the present scope. However, the sectoral approach in this volume emphasizes the significance of the service sector due to its facilitating function in the operation of market mechanisms.

Technology Diffusion, Productivity Employment, and
Phase Shifts in Developing Economies

1

Technology Diffusion: The Input-Output Ratio Approach

In DE[1] the growth mechanism of developing economies was analyzed based on the hypothesis that a nation's capability for absorbing advanced technology is the most crucial factor, although the actual process of technology diffusion was not dealt with directly. This chapter treats the issue explicitly. Two approaches are relevant here: one from the viewpoint of economic analysis and the other from the viewpoint of technology itself. These two different approaches are complementary in clarifying the process of technology diffusion. A simple formula is proposed using the input-output relation. In OK[2] the factor-input ratio, Lw/K, was used as the key term (where K is capital; L, labor; and w, wages). Here, using the conventional output-capital ratio, Y/K (Y, output), a measure of output effects on capital and the output-labor ratio, Y/Lw, is proposed to deal with the output effects on labor. For simplicity, this is called the input-output ratio (IOR) approach. Like the residual approach applied in DE, it is basically economic analysis, and no attempt is made to examine technology itself in engineering or agronomic terms.

In the residual growth approach, the measured residual or total factor productivity (TFP) alone was taken to represent technological advance, and even at present this approach is often used in so-called source analysis of growth. The assertion in DE was that the output effects of nonconventional factors can only be measured as a whole, and the output-input relation of the respective factors cannot be

[1] Kazushi Ohkawa in collaboration with Katsuo Otsuka and Bernard Key, *Growth Mechanism of Developing Economies: Investment, Productivity and Employment* (Tokyo: International Development Center of Japan, 1993).

[2] Kazushi Ohkawa and Hirohisa Kohama, *Lectures on Developing Economies: Japan's Experience and Its Relevance* (Tokyo: University of Tokyo Press, 1989).

singled out. Thus, the effects of technological advance cannot be separated from the effects of other factors such as changes in the level of human capability, social organization, institutions, etc. It is important to recognize that the common effects of these non-conventional factors as a whole are measured by market price evaluation. In other words, the residual measures all the output effects of the input factors not taken into account by market price evaluation. The idea of social capability (SC) was proposed in *DE*; it is the conceptual view that leveling SC permits realization of residual growth, including technological advance, not vice versa. Empirically the measured residual growth is sizable, and SC level changes are crucial in analyzing technology diffusion in developing economies.

This approach has both advantages and disadvantages. The advantage is that it treats the mechanism of technology diffusion in an overall framework of SC, but the disadvantage is that direct treatment of the actual process of technology diffusion is not possible. It has often been asserted that this disadvantage stems from the equilibrium analysis applied in the measurement of the TFP or residual. This is acceptable so far as the neoclassical approach is concerned, but the residual can also be assessed in the framework of a disequilibrium process. This is the essential approach in *DE*. The disadvantage stems from the lack of explicit treatment of terms directly relevant to the actual technology diffusion process and mechanism. The formula proposed here is intended to deal with the processes and patterns of technology diffusion, but differs from the technology approach in depending solely on the use of economic terms to link it conceptually with the residual approach. In other words, it attempts to clarify the technological aspects of residual measurements. The input-output formula is simplified as explained below; its disadvantage in the treatment of the complex process of technology diffusion should be recognized.[3]

Section I makes factual observations on postwar developing economies. From the empirical knowledge thus obtained a simplified

---

[3] Yukihiko Kiyokawa recently presented a comprehensive review of studies on this theme. The present formula is more "simplified," even if the scope of observation is confined to economic analysis. A number of further studies are required in light of his review. His conceptual framework, however, seems to endorse the basic notion stated earlier that the process of technology diffusion can and should be assessed from two aspects: one is economic and the other is technology itself. Yukihiko Kiyokawa, "Economic Analysis on the Diffusion of Technological Innovations—A Survey" (in Japanese), *Keizai Kenkyu (The Economic Review)*, Vol. 42, No. 4 (Tokyo: Economic Research Institute, Hitotsubashi University, October 1991).

formula is derived to deal with this problem at the macro level. A hypothesis is then given in a model consisting of key terms essential in treating the process of technology diffusion. Special consideration is paid to its dualistic structure. In section II, further interpretation of the orientation and implication of the current approach is made in light of a selected review of economic theories and approaches relevant to technology transfer and diffusion.

I. Contemporary Developing Economies: Proposal and Hypothesis

Incremental Changes in Key Terms and Proposed Formula
In chapter 1 of *DE*, residual growth was measured first in terms of investment and second in terms of output. Relevant incremental terms were measured but not fully discussed. In dealing with technology diffusion, the significance of incremental performance should be more fully elucidated, since the process is one of disequilibrium moving toward equilibrium. Table 1.1 summarizes key terms estimated for selected groupings of countries. In addition to the average for the group (Roman numerals) classified by product per worker (Y/L) level, investment efficiency $(\Delta Y/I)$ by subgroup is listed. The groupings are as follows, with Y/L levels in US dollars for 1970 in parentheses:

Group I
- A: Burkina Faso (Upper Volta) (116), Mali (142), Malawi (148), India (240), Burma (177), and Tanzania (179);
- B: Ethiopia (124), Niger (158), Nepal (168), Benin (176), Somalia (253), and Madagascar (272).

Group II
- A: Kenya (324), Thailand (366), Cameroon (473), Pakistan (519), Philippines (524), Ivory Coast (542), and Bolivia (737);
- B: Sierra Leone (365), Mozambique (388), Sudan (431), Senegal (452), Sri Lanka (459), Congo (520), and Liberia (729).

Group III
- A: Republic of Korea (754), Turkey (787), Paraguay (802), Morocco (977), Malaysia (1,087), and Syrian Arab Republic (1,146);
- B: Egypt (767), Tunisia (786), El Salvador (869), Honduras (913), Colombia (1,195), and Nicaragua (1,255).

Table 1.1
Key Terms Relevant to Technology Changes: Developing Economies, 1960–1985

(A): In growth terms

Groups	GY	GL	Gy(GY – GL)	GK	Gk(GK – GL)	GR	GY – GK	(Gw)	(Gk – Gw)	(Gy – Gw)
I	3.1	2.4	0.8	3.1	0.7	0.37	0.0	0.5	0.2	0.3
A	3.9	2.5	1.4	3.9	1.4	0.94	0.0			
B	2.4	2.2	0.2	2.4	0.2	-0.21	0.0			
II	4.0	2.4	1.6	3.5	1.1	1.08	0.5	0.8	0.3	0.8
A	5.0	2.6	2.4	4.0	1.4	1.72	1.0			
B	3.0	2.1	0.9	3.0	0.9	0.44	0.0			
III	5.5	3.1	2.4	4.6	1.5	1.68	0.9	1.3	0.2	1.1
A	6.5	3.0	3.5	4.4	1.4	2.77	2.1			
B	4.4	3.1	1.3	4.9	1.8	0.39	-0.5			
IV	4.0	1.9	2.1	4.4	2.4	0.90	-0.4	1.5	0.9	0.6
A	4.7	2.1	2.6	5.3	3.2	1.05	-0.6			
B	3.2	1.6	1.6	3.4	1.8	0.74	-0.2			
V	3.6	1.2	2.4	4.1	2.9	1.51	-0.5	2.1	0.8	0.3
A	4.1	1.2	2.9	4.1	2.9	1.99	0.0			
B	3.1	1.1	2.0	4.1	3.0	1.06	-1.0			

(B): In incremental terms

Groups	ΔY/ΔK	wΔL/ΔK	r	ΔR/ΔK	ΔR/ΔY	wΔL/ΔY	rΔK/ΔY
I	27.3	9.8	14.4	2.71	7.7	35.9	54.3
A	31.0	9.6	14.1	7.45	24.0	31.3	44.5
B	23.7	10.2	15.2	-2.04	-8.6	40.5	64.1
II	31.7	8.6	14.4	8.36	24.1	27.8	46.3
A	39.0	9.0	16.6	13.16	33.7	23.3	42.6
B	24.6	8.1	12.3	3.55	14.4	32.3	50.0
III	32.9	8.2	15.5	9.88	25.9	25.5	50.0
A	40.4	8.4	16.4	17.47	42.6	19.6	40.6
B	25.3	8.0	15.0	2.29	9.1	31.3	59.3
IV	25.4	5.7	13.9	5.77	23.7	22.7	54.2
A	30.0	6.5	16.4	6.82	24.7	21.7	54.8
B	20.7	4.9	11.2	4.71	22.8	23.3	53.6
V	28.2	5.6	10.7	12.01	41.6	19.9	38.9
A	33.7	6.0	11.3	16.34	48.5	17.5	33.5
B	22.8	5.1	10.1	7.67	33.6	22.2	44.3

Notes: Y, product (GDP); L, labor; K, capital; R, residual; w, wages; r, rate of return on capital; G, rate of growth (average annual rate); Δ, incremental increase.

Source: DE, Chapter 1, Table 1.1

Remarks: i) For technical details, see the relevant parts in *DE,* Chapter 1. The basic definition is $\Delta R = \Delta Y - \Delta Y^*$, and ΔY^* is evaluated by the conventional costs of the base year, under the assumption of no technological organizational advance.

ii) L is the "economically active population" (ILO data), with a broader meaning of the labor force employed. This is used assuming no serious problems in growth terms on long-term average.

iii) K, capital stock, is not estimated. GK is estimated together with the rate of return on capital r using Japan's historical data on average capital stock. In order to be consistent with GR in this table, the length of duration is reduced by 10% from the original estimates. See Technical Notes.

iv) Gw is estimated by specific assumptions for the group average. See Technical Notes.

v) The sum of wΔL/ΔK, r, and ΔR/ΔK does not necessarily add up exactly to ΔY/ΔK due to approximated calculations.

Group IV
  A: Dominican Republic (1,284), Brazil (1,450), Peru (1,780), Portugal (1,829), Mexico (2,455), and Greece (2,920);
  B: Yugoslavia (1,475), Costa Rica (1,855), Jamaica (1,975), Uruguay (2,209), Argentina (2,496), and Singapore (2,606).
Group V
  A: Japan (3,822), France (6,532), Denmark (6,649), Netherlands (7,047), Belgium (7,098), Canada (9,476), and USA (11,335);
  B: UK (4,792), Finland (4,853), New Zealand (5,743), Switzerland (6,771), Germany (6,893), Norway (6,956), and Sweden (9,390).

The IOR formula used here pertains to $w\Delta L/\Delta K$, $\Delta Y/\Delta K$, and $w\Delta L/\Delta Y$, the combined results of the two (all in Table 1.1 B). It is widely accepted that advanced technological knowledge borrowed from developed economies requires capital intensification for domestic absorption by developing economies. The variation of $\Delta K/w\Delta L$ expresses the performance of capital intensification. The inputs, a combination of capital and labor, determine the magnitude of the output effect $\Delta Y/\Delta K$, although the value actually realized may deviate. The relation of inputs and outputs can also be felt in the performance of $\Delta Y/w\Delta L$. Incremental changes in these terms, shown in Table 1.1 B, together with other relevant terms, illustrate capital intensification vividly.

Two aspects must be considered: the relation to the residual approach and examination of the possibility of alternative procedures. The former is needed to link the results of analysis presented in *DE*, while the latter is needed to clarify the IOR formula in a comparative sense. In the residual approach, technological advance (in which organizational change and other factors are inseparably combined) is usually indicated by $\Delta R/Y$, that is, the ratio of incremental residual growth to the level of product in the base year, and this is conventionally expressed by GR (Table 1.1 A). By group the Y/L level shows a distinct tendency to increase, but decreases from III to IV, followed by another increase toward V. Instead of analyzing the factors responsible for this pattern, examine $\Delta R/\Delta Y$ in Table 1.1 B, which represents the ratio of residual to product at the incremental level. The average of groups by Y/L level reveals a distinct tendency to increase throughout I to V (with a dip in IV). Change in the ratio GR/GY has often been used as a representative indicator of technology change. This is actually equivalent to

ΔR/ΔY (ΔR/Y/ΔY/Y), an incremental ratio. By definition ΔY = ΔR + rΔK + wΔL, where ΔR = ΔY − ΔY* (the increase of output assumed to take place in case of no change in technology organization). The following relation is thus obtained:

$$\Delta R/\Delta Y = 1 - \{(r\Delta K/\Delta Y) + (w\Delta L/\Delta Y)\}. \tag{1}$$

This is transformed to

$$\Delta Y/\Delta K = (\Delta R/\Delta K) + r + (w\Delta L/\Delta K). \tag{2}$$

Using formula (2), the incremental output-capital ratio, ΔY/ΔK, is decomposed into three components: the rate of capital return r; factor input ratio wΔL/ΔK; and the residual term ΔR/ΔK. The numerical values of all these terms are given in Table 1.1 A. The relationship found between (1) and (2) first requires comparison of ΔR/ΔY and ΔR/ΔK. The difference corresponds to the alternatives of selecting output effects on labor or capital. The pattern of ΔR/ΔK as seen in the group averages appears broadly similar (a tendency to increase with a dip at IV), but the difference found between the two indicates the difference in evaluating the speed of residual change. Second, different performance is found between the components in the two formulas. Formula (2) is appropriate for measuring output effects on capital since it is consistent with measures of incremental residual growth due to investment. For measuring the output effect on labor, the term ΔY/wΔL (reciprocal) is a component of formula (1) along with rΔK/ΔY. In comparing the group average performance of wΔL/ΔY and rΔK/ΔY a problem of "alternative" procedure occurs. In theory, either wΔL/ΔY or rΔK/ΔY can be adopted. The former is adopted here since it more conveniently illustrates the process of technology diffusion by the IOR formula. The magnitude of wΔL/ΔY shows a distinct tendency to decrease, whereas for rΔK/ΔY there is no clear trend of increase or decrease. This difference is substantive. The reason for it is found in the relation of the components in formula (2). We can write

$$w\Delta L/\Delta Y = w\Delta L/\Delta K/\Delta Y/\Delta K, \quad \text{or} \tag{3}$$

$$\Delta Y/w\Delta L = \Delta Y/\Delta K \cdot \Delta K/w\Delta L. \tag{3'}$$

It is interpreted that the distinct tendency to decrease found for wΔL/ΔY is the combined result of two different patterns: a relatively high magnitude in the former segment and a low magnitude in the latter segment for wΔL/ΔK and an inverse U-shaped pattern of ΔY/ΔK, with a dip at IV. Formula (3') is also appropriate for subsequent treatment. In this case, the tendency for a distinct increase in $\Delta Y/w\Delta L$ is expressed as the combined result of $\Delta Y/\Delta K$ and $\Delta K/w\Delta L$. Likewise, the alternative pattern of $r\Delta K/\Delta Y$ is the combined result of movement of $\Delta Y/\Delta K$ and r. In the former segment a moderate tendency for an increase in $\Delta Y/\Delta K$ is cancelled by a moderate increase in r, and in the latter segment a dip in $\Delta Y/\Delta K$ at IV raises the level of $r\Delta K/\Delta Y$ particularly high. It should be noted that in group IV, $w\Delta L/\Delta Y$ shows no bias from the group trend to decrease but in the alternative case its bias is noticeable. The present discussion does not proceed further using the alternative $\Delta Y/r\Delta K$ to examine the output effect by capital because the conventional term $\Delta Y/\Delta K$ is used. The performance of $\Delta Y/w\Delta L$ is most influential on the incremental pattern of growth, and its trend of increase (decrease in $w\Delta L/\Delta Y$) is due to a greater increase in $\Delta Y/\Delta K$ relative to an increase in $\Delta K/w\Delta L$ (decrease in $w\Delta L/\Delta K$). This provides the empirical basis for adopting $\Delta Y/w\Delta L$ as the appropriate term in dealing with the process of technology diffusion. This is discussed in detail after explaining the comparative performance of subgroups.

In the present framework, subgrouping is essential because without it what is called "nonassociated" movement cannot be grasped. Technology advance does not proceed based on the process of leveling up Y/L alone. Instead, factors not associated with the level of Y/L must be significant. As described above, the performance of residual growth is associated with differences in Y/L level to a certain extent, and its significance is undeniable. However, among nations with essentially the same Y/L level, performance in technology diffusion appears to vary widely. The criteria used for subgrouping depend upon the analytical purpose. In this volume, A–B subgroups are classified in terms of investment efficiency $\Delta Y/I$, because this term is most relevant to the present analysis. Other criteria, for example rate of labor productivity growth, cannot be rejected, however.

In Table 1.1 A, the difference in growth performance between groups A and B is shown by the conventional indicator of residual growth GR together with relevant terms. GR is greater in A than in B in all groups without exception. The magnitude of difference is generally sizable, particularly during the former segment, in comparison with the group difference magnitude. For example, the GR difference in the subgroups in II is 1.28 (A, 1.72; B, 0.44) versus 0.57 for the group average (1.65, III; 1.08, II). In the latter segment, however, this is not necessarily the case. For example, the GR difference in the subgroups in IV is 0.31 (A, 1.05; B, 0.74) versus 0.57 (V, 1.51; IV, 0.92). The reason for such variation is one of the problems to be clarified later. In Table 1.1 B, incremental values of residual growth are shown by $\Delta R/\Delta Y$ and $\Delta R/\Delta K$. As stated earlier, group averages of $\Delta R/\Delta L$ and $\Delta R/\Delta Y$ show a tendency to increase with a dip at IV. Its subgroup differences are sharper, particularly in the former segment. In comparing subgroup A in all groups by Y/L level, a distinct tendency to increase is revealed (with a dip at IV) for the group average. However, a similar comparison of group B shows no analogous performance. The magnitude is much lower than that in subgroup A (and negative in I), but no tendency to increase is seen during the former segment. In the latter segment, however, the subgroup difference becomes much narrower. The reason for such variance requires clarification because although the present estimates indicate regularity of residual growth, no straightforward generalizations are possible.

Applying formula (3) or (3′), the level of $w\Delta L/\Delta Y$ is smaller in A than in B throughout all groups without exception. In other words, the level of $\Delta Y/w\Delta L$ is higher in A than in B even for group IV, in which a dip is often observed. This is important. The magnitude of $\Delta Y/\Delta K$, on the one hand, is higher in A than in B throughout all groups. On the other hand, the level of $\Delta K/w\Delta L$ (reciprocal of $w\Delta L/\Delta K$ shown in Table 1.1 B) tends to be lower in A than in B in all groups with the exception of group I. The subgroup difference is particularly moderate during the former segment. In light of the tendency for an increase in $\Delta K/w\Delta L$ with respect to the group average (moderate in the former and accelerated in the latter segment), this subgroup phenomenon deserves special attention. Using formula (3′), the higher level of $\Delta Y/w\Delta L$ in A than in B is due to the combined effects of higher $\Delta Y/\Delta K$ and higher $w\Delta L/\Delta K$ (except in I). This may be contrary to the usual expectation, but the following interpretation can be made. First, there is a technical relation between incremental and average terms as follows:

$$w\Delta L/\Delta Y = (Lw/Y) \cdot (GL/GY), \qquad (4)$$

in which Lw/Y (β, labor's income share) is assumed to be equal between subgroups A and B. Based on accounting concepts, Y from the production aspect is different from that of distributed income. For simplicity, this is ignored for the time being. The magnitude of the ratio GL/GY as shown in Table 1.1 A in the right-hand column is distinctly smaller in A than in B throughout all groups without exception. Therefore, the incremental value of β (say, $\Delta\beta$) must be smaller or that of the reciprocal, $\Delta Y/w\Delta L$, must be greater in A than in B. If β were higher in B than in A, modification would be needed, but no data are available to do so. Estimates should therefore be taken with some reservation. The pattern of $w\Delta L/\Delta K$ found above is close to reality as long as $\Delta Y/\Delta K$ is estimated reliably because formula (3) or (3') is an identity. Second, the factor input ratio at its incremental level, $\Delta K/w\Delta L$, indicates that technology adopted in A is of more labor-intensive type than that in B. This is an important suggestion in revealing the basic problems pertaining to the technology diffusion process of developing economies. In order to endorse its validity, sector and subsector analysis is needed. The concern here is to provide a plausible overview.

Taking group and subgroup observations together gives an empirical background for treating formula (3') or (3) as a behavioristic relation, as follows. Entrepreneurial investment is made to incorporate advances in a certain type of technology, and the economic indicator for this is given by the factor input ratio $\Delta K/w\Delta L$. A certain output effect, $\Delta Y/\Delta K$, is expected to be sufficiently profitable. Although the expected output effect may be less than sufficient, the *ex post* data show it is generally plausible as suggested by the pattern of $\Delta Y/w\Delta L$. Its tendency to increase through groups and its subgroup difference should be noted in this regard. As illustrated by group IV, unless $r\Delta K/\Delta Y$ has significant effects, this indicator potentially indicates the magnitude and speed of technology advance realized. $\Delta Y/w\Delta L$ is not the behavioristic target of investment but can be assumed to indicate technological advance.[4]

Finally, taking all these factual observations into consideration, formula (5) is presented to show another relation between the IOR formula and the residual approach.

$$\Delta Y/w\Delta L = \Delta R/w\Delta L + r\Delta K/w\Delta L + 1. \qquad (5)$$

This is directly derived from the original formula $\Delta Y = \Delta R + r\Delta K + w\Delta L$. The term $\Delta Y/w\Delta L$ is proposed as the basic means of understanding the technology diffusion process as the combined results of $\Delta K/w\Delta L$ and $\Delta Y/\Delta K$. It is composed of two terms, the residual per labor input ($\Delta R/w\Delta L$) and the factor input ratio (capital/labor), apart from unity. The former is not the conventional method

---

[4] Individual entrepreneurial behavior concerns capital formation and in conventional project appraisal capital itself is treated with time discounting. Here, in macrosectoral assessment, the capital accumulation at enterprise base is treated as new investment, ΔK, an addition to total capital stock. Assessment by "average" magnitude is illustrated in chapter 2.

of treating the residual, but its meaning can be easily understood. The residual approach measures $r\Delta K/w\Delta L$ in order to derive $\Delta R/w\Delta L$, whereas the IOR formula attempts to treat the sum of the two terms together. The former pertains to accounting in terms of market prices, but the latter aims at clarifying technology performance: the relation between certain capital-labor combinations and output effect, including the residual. The relation between $\Delta Y/w\Delta L$ and $r\Delta K/w\Delta L$ should not be assumed to be the same since it varies between different kinds of technology, e.g., traditional versus modern, as will be explained later. The elucidation of this variance is very important in analyzing the technology diffusion process. The usual assumption of homogenous diffusion of technology in the same category is far from the development path reality.[5]

Model of Dualistic Development: Hypothesis
The substantive aspects of development should be examined more closely in order to clarify the problems addressed in subsequent discussion. For this purpose, the conventional approach in growth terms is adopted, referring to Table 1.1 A. The significance of the IOR formula has been demonstrated by presenting the incremental performances of relevant terms. To apply the IOR formula to the growth path, the numerical procedure is $(\Delta Y/\Delta K)/(Y/K) = GY/GK$, for example. It is desirable to give an overview by presenting a model of growth performance which can incorporate the hypothesis that the crucial elements forming the process of technology diffusion operate through the changing path of development in a dualistic structure (modern versus traditional), as explained below.

It is common knowledge that advanced technological knowledge borrowed from developed economies requires capital intensification for its domestic absorption by industries in developing economies. This recognition provides an analytical basis, often assuming that a certain type of production function has international commonality for both predecessors and latecomers in the technology diffusion

---

[5] The conventional formula for measuring total factor productivity (TFP) is given in its essence by

$$\alpha(GY - GK) + \beta(GY - GL),$$

which implies $\alpha GY + \beta GY = GY$ (assuming $\alpha + \beta = 1$).

Incremental changes are involved but not treated explicitly. Conceptually, one can say that when and where $GY - GK$ is much smaller than $GY - GL$, if not $GY = GK$, the Harrod neutral, a dominant role is expected to be played by the labor term.

process. That approach is not followed here, although capital intensification is an indispensable technological requirement that has
been fulfilled vigorously in postwar developing economies. However, too much capital intensification has often been criticized due
to the need for labor-intensive technology in labor-surplus economies.
This suggests the basic issues involved.

The figures listed in Table 1.1 appear not to endorse a simplified
view. For example, in Table 1.1 A the rate of increase in capital intensity, $GK - GL$, is surprisingly small in the former segment,
although toward the latter segment it becomes noticeably larger.
The measurements are focused on incremental changes and the estimate of GK is conditional, yet this does not stem from underestimates of GK, although some distortions may be allowed.[6] What is
more important is the adoption of the term $GK - (GL + Gw)$ in the
dualistic structure framework of the traditional and modern sectors,
that is, measures of the growth term of $\Delta K/w\Delta L$, the performance
of which was discussed earlier in terms of its reciprocal. The estimated magnitude of $GK - (GL + Gw)$ is listed in the right-hand column of Table 1.1 A. This magnitude is extremely small, although
larger for the latter segment. The available data for Gw are limited
but approximated by assuming $Gw = Gk$ for the traditional sector.
(Due to this rough approximation it is not possible to treat subgroup
performance.) The average pattern of Gw is very small, being under
unity during the former segment, although it has a clear tendency to
increase through groups toward the latter segment. This corresponds to its incremental performance, $\Delta K/w\Delta L$, the reciprocal of
which is shown in Table 1.1 B. Thus, $GK - GL(Gk)$ is very small
and very close to the smaller value of Gw. It can be said that this
suggests an overly labor-intensive path, while making the effects of
advanced foreign technology appear too limited. It also raises
another question: If this quantification mirrors reality, why does the
rate of residual growth increase so remarkably, in particular during
the former segment?

Such questions are an important challenge to the present analysis.
In responding, we note the implication of the hypothesis with regard
to the variance of technology. It is composed of two categories:
modern and traditional. The former is international and the latter
national or indigenous to developing economies. For the factor-
input ratio, as stated above, the former is characterized by
$GK > GL + Gw$, whereas the latter is essentially characterized by

---

[6] Regarding the estimates and relevant points, see Technical Notes.

GK = GL + Gw, that is, the factor-input ratio remains unchanged. At a given time macro performance is provided by the weighted sum of these two elements. As the weight of the modern tends to increase along with development, the macro pattern may increase the inequality GK > GL + Gw, but the path proceeds at a moderate pace since the traditional element still plays an important role until a certain point. Modern technology itself becomes more capital-intensive, as is roughly illustrated by the change in the relevant terms from III to IV, demarcating the former segment from the latter, in which the traditional element becomes increasingly minor; it is near zero in V.

What requires special explanation is the role of traditional technology. GK − GL = Gw in this sector means an equal rate of change in the capital-labor ratio and wages, instead of assuming lack of constancy in either K/L or wages. Substantively, the two tend to be equal at very low levels—the level determined indigenously by each nation's historical sociocultural system. It is assumed in the present hypothesis that if this type of factor-input ratio remains, traditional technology can raise its output effects, achieving a pattern of increased output-capital ratio, Y/K, the incremental magnitude of which, $\Delta Y/\Delta K$, is illustrated in Table 1.1 B. Why is this possible? The answer should include the effectiveness of current (intermediate) inputs, instead of capital inputs. This is most amply illustrated by agricultural production, but small-scale handicraft production in manufacturing serves as well, as explained in chapter 2. The view that simply assumes that modern technology diffusion is a straightforward process replacing indigenous technology is not shared by the present authors. While many traditional establishments or firms have been replaced by modern ones based solely on superior competitive efficiency, the present hypothesis implies that the resistance force applied by indigenous production activity should also be appropriately evaluated.

The interactive mechanism between international and domestic elements thus becomes an important aspect of diffusion process analysis. This is a derived proposal of the present hypothesis. The interaction covers a variety of issues, including organizational changes exceeding the "hybridization" of traditional and modern elements of technology advance.

Qualifications and/or reservations are needed in the terminology to define categories of technology. Traditional versus modern are used in historical terms, with an assumed correspondence between national versus international. This is too simple and misleading.

First, such terms pertain to production activity. As explained in chapter 5, agricultural development depends upon the borrowing of advanced technological knowledge and to that extent an international element is involved, although the production system may remain traditional. Small-scale manufacturing firms also use modern elements of technology to a certain extent. These examples suggest that the terminology used tends to emphasize production organization. Second, by definition category, as distinguished from type, of technology in the neoclassical sense concerns disequilibrium process performance between output effects and factor-input combinations. This does not pertain to technological change in the conventional sense, however. As touched upon above, the intention here is to distinguish the present approach from accounting measurements by focusing on the aspect of technological requirements.

Corresponding to the previous discussion of factor-input aspects, output effects, as indicated by $GY - GK$ in Table 1.1 A, should be discussed here. As in the case of factor inputs, which demarcate the former and latter segments, $GY - GK$ tends to increase in the former segment, followed by a decrease in the latter segment. The performance of the traditional sector influences this pattern, as suggested previously for the former segment. The pattern $GK > GY$ in the modern sector becomes dominant toward group V. The two key terms, $GK - (GL + Gw)$ and $GY - GK$, operate together to form $GY - (GL + Gw)$, the growth term of Y/Lw through groups as shown in the last column of Table 1.1 A. It tends to increase in the former segment, followed by a decrease toward V.

To summarize, the present hypothesis for technology diffusion analysis is quantified. The macro pattern of key terms relevant to the process of technology diffusion can be clarified by considering the combined operation of modern and traditional elements. Numerical values given in the Technical Notes are for illustrative purposes, not genuine estimates, to present the model in quantitative terms.

Finally, the relation of the present model to the well-known models of development should be determined. The present hypothesis directly pertains to categories of technology, the economic property of which is defined simply by factor combination. Therefore, factor prices, particularly wages, are not treated as a primary factor in determining the pattern and mechanism of development. However, the authors believe that no contradiction exists between the so-called classical model of unlimited supplies of labor and the present hypothesis. Rather, a model derived from this hypothesis may include the case of unlimited labor supplies, that is, unchanged real wages for unskilled labor in the former segment (before the turning point). Data on wages include those for skilled and semi-skilled workers, so that a very moderate magnitude of Gw may imply constant wages for unskilled workers as an extreme case, although no precise measures can be given. What is intended here is to give the relation of wages to technology. The pattern GK = GL is often called capital widening in this type of approach. If this terminology is used, the pattern of GK = GL + Gw can likewise be called capital widening but in a specified sense, e.g., taking wages as capital measurement unit. However, in such a comparative clarification of concepts, the characteristics of the hypothesis proposed here should be viewed from the following two aspects. First, factor combination is not primarily induced by factor prices in a traditional economy. A type of balanced linkage is historically established between the level of productivity and the people's standard of living (subsistence level in classical terminology) by use of production means (instruments, buildings, etc.) measured as capital stock, K. Human experience based on technology and traditional wages are thus viewed in terms of historical linkage. Second, in dealing with open economies not only outputs and inputs but also technological knowledge are indispensable elements. "Capital deepening," in contrast to "widening," reflects linkages with indigenous systems of production technology.

Technical Notes

1) GK and r. The rate of return on capital, r, is estimated by $\alpha = rK/Y$, in which $K/Y = K/D \cdot D/Y$ (where D stands for depreciation allowances). Average capital life is approximated by K/D. $GK(\Delta K/K)$ is derived from $\Delta K/Y \cdot Y/K$, in which ΔK is estimated from investment (I) using the average replacement coefficient. The term K/D is estimated by the use of Japan's historical data as follows (in number of years):

I	II	III	IV	V
49.5	45.0	38.7	31.5	22.5

For details, see *DE*, chapter 1, Technical Notes.

2) Gw. Data for estimating the rate of changes in wages are not available for international comparisons at the macro level. However, general knowledge of Gw performance is indispensable for analytical purposes. By making the specific assumptions below, Gw is estimated for the group average and listed in the right-hand column in Table 1.1 A in parentheses. Assumptions for such estimates are specified by the supposed dualistic structure consisting of the traditional (T) and modern (M) sectors. These are explained in detail in the main text. First, changes in the structure of the economy are represented by changes in the share of labor employed by T and M. Generally, T consists of agriculture and M of industry, assuming that the part of agriculture in M corresponds roughly to the part of industry in T. The service sector is a mixture of T and M. In this sector, the ratio is assumed simply to be T, 1 : M, 2. The numerical values are as follows (1960–1980 average, %):

	I	II	III	IV	V
T	86.8	78.1	61.3	49.7	23.7
M	13.2	21.9	38.7	50.3	76.3

Source: *DE*, Table 4.10.

Second, with respect to T, the assumption Gk = Gw is applied through all groups. The annual average rate of growth is assumed to be a flat 0.5%, close to the aggregate rate of group I, assuming this has almost no influence on the other groups. Data on macro Gk are given in Table 1.1 A so that by using weighted shares the magnitude of Gk for sector M can be derived as follows:

I	II	III	IV	V
0.7	1.1	1.5	2.4	2.9

With respect to sector M, it is assumed that Gw is equal to the rate of productivity growth as an average of Gy_1, that of industry, and Gy_2, that of services. This simple assumption is consistent with the estimate of the constant relative income share of labor in industry and services covering the interval under review. It is estimated as follows, with adjustments, for 1960–1985:

I	II	III	IV	V
0.83	2.23	2.43	3.00	2.64

Source: Gy data, *DE*, Table 4.9.

Using these weights macro values of Gw can be derived as follows (listed in rounded figures in the righthand column of Table 1.1 A), together with sector M and sector T components.

	I	II	III	IV	V
Macro	0.54	0.79	1.25	1.76	2.13
M	0.11	0.40	0.94	1.51	2.01
T	0.43	0.39	0.31	0.25	0.12

It should be noted that the figures for Gw thus obtained are not "estimated" in the conventional sense but incorporate the hypothesis underlying the present model. The figures cannot be used to test the hypothesis in a genuine sense, although it is expected that they will be useful to describe possible patterns in developing economies.[7]

II. Selected Review of Relevant Theories and Approaches

The proposal of the simplified formula in section I was deduced from the results of empirical studies. This section explains its relation to the theories and approaches relevant to the conceptual framework of the proposed formula by presenting a broadly selected review.

Technology Advance in Modern Economic Growth
Technology advance is one of the most important factors in modern economic growth. Only since the industrial revolution in England in

---

[7] The procedure for estimating Gw adopted here is not consistent with the original definition $\Delta Y = \Delta R + \Delta Y^*$ because wages pertain to ΔY^*, not to ΔY. It is not possible to obtain an adequate estimation based on ΔY^*, but the authors believe no substantive inconsistency is implied, however.

the latter half of the 18th century—in other words, in the past 200 years or so—has any remarkable economic development been achieved owing to the invention of new technologies. The world economy before that, whether in terms of increased productive capacity or of population, manifested very slow growth, with per capita output remaining almost constant. It was thus not possible for such classical economists as Smith, Ricardo, and Malthus to envisage rapid economic growth. Their predictions foresaw the continuation of the so-called stationary state of the economy.[8] Although they recognized that capital accumulation and increased productivity would occur in national economies during the process of industrialization, they expected continuous, sustained advancement of modern economic growth. In the agricultural sector a tendency toward diminishing returns on land together with less technical progress was noted, while a tendency toward increasing returns on capital was anticipated in the industrial sector. Classical thought held that the process of capital accumulation which creates economic development would not last forever, but would induce a fall in the profit rates of production factors, eventually placing the economy in a "state of constancy" where both capital and income per person would not increase substantially. If this occurred, it would become impossible to feed the growing population and, as a result, population growth would also cease.

It was inconceivable for the classical economists that an economy could sustain its development and prosperity over a long period of time. Marx, who was strongly influenced by the classical school, envisaged an intensification of confrontations between capitalists and workers as a result of a lowering of the profit rate, the advent of economic crisis and depression, and the revolutionizing of capitalism into socialism and eventually communism.[9] It was thought that the transition from capitalism to socialism would be realized in a capitalist economic society at the peak of maturity.

In the history of modern economic growth, however, economic development has never achieved a stationary state, and no mature capitalist economy has made the transition to a socialist economy.

---

[8] Ricardo compiled classical economic theories. He believed that a stationary state is the final resting point of economic development, although he recognized the advance of technology itself. David Ricardo, *On the Principles of Political Economy and Taxation* (John Murray, 1821).

[9] Although Marx wrote many books, *Das Kapital* is appreciated as his representative work. Karl Marx, *Das Kapital: Kritik der Politischen Ökonomie* (Otto Meissner, 1884–1867).

Instead, both national incomes and population have increased remarkably. The main contributing factor to these increases was technological innovation.

Schumpeter argued that it was possible for a capitalist economy to continue developing through technological innovation. He believed that economic development could be attained through the intermittent emergence of new production methods called "new combinations."[10] Those who promote this process were called innovative entrepreneurs, and entrepreneurs who attempted technological innovation using new combinations earned profits and became leaders contributing to the growth of economic society. It was believed that as long as innovation occurred economic progress would continue. Technology to promote economic development gained greater recognition as the world economy developed from the 19th century through the 20th century, until it finally began to be taken seriously in theories of economic development and growth.

Kuznets introduced the concept of "modern economic growth (MEG)" and attempted a comprehensive, quantitative analysis of the process of world economic development after the industrial revolution.[11] He asserted that modern economic growth was characterized by sustained growth of production and population, changes in industrial structure, and enhanced international interchange, and that improving production capacity by introducing modern technology based on the utilization of modern scientific ideas was a prerequisite to attaining such modern economic growth. This subsection follows the concepts of Kuznets.

Analysis of economic growth gained momentum after World War II, and academic economists devised elaborate methods for explaining the mechanism of economic growth. This pursuit eventually resulted in the theory known as the modern theory of economic growth. As economic growth models representing the advance of the modern theory, the Harrod-Domar growth model and the neoclassical growth model can be cited.[12] The modern theory of economic growth emphasized the role of "technological progress," and

---

[10] Joseph A. Schumpeter, *Theorie der Wirtschaftlichen Entwicklung: Eine Untersuchung über Unternehmergewinn, Kapital Kredit, Zins und den Konjunkturzyklus,* 5 Auf 1. (Dunker & Humbolt, 1985).

[11] Simon Kuznets, *Modern Economic Growth: Rate, Structure and Spread* (Yale University Press, 1966).

[12] As an introductory textbook that explains and comments on the modern theory of economic growth, the following is cited: H.G. Jones, *An Introduction to Modern Theories of Economic Growth* (Thomas Nelson, 1975).

produced various analytical methods with which theoretical and empirical studies of the magnitude and type of technological progress were actively pursued. In 1957 Solow published a paper in which he used a neoclassical growth model to measure the growth rate of per capita output of the nonagricultural sector in the USA during the period between 1909 and 1949 and derived the shocking conclusion that nearly 90% of that growth in per capita output could be ascribed to the contribution of technological progress.[13] Since then, attempts to measure technological progress have been made in other Western countries by expanding on the "source of growth" approach presented by E.F. Denison.[14]

A study by Ohkawa and Rosovsky of Japan found that nearly 50% of the growth in output of the nonagricultural private sector during the high-growth period between 1955 and 1964 was accomplished by the "residual," suggesting that the role of technological progress was crucial.[15]

Solow made an empirical study of technological progress using the general form of aggregate production function, $Q = f(K, L, t)$, where Q, K, and L represent output, the input of capital, and the input of labor, respectively, while t is a parameter indicating the time necessary for technological change. When the above general form is rewritten in a formula that shows dynamic change, assuming that neutral technological change is in progress, it becomes:

$$\dot{Q}/Q = \dot{A}/A + \alpha\dot{K}/K + \beta\dot{L}/L \qquad (6)$$

where A is a constant term by which the function shifts with time; α and β represent, respectively, relative shares of output to capital and labor, while $(\cdot)$ is a derivative with respect to time. Solow's view was that if time-series values of Q, K, L, and α and β were obtainable, then the shifting term $\dot{A}/A$ of the production function, or the rate of technological progress, would be measurable as a residual. The rate of technological progress thus derived contains some theoretical problems. For example, it appears that the interconnection between the effect of technological progress and the

---

[13] Robert M. Solow, "Technical Changes and the Aggregate Production Function," *Review of Economics and Statistics*, 1957.

[14] Edward F. Denison, *Why Growth Rates Differ: Postwar Experience in Nine Western Countries* (Brookings Institution, 1967).

[15] Kazushi Ohkawa and Henry Rosovsky, *Japanese Economic Growth: Trend Acceleration in the Twentieth Century* (Stanford University Press, 1973).

trend of capital accumulation is ignored while so-called unembodied technological progress is taken into account. Attempts have been made to measure the rate of technological progress based on the idea that it is achieved through the investment of new capital. As theoretical and empirical studies on technological change have progressed, the relationship between economic growth and technology has become clearer.

To be accurate, "technological progress" in the modern theory of economic growth is measured by residual or total factor productivity, which includes everything used to increase output except contributions made by such conventional production factors as capital and labor. In other words, the "residual" is composed of various factors including the improvement of the quality of labor, improvement of management techniques, realization of economies of scale, effects of external economies, and changes in industrial structure, in addition to technological progress in the true sense. Therefore, in measuring the rate of technological progress it is necessary to interpret carefully the contents of advances, as in the "source of growth" approach that attempts to decompose the effects of nonconventional factors.

Transfer and Diffusion of Technology

Technology plays an important role in modern economic growth in developed economies. Advanced technology is usually transferred from high-income countries (or areas) to low-income ones because the former have achieved economic growth by adopting more advanced, more productive technology. Developing countries are eager to increase the level of productivity as well as production scale by transferring modern technology from developed countries, an aspect that has become increasingly important.

The concept of technology transfer is generally used to mean technology transferred to developing countries and it is defined as the international propagation of technology. Technology transfer refers especially to the cases where technology from advanced economies is propagated among developing economies. However, technology diffusion can have a wider concept in which technology is spread not only from one country to the other but also within a country. In this study emphasis is placed on the pattern of propagation of technology within a country, as it is becoming an important issue in developing countries how to make better use of the technologies transferred from developed countries. Unless there is a pool of people in developing countries who can utilize technologies effectively, no rise in technology level and productivity can occur in a national economy.

The most noteworthy study on international movement of technology was the *Report of the Pearson Committee* in 1969.[16] The Pearson Committee, headed by former Prime Minister of Canada L.B. Pearson, was established in August 1968 at the request of the World Bank to study and evaluate the results of development aid during the previous 20 years and to recommend how future development aid should be disbursed. In the report it released at the annual general meeting of the World Bank in the following year, the committee positively evaluated technology transfer, and pointed out that the inducement of technology is indispensable in promoting economic growth in developing countries and that it was necessary for advanced countries that transfer technology to offer aid with circumspection. Ever since, technology transfer has been an established term in discussing development aid. UNESCO, UNIDO, UNCTAD, and various other UN organizations and the OECD have actively addressed this issue and studied how to realize technology transfer to north-south disparities.

The first international conference on technology transfer was the Istanbul Seminar, held in October 1970 under the sponsorship of the OECD. At that conference various problems, such as importing technology through direct investment, substantiation of R&D by the recipient country, improvement of the ability to collect information and data, and the way technical assistance should be offered by advanced countries were discussed. In August 1974, the Technology Transfer Committee was inaugurated as a permanent organ of UNCTAD, and research on various measures to promote technology transfer was formally launched.[17] Thus, international organizations have played a central role in active discussion of technology transfer issues to date.

From the mid-1960s the term "technology transfer" began to be used in analysis of economic development, and a number of views have been presented on the concept of technology transfer. According to Rosenbloom, it means that technology is acquired in a context different from that of its country of origin, developed, and

---

[16] Lester B. Pearson, *Patterns of Development: Report of the Commission on International Development* (Praeger, 1969).

[17] On the theory of technology transfer studied at UNCTAD, refer to *Technology Transfer and Multi-national Enterprise: United Nations Report* (Japanese version).

utilized.[18] Spencer referred to any systematic, rational movement of technology or information necessary to accomplish a certain task as technology transfer.[19] Bradbury's definition was stricter. Specifically, he defined the process from basic research to development as "vertical technology transfer," the process of applying a technology to a different realm by new development or improvement as "horizontal technology transfer," and the process during which a technology is adopted within a certain group as "propagation." He interpreted the entire process of those transfers as the "transfer process of technical change."[20] Vertical and horizontal technology transfer is closely related to R&D, and the speed with which technology transfer is accomplished is determined according to the efficiency of R&D, depending on whether the technological innovation has a great or small potential.

Upon analysis, the problems of technology transfer broadly consist of two major aspects. One is problems with the providers of technology, and the other, problems with recipients. Recipients desire smooth transfer of technology, but if the holder of technology desires to monopolize or hide it, free movement is hampered. Magee pointed out that there is a strong tendency among multinational corporations engaged in technological development to monopolize or hide technology and that this precludes technology transfer from being realized as smoothly as might be wished.[21] As the technologies developed by multinational enterprises are complex and highly advanced in content, it is not easy for others to imitate them. Hymer also noted that multinational enterprises have a propensity to hide their technologies through internationalization of the market.[22] Another problem in addition to the problems of monopoly and secrecy is the use of technology to control the market or control affiliated enterprises. The possessor of technology not only provides advanced technology under sales contracts but occasionally attempts to strengthen its domination of the market indirectly by utilizing the financial resources and managerial competence of its

[18] R.S. Rosenbloom, *Technology in the Twentieth Century* (Oxford University Press, 1967).

[19] D.L. Spencer, *Technology Gap in Perspective* (Spartan Books, 1970).

[20] F. Bradbury (ed.), *Transfer Process in Technical Change* (Sijthoff and Noordhoff, 1978).

[21] S.P. Magee, "Information and the Multinational Corporation: An Appropriability Theory of Direct Foreign Investment." in T. Bhagwati (ed.), *The New International Economic Order* (MIT Press, 1977).

[22] S.H. Hymer, *The International Operations of National Firms: A Study of Direct Foreign Investment* (MIT Press, 1976).

licensees or to regulate the business activities of licensees by making them affiliates.

The foregoing problems are related to technological transfer effected by private enterprises, but similar problems occur in effecting technology transfer under government leadership. For an advanced country that attempts technology transfer in the form of technical cooperation, it is impossible to provide a developing country with the technology that it desires immediately or unconditionally. The technology to be provided is chosen only after strict screening, and it is probable that the technology chosen to be transferred will reflect the will of private enterprises in the providing country.

Developing countries that receive technology often complain that one of the reasons why technology transfer does not proceed smoothly is that the advanced country imposes various restrictive conditions. This specifically refers to the providing country's restrictive trade practices, restrictions on improving the technology transferred, the package method which aims at making tie-in sales of unnecessary technology, restrictions on export of products produced by the transferred technology, etc. Since these restrictive conditions limit the activities of recipient countries, it is desirable that they be alleviated.

For the countries that receive technology, the problem is how much profit can be generated using the technology transferred. Enterprises or governments of technology recipient countries try to enter new fields or use the technology in existing fields to new methods of production to improve productivity and enhance profitability. Therefore, for private enterprises the question is how much demand they can anticipate for products resulting from the transferred technology and what the profits will be. The trend of demand for any new product can be grasped only gradually. However, even if the prospect for growth in the market may appear bright, the difficulties that must be overcome to improve productivity and increase profit by applying a received technology are many. First, there is the problem of how to raise the necessary investment funds. Second, the managerial competence of entrepreneurs and the technical skill of workers may not be adequate to utilize the technology effectively. Unless these problems are resolved, smooth technological transfer is not possible.

Mansfield and Rogers proposed the idea of explaining the process of technology transfer using a logistic curve.[23] If the number of en-

---

[23] E. Mansfield, *Industrial Research and Technological Innovations* (W.W. Norton & Co., 1968). E.M. Rogers, *Diffusion of Innovation* (Free Press, 1962).

terprises introducing new technology is plotted on the vertical axis and the period that has elapsed since development of the technology on the horizontal axis, an S-shaped logistic curve can be drawn. In other words, their view is that the number of enterprises introducing technology begins to increase sharply after a certain period of time. The trend of increase and decrease in profit is relevant to the occurrence of this change.

Another view of the process of technology transfer considers the stage of transplanting technology as the basic transfer and distinguishes it from the stage of propagation of technology, which is considered the secondary transfer.[24] According to this view, it is only when successful secondary transfer has been effected that the diffusion of technology becomes possible and effective application of technology is able to evolve and become widespread within industry. Accordingly, the most important task in effective technology transfer is the smooth transition from basic to secondary transfer. In this regard, attention should be drawn to Kiyokawa's "hypothesis of the technology gap." He demarcated three phases of technology diffusion: initial introduction, promulgation, and efficiency upgrading. The pattern is more distinct when the technology gap is wider and less distinct when the gap is smaller.[25]

The actual pattern and process of technology transfer and diffusion are complex not only for developing nations but also for the providers of advanced technological knowledge. Methods used to examine the process should be operational without obscuring the general nature of the phenomena involved, which requires a conceptual and theoretical framework. It is not easy to measure precisely the degree of technology diffusion using quantitative data, and thus a conceptual framework as a theoretical basis for measurement is necessary.

There are several theories that attempt to interpret the effects of technology diffusion. Among them, Vernon's product cycle theory appears noteworthy, as it explains why a number of countries have changed the choice of technology to be acquired during the process of economic development.[26] Vernon asserted that a country that

[24] Tatsuya Kobayashi, *Technology Transfer: Historical Review—America and Japan* (Bunshindo, 1981, in Japanese).

[25] Yukihiko Kiyokawa, "Technology Advance in Japan: Its Characteristics and Implications," chapter 14 in Ryoshin Minami and Yukihiko Kiyokawa (eds.), *Industrialization and Technological Progress in Japan* (Toyokeizai Shimposha, 1987, in Japanese).

[26] Raymond Vernon, "International Investment and International Trade in the Product Cycle," *Quarterly Journal of Economics*, 1964.

achieves technological innovation subsequently wields stronger power in the international market by utilizing new technology to become the first exporter of its products. As the export volume from the country increases, however, competitors appear who have imported the new technology, and severe competition takes place in the world market. Favorable conditions for the innovator continue as long as a technology gap exists. In the second stage, the innovator gradually loses comparative advantage for the new products, and imitators emerge. When imitators can make products of similar quality at lower production cost than the innovator, the obvious technology gap ceases to exist.

It is an advantage for developing countries to utilize cheap labor. If the transfer of technology to a developing country is smooth, it can become an exporter of its products by expanding the production scale. This leads finally to decreased production by the innovator country, which no longer enjoys a comparative advantage on the world market. From the viewpoint of the country introducing a new technology, there is a cycle of production, from the period of importation to that of domestic production expansion and then to export promotion.

Concerning the relationship between the technology gap and economic development, Gerschenkron's theory of the advantage for latecomer countries is worth noting.[27] The theory states that any country starting modernization relatively later has the chance to proceed to industrialization quickly by importing and utilizing modern technology developed in more advanced countries. Developing countries do not bear the development expenses but can utilize "borrowed technology" and thus enjoy the advantage of latecomers to economic development. The larger the technology gap between developing and developed countries, the more rapid industrialization and economic growth will be due to the effect of that advantage.

These well-known theories are illuminating so far as the general interpretation of technology diffusion and promulgation is concerned. However, these are not sufficient for the present analysis. Although a potential advantage may exist for all latecomers, some succeed in economic development while others do not. Therefore an important question is why such differentials occur among countries, and what is the decisive factor in the success or failure of latecomers.

---

[27] Alexander Gerschenkron, *Economic Backwardness in Historical Perspective: A Book of Essays* (Harvard University Press, 1962).

Nakaoka pointed out that many developing countries cannot make use of modern technology transferred from advanced countries, and maintain very low rates of utilization of capital equipment.[28] On the basis of his empirical research, the utilization rates of new steel plants in Mexico in 1989 were less than 30%. The technology in those plants was imported from abroad and was the most modern in the world at that time. This illustrates the fact that a developing country does not always enjoy the latecomers' advantage in development, contrary to Gerschenkron's view. Through study of the Mexican steel industry, Nakaoka found that factors contributing to an unfavorable situation for developing countries included low worker skill levels, poor maintenance of capital equipment and machine parts, insufficient supply of raw materials and energy, lack of communications and transportation systems, underdevelopment of related industries, and cultural and political problems. Such factors are summarized as "low technical capability of the society." Nakaoka emphasized that differences between the level of technology introduced and the technical capability of the society should be particularly noticed in discussing the economic development in developing countries. The greater the difference, the more difficult technology transfer becomes, and therefore the advantage effect for latecomers does not apply.

The study group on "technology formation" under the leadership of Nakaoka conducted a detailed study on the technical capability of societies.[29] This study noted that it is useful to define the technical capability of a society from two different points of view: static and dynamic. The static aspect refers to the ability to maintain and reproduce the present level of such economic activities as production, distribution, and consumption. Technical capability in the static aspect includes the skill of workers, talent of engineers and managers, quality of machines and equipment, maintenance capability, acquisition of raw materials and parts, demand, market scale, social capital, economic and social systems, and foreign trade structure. The technical capability of a society from the dynamic viewpoint is explained by factors that can foster a continuous process of innovation of production activity by increasing types and quality of various outputs, and by decreasing their costs. These factors consist of the ability to imitate and improve on technology, the effect of learning by making, ability to lower production costs, capacity to invent and

---

[28] Tetsuro Nakaoka (ed.), *International Comparison of Technology Formation—Social Capability of Industrialization* (Chikuma Shobo, 1990, in Japanese).

[29] Nakaoka, *op. cit.*

develop new products, ability to find new markets, and so on. In short, this capability can be summarized as the capability of a society to adapt to changes in the economy, identify problems, and eventually solve them.

The present authors have proposed a concept to explain the abilities of society to contribute to economic development and called it "social capability."[30] The idea developed by Nakaoka and his colleagues is closely related to this in the sense that national capability differences are endogenous factors that create national differentials in the process of technology transfer. Their concept, however, appears too broad to use for empirical analysis in operational terms. While it is useful to discuss social aspects generally, study based on a specified framework of analysis with regard to the relationship between technology diffusion and social capability is desirable.

Social capability consists of two mutually interrelated ingredients: individual human capability and institutional-organizational capability. Individual human capability is connected with levels of school education, vocational training, and learning by doing, and thus workers' skill and managerial competence must be examined. It can be defined in developing economies as the ability of human resources to perceive, absorb, and utilize transferred modern technological knowledge so as to make economic growth possible. Institutional-organizational capability resides in the various systems and organizations in the society in relation to production activity. Such employment systems as lifetimes and seniority wages are examples.

It is not the present objective to measure social capability level directly, since precise measurement is almost impossible. The main objective is to determine the relationship between technology diffusion and social capability. It is necessary for developing economies to increase social capability to enable smooth transfer of modern technology. If, for example, the worker skill level is low due to poor school education and vocational training, it will not be possible to attain satisfactory results. Likewise, inferior institutional and organizational systems will result in inefficient learning by doing.

Framework of the Simplified Approach

An analytical framework concerning technology use for empirical study of the relationship between technology diffusion and social

---

[30] Originally, Ohkawa and Rosovsky, *op. cit.*, and recently, Ohkawa and Kohama, *op. cit.*, lecture 6.

capability is needed. Various frameworks can be suggested. The approach in this volume begins with the most general version of the aggregate production function incorporating technological progress:

$$Y = F(K, L, t). \tag{7}$$

An increment in output ΔY can result from an increment in capital stock ΔK, an increment in labor force ΔL, and the effect of technological progress which would be better called "residual." If the capital stock increases by increment ΔK, then the incremental output will equal the incremental capital multiplied by capital's marginal productivity in producing output. In the same way, an incremental labor force will generate an incremental output equal to the marginal product of labor multiplied by the additional labor force. If the market conditions of production factors are near the competitive level, the marginal products of capital and labor become nearly equal to the prices of these production factors, that is, the rental rate of capital and the wage rate. Then, the following equation for the total effect of the production factors leading to an increment in output is obtained:

$$\Delta Y = \Delta K \times r + \Delta L \times w + \Delta R \tag{8}$$

where r and w represent the rental rate of capital and the wage rate, respectively, and ΔR denotes the increment of output stemming from the effect of the other factors, that is, the residual.

Equation (8) can be divided by Y (output), and is written as

$$\Delta Y/Y = \alpha \times \Delta K/K + \beta \times \Delta L/L + \Delta R/Y$$

or

$$G(Y) = \alpha G(K) + \beta G(L) + G(R) \tag{9}$$

where α and β represent the income shares of capital and labor, respectively, that is, $\alpha = rK/Y$, $\beta = wL/Y$, and $G(Y)$ stands for denoted growth rate. Thus, the growth rate of output is explained by the contribution of the growth of capital and labor and by the effect of the residual. The residual is estimated as the difference between the growth rate of output and the contribution of the growth of capital and labor when data on these factors (Y, K, L, α, β) are obtained. This is the most common way of estimating the residual in the modern theory of economic growth as referred to in formulas (1) and (6).

The present approach is different. It is impossible to observe directly the effect of efficiency of capital from Equation (9). Capital investment is essential for economic growth, particularly in developing economies where capital stock is relatively scarce. An important issue is whether the capital invested is used efficiently or not, and thus the efficiency of capital investment should be investigated explicitly. If the effect of the residual with regard to investment, unlike that with regard to output indicated in Equation (9), could be estimated quantitatively, discussion of economic development and its planning would become more significant and useful.

These issues cannot be addressed using the conventional procedure based on the concept of sustained process in an "equilibrium state," upon which Equation (9) depends. In theory, the investment approach pertains to the process of disequilibrium, although it is recognized that forces operate toward the state of equilibrium. The definition of the residual needs the specific assumption that the incremental output (ΔY^*) is realistically conceivable for the hypothetical case of no changes in technology-organization between the intervals being compared. Thus $\Delta R = \Delta Y - \Delta Y^*$ is presented in Equation (8) above.

When Equation (8) is divided by I (investment) instead of by Y, the following equation is obtained:

$$\Delta Y/I = r\Delta K/I + w\Delta L/I + \Delta R/I. \qquad (10)$$

In this equation, $\Delta Y/I$ can be assumed equivalent to the reciprocal value of the incremental capital-output ratio (ICOR), which was originally used in the Harrod-Domar growth model and defined as the actual rate of change in capital stock (i.e., actual investment) related to the actual rate of change of national income. The ICOR indicates the relation between investment and output and is understood to show the efficiency of capital investment. Since the increment of capital stock can be assumed to be equivalent to investment by counting the replacement ratio, Equation (10) is rewritten as

$$\Delta Y/I = r + w\Delta L/I + \Delta R/I. \qquad (11)$$

This is the formula that decomposes the ICOR (actually its reciprocal) into three terms: the rate of investment return, the incremental increase in the wage payments per investment, and the incremental increase in the residual per investment.[31] It should be noted that it becomes possible to discuss the effect of capital efficiency and the residual growth simultaneously on the basis of Equation (11). It may be reasonable to assume a positive correlation between capital

[31] See Ohkawa and Kohama, *op. cit.* (*OK*), lecture 5.

efficiency and the residual, that is, when the residual is high, the ICOR becomes low. The term $w\Delta L/I$ is the incremental term of wL/K, which is defined as "factor-input ratio (FIR)," the economic indicator of technological characteristics of industries. If this term is greater (smaller) or more labor intensive (capital intensive) in the present sense, investment productivity ($\Delta Y/I$) will be higher (lower). Thus, the ICOR cannot be treated independently of the technology type involved.

Equation (11) suggests several significant points in the analysis of economic development and technology diffusion. First, although the estimation of the residual is necessary, it is actually difficult to apply the widely utilized Equation (9) of the economic growth model to many developing countries due to the scarcity of capital stock data. Thus the effect of the residual is measured in the present equations in terms of investment, instead of capital stock, data. Beyond this problem, the incremental residual per investment is more important than the residual per output from the viewpoint of economic development, as in Equation (9). This is because capital investment is considered the main factor, from an economic perspective, in achieving the goal of economic growth in developing economies.

Second, the relation between the ICOR and the residual is observed easily from a single equation. The ICOR denotes capital efficiency in a loose sense so that it is regarded as an indicator of the output effects of economic growth. It includes all output effects of the nonconventional factors of production, as distinguished from the output effects of the conventional factors of capital and labor. It is useful to compare the value of the ICOR with that of the residual in order to elucidate the relationship between the two. The value of ICOR is changeable, like that of the residual, over time. This is contrary to the conventional idea of its constancy as used in the Harrod-Domar model. According to Equation (11), if the rental rate of capital and the FIR tend to be unchanged, the ICOR has a direct correlation with the residual.

Third, since the FIR represents the technological characteristics of industries, technology type can be examined. In the study of technology diffusion, the type of technology to be adopted becomes an important issue, and the relation between the technology adopted and the residual must be analyzed. Generally speaking, developing countries have the advantage of cheap labor, and labor-intensive technology may be a suitable technology choice. Yet the effect of the residual needs to be examined at the same time, as it is the most representative indicator of efficiency in an economy and the importance of efficiency should be emphasized in order to achieve better economic performance.

Fourth, the equations above deal with changes in both output and input with regard to investment in the macroeconomy. In micro-project appraisal, the central concern of analysis pertains to the difference between benefit and cost, and the rate of expected return on capital is at issue. There have been no consistent approaches that reconcile the formulae for macroeconomic planning and micro-project appraisal. Equation (11) suggests a bridge between the two, as the output effects with regard to capital investment are noted in the analysis of the macro (and sectoral) economy. This in turn makes it possible to modify the method of project appraisal to maintain consistency with the macroeconomy.

A different aspect of the problem is how to grasp the actual process of technology diffusion, rather than an analysis of the resultant effects of technology advance. According to the conventional view, the process can and should be analyzed in terms of profit behavior so far as the economy is based on the operation of market mechanisms. This view can broadly be described as follows. There may be various reasons for entrepreneurs in each industry in a country to adopt new production methods. Among them, the pursuit of higher profits is a central motive. This is an understanding of technology adoption from the microeconomic viewpoint. From the macroeconomic viewpoint, technology diffusion is a process that reduces gaps in the profit rates between industries or firms. As long as such gaps exist, technology diffusion will occur from places of higher profit rate to those of lower profit, so that profit rates show a tendency of equalization in the economy.

If this model is followed, the central issue must be the process of equalization of the profit rate. For example, if there are two kinds of technology (traditional and modern) in an economy (or industry) and profitability is different between the two, the rate of return on capital is adopted as an indicator to measure profitability and to analyze the process of technology choice and diffusion. In this conventional approach, the rate of return on capital is expressed in the following formula:

$$\pi = (Y - wL)/K \qquad (12)$$

where π represents the rate of return on capital. This is rewritten as

$$\pi = Y/K - wL/K. \qquad (13)$$

Formula (13) means that the level of π is determined by the reciprocal value of the capital-output ratio and that of FIR. This measures the "rate of return" on capital pertaining to production activity; it cannot be precise in the accounting sense since, for example, the effects of varied duration of capital service life are not counted in comparing the rate of return. However, for the present purpose of dealing with the process of technology diffusion, this simple formula is acceptable. In the above illustration, for example, if π of the traditional sector is lower than that of the modern sector, technology in the modern sector will diffuse into the traditional sector and eventually π equalization occurs, although not precisely in the accounting sense. Yet π can be used as a simple indicator. The real issue is whether this is sufficient to clarify the real problems that emerge in the complex process of technology diffusion.[32] The additional proposal presented here is a selected partial device that is the direct observation of the components in the right-hand side of Equation (13), that is, Y/K and wL/K. In incremental terms these are $\Delta Y/\Delta K$ and $w\Delta L/\Delta K$. The latter is assumed to represent the investment activity of entrepreneurs and the type of technology incorporated whereas the former represents the output effects expected. The relationship between changes in FIR and changes in the capital-output ratio is crucial. The simple ratio of the two is $\Delta Y/w\Delta L$ (Y/Lw).

Two points may need amplification: the relation of the formula with the residual approach represented by Equation (11) and the implication of Y/Lw. With regard to the relation with Equation (11), the interconnection between the two must be viewed in the long term, which requires elaborate analysis. The focus here is concerned more with the different analytical aspects of the two approaches. The simple formula under discussion pertains specifically to the process and pattern of technology diffusion, whereas the residual approach deals with the general effects of nonconventional factors and incorporates technology advance. Equation (11) is a decomposition of the ICOR, while Equation (13) implies the relation with FIR, and can be rewritten as follows to deal with Y/Lw explicitly:

$$\pi = wL \times YwL - wL/K = wL/K(Y/wL - 1). \qquad (14)$$

It can be asserted that the reciprocal of Y/Lw is the labor income share. Ignoring the conceptual differences (production, gross market prices versus income distribution at factor cost, etc.), this assertion

[32] For details, see chapter 2, section I.

holds true. Nevertheless, this term is essentially treated as a resultant, changing variable in the framework of the independent variable FIR, instead of being given at the equilibrium state. The labor income share is not treated as indicating the elasticity of output with respect to labor.

According to the neoclassical growth model, it is understood that an equilibrium condition can be achieved through smooth substitutions of such production factors as capital and labor during a dynamic process of economic activity. Thus it concentrates on analysis of the equilibrium state, instead of disequilibrium analysis. The present authors believe that technology diffusion is a disequilibrium phenomenon, and therefore differences in methodology are inevitable.

2

Technology Diffusion: Empirical Studies

The hypothesis proposed here is deduced from factual observations at the macro level, not based on theoretical reasoning. In applying the input-output ratio (IOR) approach, the actual behavior of key terms should be investigated comprehensively at the sectoral-micro level, which is beyond the present scope. Rather than testing the hypothesis, partial data for selected illustrations are given below. Three aspects are examined through empirical studies: the Japanese experience in modern manufacturing (section I); the patterns of manufacturing technology diffusion in contemporary developing economies (section II); and small-scale firms in manufacturing and family farming in agriculture, which pertain to the traditional sector (section III).

I. Manufacturing in Japan

Data from Japan are arranged to be comparable to those in the treatment of contemporary developing economies. The performance of manufacturing enterprises is viewed from the micro aspect. A simplified approach is formulated and applied to selected contemporary developing economies in section II. The procedure is given by converting formula (3) or (3') presented in chapter 1, section I, in average incremental terms as follows. At enterprise level this is acceptable so far as the simplified procedure is concerned. Entrepreneurs aim to increase capital stock per unit of labor employed (K/Lw) while expecting output effects indicated by Y/K. To what extent Y/Lw can be increased is discussed, along with K/Lw performance. This represents the IOR formula in average terms.

Specific Interval of Postwar Growth, 1957–1966
Japan's historical experience provides rich sources for studying the process of technology diffusion. Representative examples are given

to illustrate subsector performance below. First a comprehensive treatment of the manufacturing sector is needed, although long-term historical data are difficult to obtain. The results of special manufacturing surveys conducted for the years 1957 and 1966 were thus used, since that interval included noticeable changes in technology diffusion due to "simultaneous infusion," as explained by Ohkawa and Rosovsky:

> Technological backwardness in the late 1940's and early 1950's was made up of two parts. Japan found itself behind leading world levels in a range of older and well-established techniques. During the isolation and war the quality of the base had deteriorated. These were the activities in which a prewar base had existed. . . . Japan was lagging even further behind in 'new' activities that were born in the leading countries between the late 1930's and early 1950's. Television, many synthetics and most other science-oriented technologies lacked a prewar base altogether. . . . According to calculations of the Government's Science and Technology Agency, simultaneous infusion was in full swing in 1956. About half of the imported technology was brought forth to improve prewar-originated activities. By 1966 the situation had been fundamentally altered. Prewar-based activities had caught up, and imports concentrated overwhelmingly on continuing to bring in what was new.[1]

The manufacturing surveys present data classified by size of establishment in terms of the number of workers employed. This is convenient for the present purposes, if not the best tabulation for analyzing the varied behavior of enterprises. Exact comparison with the macro data in chapter 1, section I, classified in terms of Y/L, is desirable in time series, but that is impossible. Based on the 1966 survey, the broad distribution patterns of the key terms for establishments by number of employees were presented in *OK*,[2] Tables 3.4 and 3.5. Here, detailed observation of the original data[3] is required to reveal the performance of Lw/K through increasing scale since this is a cru-

[1] Kazushi Ohkawa and Henry Rosovsky, *Japanese Economic Growth: Trend Acceleration in the Twentieth Century* (Stanford, CA: Stanford University Press, 1973).

[2] Kazushi Ohkawa and Hirohisa Kohama, *Lectures on Developing Economies: Japan's Experience and Its Relevance* (Tokyo: University of Tokyo Press, 1989).

[3] Shokichi Motai and Kazushi Ohkawa, "Small-scale Industries: A Study on Japan's 1966 Manufacturing Census," *IDCJ Working Paper Series No. 11,* December 1978.

cial term in the present approach. An important finding is that Lw/ K performance can be demarcated into three ranges through 18 subsectors of manufacturing: near constant; moderately decreasing; and distinctly decreasing (Table 2.1). The third range is distinctly demarcated from the second, and although the border between the first and the second range may not be as clear-cut, a line can be drawn between 5 and 6. Performance differs among subsectors; for example, the first range is wider in the traditional light industries and narrower in the heavy industries, with machine industries in between. Here average performance alone is considered, and the significance of industrial variance is discussed below.

First, it is seen that in 1966 the first range of near constant Lw/K existed in a considerable proportion (38.7%) of total manufacturing employees as against 33.4% in the second range and 27.9% in the third range. In 1957 (Table 2.1 B) a similar pattern appears to exist for the first and second ranges, although somehow blurred, but a reverse trend is witnessed for the third range. Without treating such different performances by scale range, the problem of technology changes cannot be grasped realistically. The performance in the first range should be relevant to the pattern of near equality between GK − GL and Gw, which was assumed in the model in chapter 1 with regard to the traditional sector of contemporary developing countries, although direct correspondence cannot be assumed as the former pertains to the scale range in cross-section and the latter to the Y/L range of change over time. In 1966[4] Japan was generally in the phase of secondary export substitution and moving toward narrowing wage differentials between unskilled and skilled workers. Attention must be paid to these different conditions. Significant relevance is seen, however, in the sense that developing economies must have a range of nearly constant Lw/K, where a "capitalwidening" pattern of traditional technology is dominant as manufacturing develops.

Second, it should be confirmed that the tendency for a decrease in Lw/K to occur during the second range was similar in both 1957 and 1966. This is relevant to the pattern of internal diffusion of modern technology according to the present hypothesis. The problem at

[4] Employment distribution by scale did change over time but not drastically. In terms of small (fewer than 50), medium (50–499), and large (500 and over): in 1909 S (45.7), M (33.6), L (20.7); in 1931 S (37.6), M (36.7), L (25.7); and in 1958 S (43.1), M (33.8), L (23.1). Kazushi Ohkawa and Mutsuo Tajima, "Small–Medium Scale Manufacturing Industry: A Comparative Study of Japan and Developing Nations," *IDCJ Working Paper Series No. A-02,* March 1976, Table 1.

Table 2.1
Patterns of Key Terms by Firm Scale, Total Manufacturing, Japan, 1957 and 1966

A: 1966

Scale (no. of workers)	Lw/K	Y/K	Y/Lw	K/L	w	π	Distribution of workers (%)
1 (1–3)	0.90	0.80	0.89	49	44	0.11	4.1
2 (4–9)	0.81	1.35	1.67	43	35	0.54	10.8
3 (10–19)	0.88	1.76	2.00	42	37	0.88	10.3
4 (20–29)	0.91	1.98	2.17	43	39	1.05	6.1
5 (30–49)	0.89	2.00	2.22	44	39	1.12	7.6
6 (50–99)	0.79	1.81	2.27	52	41	1.02	9.7
7 (100–199)	0.69	1.69	2.44	62	43	1.00	8.4
8 (200–299)	0.63	1.65	2.63	72	45	1.02	4.1
9 (300–499)	0.53	1.44	2.70	90	48	0.91	5.2
10 (500–999)	0.52	1.29	2.50	115	60	0.77	5.8
11 (≥1,000)	0.32	1.03	3.23	177	56	0.68	27.9
Average	0.51	1.29	2.50	91	46	0.77	100.0

B: 1957

Scale (no. of workers)	Lw/K	Y/K	Y/Lw	K/L	w	π
1 (1–3)	1.65	2.70	1.64	69	114	1.05
2 (4–9)	1.74	3.70	2.13	78	136	1.96
3 (10–19)	1.59	3.83	2.41	91	145	2.24
4 (20–29)	1.39	3.51	2.53	120	157	2.12
5 (30–49)	1.04	2.97	2.86	166	172	1.93
6 (50–99)	0.89	2.70	3.03	209	187	1.81
7 (100–199)	0.66	2.25	3.41	309	205	1.59
8 (200–299)	0.56	1.91	3.41	408	230	1.35
9 (300–499)	0.44	1.57	3.57	589	259	1.13
10 (500–999)	0.47	1.50	3.19	687	301	1.03
11 (≥1,000)	0.51	1.37	2.69	658	287	0.86
12 (≥10,000)	0.51	1.54	3.02	651	329	1.03
Average	0.62	1.79	2.91	289	194	1.10

For A:
Source: See footnotes 3 and 4 to the main text.
Remarks: K/L and w (per year) are in tens of thousands per worker. $\pi = Y/L - Lw/K$.
For B:
Source: Economic Research Institute, EPA, Study Series No. 6, *Shihon kozo to kigyokan kakusa* (Capital structure and enterprise differentials by firm size), Appendix Table II.
Remark: Units for K/L and w are ¥1,000 (per year).

issue concerns the third range. As mentioned previously, the pattern of Lw/K change in the third range in comparison with the second range appears quite different: in 1966 it shows a distinct decrease whereas in 1957 it presents a clear increase. Why did such a reversal occur? The answer is essentially found in what is called "simultaneous infusion." The infusion of new technology was largely completed in 1966, but in 1957 infusion was underway in the important subsectors of manufacturing. The technological requirement for leveling up K/Lw was not yet realized, while in 1966 it was nearly fulfilled. In Japan's case the time lag was due to the aftereffects of the war, but analogous time lags with increasing K/Lw can take place in the usual peacetime development path, since large-scale enterprises are most involved in the process of absorbing advanced foreign technology. In recognition of that significance the third range is distinguished conceptually from the second. This cannot explicitly be identified by observing total manufacturing; it is involved in the estimated pattern of increasing Gk − Gw in the modern sector, although it cannot be specified separately here (see section III of this chapter).

Table 2.1 lists two other terms, Y/K and Y/Lw. Corresponding to the factor input ratio, Lw/K, these two are output-input ratios in terms of capital and labor, respectively. The former is a reciprocal of the capital-output ratio and the latter a reciprocal of β. In order to complete the IOR approach, the performance of these terms and its relation to that of Lw/K must be determined. A tendency to increase is noted for Y/Lw in 1966 throughout the entire range (with a slight exception of 10). A similar pattern is seen for 1957 but with a notable exception for the third range. Y/K behaves differently: it shows a tendency to increase in the first range and a tendency to decrease through the second and third ranges, with no differences between 1957 and 1966. Thus with regard to the first range, peculiar characteristics are recognized: both Y/Lw and Y/K tend to increase despite the near constancy of Lw/K. Through the other ranges Y/K tends to decrease as Y/Lw increases (again with the exception of the third range in 1957). This is the "normal" pattern expected in principle from the simplified formula presented in incremental terms in chapter 1, section I.

In the second range, "capital-deepening" in a specified sense continues. The basic pattern is indicated by a tendency for Lw/K and Y/K to decrease accompanying a continuous tendency for Y/Lw to increase, following the pattern of the first range. Changes in Lw/K and Y/K interact to maintain the tendency of Y/Lw to increase. Can its performance be further interpreted in this particular range? The answer is affirmative. To attain technological requirements, enterprises behave competitively in response to market mechanisms. Therefore the simple formula $\pi = Y/K - Lw/K$ has often been used to measure the rate of return on capital. Estimated values of π are listed in Table 2.1 for 1957 and 1966. A similar inverse U-shaped pattern is discernible. It generally tends to increase in the first range; the high level is more or less sustained in the second range (with decreases in 1957); toward the third range it begins to decrease, although the turning point does not necessarily coincide exactly with the range demarcation. Interpreting this performance is an analytical problem. If it is simply assumed that an equality in π indicates a competitive situation, the second range appears competitive, particularly in 1966. This is an acceptable approximation that does not detract from the usefulness of the formula. In that case, however, can the π performance in the other two ranges be interpreted? Is it possible to say that a lower level of π in the third range is due to undercompetitive activity and that the tendency to increase rapidly in the first range can be explained by changes in the degree of competitiveness consistent with the peculiar characteristics pointed out earlier? These queries are examined in detail below. What is clear here is the fact that the term π cannot serve the sole basic indicator applied over the entire range of all enterprises so far as the technology assessment aspect is concerned.[5]

This stipulation pertains to the basic concept of the π formula, which is essentially based on the equilibrium concept and does not deal primarily with the process of disequilibrium that emerges in modern technology diffusion. It can deal with the disequilibrium process by identifying lower values of π than its prevailing level for certain enterprises attempting to adopt advanced technology. The conventional comment on such phenomena is that when π becomes equal to the prevailing level through further efforts by firms, the target technology can be judged as absorbed. As discussed below, such phenomena deserve attention as indispensable processes in modern technology diffusion. However, the concept of disequilibrium should be emphasized over that of equilibrium to deal with in-

---

[5] Viewed from the accounting approach other issues could be raised, including the difference in service life of capital stock, requirement of nonphysical, financial capital, etc. As discussed later, in the third range the longer life of capital stock is particularly at issue. Stock as a whole is indispensable for annual production, which characterizes the production assessment.

novative processes in technology change. At the same time, the basic forces operating toward a state of equilibrium are recognized as market mechanisms. In this respect, the significance of residual growth dealt with in chapter 1 should be remembered. The micro approach in average terms does not permit direct comparison, but it can be assumed conceptually that the term π contains not only r but also positive and negative ΔR. Possible wide variation in ΔR is indicative of a disequilibrium process. Thus the π formula does not deal with the innovative process explicitly. These comments on the π formula, however, do not necessarily imply that the conventional procedure is useless. The formula was applied in *OK* to a limited extent. With respect to the second range, the performance of π appears plausible and acceptable for 1966, although it tends to decrease faster than expected. It is simply asserted here that the π formula is not adequate to deal with the technology diffusion process over all ranges.

The crucial term proposed here in this respect is Y/Lw, which increases due to the combined result of the decreasing tendency of Y/K and a stronger decreasing tendency of Lw/K through the entire second range. To achieve the leveling up of production technology, which requires further capital deepening, it is necessary to decrease Y/K to less than Lw/K. In enterprise comparisons the growth term may not be acceptable, but for the sake of convenience the following expression can be used to represent the required condition:

$$GY - (GL + Gw) > (GY - GK) - \{(GL + Gw) - GK\}.$$

For the third range, as stated previously, the discontinuity of the changes in the magnitude of relevant terms was the basis for the demarcation. In treating the second range, it is assumed that the continuity of the differences in magnitude of the terms under consideration is an indicator of a competitive situation between different scales of enterprises. If this is valid, then the third range is characterized by the operation of factors different from those in the enterprises in the second range. Such factors may include an oligopolistic structure in market operation, various government interventions, etc. Identification of these is not the purpose here. Rather, the role and function played by enterprises in this particular range with regard to the innovative process of technology diffusion are to be identified. Japan's case in 1966 illustrates dynamic pursuit of secondary export substitution. Rapid technological progress was achieved first by the enterprises in the third range, centering on the machine industries. The conspicuous example of transportation machinery was described in *OK*, where discontinuity was easily discernible.

According to the interpretation here, the initial absorption of advanced technological knowledge of foreign origin was carried out by enterprises in the third range. Table 2.1A presents data for 1966 showing a sharp decline in Lw/K with an accompanying smaller decline in Y/K, with the effect of increasing Y/Lw as compared with the second range.[6] In characterizing the third range, however, no such generally favorable pattern is seen. Instead, possible unfavorable cases must be noted. The technological requirement for decreasing the magnitude of Lw/K is critical in absorbing foreign technological knowledge. Its realization, however, does not necessarily ensure favorable output effects to increase Y/Lw, at least given the tendency to increase indicated by the second range. Without achieving this, "absorption" cannot be realized.

The data in Table 2.1 B for 1957 can be used to illustrate "unfavorable cases" of this kind, as the original data are arranged to be comparable with those for 1966.[7] As indicated above, the performance of Y/Lw in 1957 with respect to the first and the second range is essentially the same as in 1966. The difference is distinct for the third range, however: the magnitude of Y/Lw drops from scale 9 to scale 11, with a slight increase in scale 12. The level in scale 11 is only 74.9 as against 100.0 in scale 9. Comparing the third range with the second, no decrease in Lw/K accompanies the slight decrease in Y/K to meet the technological requirement. As long as borrowed technology is not sufficiently absorbed, a smaller level of Y/Lw will be sustained for subsectors in the third range, as will be discussed further below.

In summarizing discussions testing the IOR approach in Japan's

---

[6] The discontinuity can be simply shown by the ratio of the term of scale 11 to that of scale 10 (third range) in comparison with the corresponding ratio of scale 10 to scale 6 (second range) as follows:

	Lw/K	Y/K	Y/Lw
Scale 11/scale 10	61.5	79.8	129.2
Scale 10/scale 6	65.8	71.3	110.1

[7] See also Mutsuo Tajima, "Small-Medium Scale Manufacturing Industry: Further Discussion in a Comparative Study of Japan and Developing Nations," *IDCJ Working Paper Series No. A-08*, March 1978.

case based on data from the manufacturing surveys, two points deserve particular attention. First, the formula proposed here is useful and valid at the enterprise level. Second, three ranges are distinguished in applying this formula instead of a homogenous structure. The first and second ranges confirmed the dualistic structure in the present model, but the third range, although implicitly contained in the model, emerges explicitly.

Historical Illustrations in the Primary Phase of Development

Japan's historical experience illustrates the problems and procedures in the present assessment. From the abundant research results two cases are selected: the raw silk industry and shipbuilding. These represent different patterns of interaction between the traditional and modern elements in the achievement of technological advances during the primary phase of economic development. Historical explanation in detail is beyond the present scope, and discussion focuses on observing the process of technological advance simply in terms of π and Y/Lw comparisons. Several authors[8] have made valuable contributions to measuring the rate of return on capital r (often close to π in the present terminology), and presented data for Y/Lw and relevant terms. The viewpoint is the same as in the case of overall manufacturing analysis, but the time dimension is treated as a significant factor in examining changes over time in individual industries below.

Relevant terms for the raw-silk industry are listed in Table 2.2. Indigenous technology is represented by *zakuri* (nonmechanized reeling) firms. Between 1879, the year of initiating mechanization, and 1889, some 10 years later, a major process of technology diffusion occurred. It is interesting to note the effects of mechanization by firm scale in comparison with the activity of indigenous *zakuri* firms. The scale difference broadly represents the degree of mechanization: imported machinery was used in large-scale firms (3) while so-called *kairyo* (improved) technology was generally used in medium-scale firms (2). *Kairyo* can be called "hybrid" technology; it featured partial replacement of machinery with wooden parts.

---

[8] In particular, the authors depended heavily on several papers in Ryoshin Minami and Yukihiko Kiyokawa, eds., *Industrialization and Technological Progress in Japan* (Tokyo: Toyokeizai Shimposha, 1987); and Katsuo Otsuka, *Economic Development and Technology Choice* (Tokyo: Bunshindo, 1990).

Table 2.2
Performance of Raw Silk Industry

		π(%)	Y/Lw	Y/K	K/Lw
1879					
Nagano	1) Small scale	14	1.25	0.86	1.45
(mechanized)	2) Medium scale	21	1.43	0.68	2.10
	3) Imported machinery	12	1.92	0.24	8.00
Gunma	4) *Zakuri* (indigenous)	22	1.27	1.10	1.15
1888					
Nagano	1) Small scale	19	1.22	0.97	1.26
(mechanized)	2) Medium scale	23	1.47	0.67	2.19
	3) Large scale	22	1.64	0.54	3.04
Gunma	4) *Zakuri* (indigenous)	19	1.27	0.89	1.43

Source: Otsuka, *op. cit.*, chapter 3; 1879 from Table 3.1, p. 58; 1888 from Table 3.4, p. 61.
Remarks: i) Nagano and Gunma are prefectures where silk filatures were located.
  ii) π and Y/K are reproduced from the original source. Y/Lw and K/Lw are calculated from the relevant terms.

The process of infusing modern elements into the indigenous raw silk industry is illustrated here and the use of the conventional criterion π appears to reveal broad changes over time in competitive position, shifting from traditional to intermediate and modern firms. In 1879, π is highest in *zakuri* (4) and lowest in firms with imported machinery. In 1888, it is highest in medium-scale firms (2) with that in large-scale firms close behind, while π in traditional firms is somewhat lower. In 1879 both modified machinery firms and improved *zakuri* firms developed without creating differentials in the rate of return on capital, but in 1888 the differential emerged. In 1888, however, (4) in Table 2.2 includes the effects of improving traditional methods.

The data in the table pertain also to technological aspects of the silk-reeling process, as distinguished from measuring π, rate of return on capital in the accounting approach. Therefore the figures in Table 2.2 can be used to illustrate the present procedure. In 1888, the magnitude of Y/Lw was in the order 1) < 4) < 2) < 3) resulting from operation of the simple formula (4) given in chapter 1. For example, in comparing 2) with 4), Lw/K (K/Lw reciprocal in the table) decreases by 65.3% with a smaller decrease 75.3% for the output effect Y/K. Also, in comparing 3) with 2), a 72.0% decrease of Lw/K brings forth an 80.6% decrease of Y/K. These explain, respectively, the difference in Y/Lw order mentioned above. Thus, as far as the situation in 1888 is concerned, π and Y/Lw do not appear to deviate much, although the reverse order holds [2) > 3)] for π. The deviation in 1879, however, is distinct with respect to 3), the case of firms using imported machinery. The level of π is lowest, whereas the magnitude of Y/Lw is highest, although the relation between 2) and 4) is as expected. Why is there such a deviation? A comprehensive answer is not easy to formulate. However, the deviation suggests that π cannot be the sole indicator in assessing the problem at issue. For total manufacturing in 1966 it was found that toward the third range Y/Lw tends to increase, while π tends to decrease. Technically, one major factor in the reversal of the two terms is the differing durations of service life of fixed capital stock. In the present case, an exceedingly high level of K/Lw suggests the validity of this factor.

This does not mean that general adoption of the accounting approach to replace the simplified formula is recommended, although when and where possible it is desirable to apply it for comparison of the results of the two approaches. Fortunately, Minami and Makino's detailed research[9] provides the measured performance of the rate of net return r on total capital obtained using the accounting method for the raw silk industry covering the period 1888 to 1934. For illustrative purposes 1888 figures are cited in the examples below, although the performance of this industry during subsequent years, as clarified by Minami and Makino's research, is also illuminating. Their hypothesis for dealing with technology diffusion is realization of profit maximization of modern enterprises and r is estimated to be 17.6% for mechanized as against 15.4% for the traditional *zakuri* firms (calculated from the Appendix table). This appears to endorse the previous measures using the simple π formula, and leads to the same general conclusion. However, such broad agreement cannot always be expected. In particular, the concluding remarks of Minami and Makino stated that the changes in r in this industry are affected by the quality and prices of raw material (cocoons) in addition to the major factor of upgrading reeling technology. This underlines the significance of current inputs in general, a topic covered in section III. What is suggested as important for

[9] Ryoshin Minami and Fumio Makino, "Technology Choice in [the] Raw-Silk Industry," chapter 3, in Minami and Kiyokawa, eds., *op. cit.* For the sake of convenience, the method they adopted is called "accounting" here in a broad sense, but note that it is not the same as that in the conventional project appraisal method.

Table 2.3
Performance of Shipbuilding Industry

		$\pi(\%)$	Y/Lw	Y/K	K/Lw
I) 1877–1880					
Large scale	(2)	−1.6	0.985	1.067	0.923
Medium scale	(1)	2.3	1.011	2.257	0.449
Small scale	(1)	33.1	1.163	2.355	0.494
II) 1885–1890					
Large scale	(5)	20.7	1.309	0.88	1.488
Medium scale	(6)	7.2	1.091	0.86	1.269
Small scale	(6)	30.1	1.096	3.45	0.318
III) 1902–1908					
Large scale	(1)	9.5	1.421	0.32	4.441
Medium scale–					
Small scale	(4)	6.2	1.014	4.42	0.229

Source: Otsuka, *op. cit.*; 1877–1880 from Table 4.3, p. 96, 1885–1890 from Table 4.4, p. 99, and 1902–1908 from Table 4.5, p. 100.

Remarks: i) Large-scale yards (and medium-scale in I) produce modern steel ships; small-scale yards produce indigenous wooden ships. Medium-scale yards marked in II and medium-small scale yards in III produce both steel and wooden ships.

ii) The figures in parentheses are the number of companies averaged.

iii) π (originally r) and Y/K are reproduced from the original tables; Y/Lw and K/Lw are calculated from the relevant terms.

analysis of this industry in general is that the technology and accounting aspects should be distinguished in dealing with technology diffusion.

Technology advances in shipbuilding are briefly described based on the relevant data in Table 2.3. The competitive process of indigenous versus modern shipbuilding can be assessed using the π criterion over some 25–30 years. This is distinctly shown by the cross-section comparison of π between large-scale (L) and small-scale (S) yards in Table 2.3. The performance of Y/Lw over time changed from S > L in period I, reversed to L > S in period III (although M is mixed). Through the three periods (I, II, and III), Y/Lw tends to increase in L, whereas it tends to decrease in S. The regularity of these tendencies draws attention because it operates as a distinct indicator of the technology diffusion process under review. The magnitude of K/Lw in L increases through the entire interval, and particularly sharply from II to III, whereas its magnitude in S tends to decrease without being interrupted. Thus the moderate difference between L and S in period I becomes much larger in period III.

Focusing on the tendency of Y/Lw to increase, the present formula can be applied over time as follows with regard to the accelerated process of modern technology diffusion. From period I to II, Lw/K (reciprocal K/Lw in Table 2.3) decreased by 63.4% with an accompanying 82.5% decrease in Y/K. From period II to III, Lw/K decreases further by 34.3% but that results in a 36.4% decrease in Y/K. The tendency to maintain Y/Lw increases is thus realized. However, it is again noted that the performance of π is not necessarily associated with it. The performance of middle-scale yards is impressive in the negative sense. In terms of both π and Y/Lw it is inferior to that of small-scale yards in periods I and II. This indicates that, unlike in the raw silk industry, "hybrid" technology was not developed in shipbuilding where the technological requirement represented by the level of K/Lw is extremely high. If at some point between periods II and III L had become dominant over S, the differential of K/Lw between L and S would have been much higher (roughly 20:1), in striking contrast to the case in the raw silk industry (roughly 2:1) in 1888. In short, in modern shipbuilding, the initial level of K/Lw adopted was too low but a sustained leveling-up was realized, particularly toward period III. This emphasizes the significance of the K/Lw requirement difference by industry.

The reason for proposing the term Y/Lw is explained by historical examples in two industries. Integration with the description in the previous subsection is not intended to be theoretically comprehensive beyond asserting that the actual process of technology diffusion is by nature in disequilibrium and does not permit the assumption of continuity in overall functional analysis. Market forces operate to lead the economy toward a state of equilibrium if not interrupted, but the actual process cannot be fully grasped by the conventional production function analysis.

An illustration can be given using the 1966 data for total manufacturing used previously in this section (Table 2.1A). Excluding the first range [small-scale firms 1) – 5)], a simple type of production function can be used to measure output elasticity of the factor input.[10] The usefulness of such an approach for the present purpose is limited since the constant elasticity thus measured cannot illustrate the actual performance of Lw/Y (β); for example, even within the second range, the magnitude of Y/Lw—the reciprocal shown in the table—shows considerable variance of 2.27–2.70, a much greater value of 3.23 for the third range. The conventional concept

[10] Motai and Ohkawa, *op. cit.*

of the "envelope curve" preserves the validity of applying the production function concept to individual scales of enterprises or establishments, allowing for differences in level corresponding to the possible effects of nonconventional factors. The envelope approach is not dwelt upon here,[11] although it is far superior to the production function approach in elucidating the technology variance witnessed among various scales of firms. The concept of envelope curve would be useful in the second range, where domestic forces toward equilibrium operate in a relatively effective manner. The behavioral aspect of the first range is discussed in the subsequent section. The domestic system of technology is basically formulated by the second and first ranges. The term "system" may not be appropriate, but its use emphasizes the significance of technology level and type linkages in different firm scales in total manufacturing.

Technology diffusion has an international aspect, in which the essential issue is how foreign technology is internally assimilated and absorbed into the national system of existing technologies involved in the envelope curve of individual countries. The linear, homogenous production function usually applied to both developed and developing countries is not realistic based on the interpretation with respect to the internal system.[12] Discontinuity is observed in the third range, underlining the significance of factor price differences. Although this is an important requirement, the substitution aspect is not the sole issue. Foreign technology absorption pertains also to the possibility of fulfilling the "technological requirement." The real issue is how to deal with the relation between the technological and economic requirements. A comprehensive approach is not possible here and the simplified procedure will be followed in subsequent chapters.

II. Contemporary Developing Economies: Selected Cases

In this section the simplified formula is applied to contemporary developing economies in order to elucidate the process of modern technology diffusion in manufacturing. Due to data limitations link-

---

[11] Some explanation is given in Ohkawa and Kohama, *op cit.*, chapter 4, section III.

[12] R.R. Nelson's view is followed in this respect ("International Productivity Differences," *American Economic Review,* December 1968); although the focus of discussion differs, the present authors share his essential interpretation.

Table 2.4
Indices of Output-Labor Input Ratio Y/Lw by Firm Scale Range: Manufacturing in Selected Developing Economies

		M (50–499)	M' (closest to L)	L (≥500)	Ratio L/M	Ratio L/M'
Taiwan	1971	107	111	190	179	170
Malaysia	1973	124	130	130	105	100
Pakistan	1960–1970	132	141	141	107	100
India	1954	126	130	114	90	88
Philippines	1960	140	164	123	88	75
Brazil	1960	105	108	111	106	103
Mexico	1970	103	105	102	99	97
Mexico	1975*	112	107	110	98	103
Peru	1963*	133	146	180	135	123
Peru	1973*	131	140	126	96	90
Chile	1967	104	109	81	78	74

Sources: Mutsuo Tajima, "Small-Medium Scale Manufacturing Industry," *op. cit.*, Appendix tables (arranged in indices, originally based on a manufacturing survey of each country. S (20–49) is taken as 100 for relevant terms. Cases marked * are from *Towards New Forms of Economic Cooperation between Latin America and Japan*, ECLA and IDCJ, 1980, Appendix tables. (In these cases, the base scale for indices differs but cannot be adjusted.)

Remarks: i) The figures in parentheses under M and L are numbers of employees.
ii) Indices are simple averages of the values of each subrange. Figures under M' show the level of the subrange closest to L in order to indicate the simple pattern of distribution within range M.

age of the process with that described in section I is dealt with only briefly. The actual process of technology diffusion in developing nations varies widely, especially in terms of the different time durations required to complete the entire process of technology diffusion when gaps in technology level are present.[13] Nevertheless, an attempt is made below to examine the possibility of applying the formula to selected developing economies. In Table 2.4 a summary of the relevant data for Y/Lw is given, arranged in a form generally comparable to Japan's case in order to compare the M-range (the second range) and the L-range (the third). The first range (S) cannot be included due to data limitations. As noted in the remarks to

[13] This aspect was originally developed in Yukihiko Kiyokawa, "Technology advance in Japan: Characteristics and implications," in Minami and Kiyokawa, eds., *op. cit.*, chapter 14.

Table 2.4, the range demarcation differs from that for Japan. This is acceptable in light of the actual distribution of firm scale in the countries in the table.

Conceptually it is desirable to clarify the performance of Lw/K followed by treatment of output effects Y/K and Y/Lw. Actually it is more convenient to start with Y/Lw, the combined result of Lw/K and Y/K, although the output per unit of labor is not the direct issue here. The same procedure was adopted previously in discussing the historical illustration of Japan's case.

Readily available data are used for these cases and the coverage is therefore limited and may be subject to bias. More systematic selection of recent data is desirable.[14] Nevertheless, the varied general diffusion processes can be elucidated. Three patterns of Y/Lw are witnessed in comparing scale ranges: $L > M$ (I), $M > L$ (II), and $M' \leq L$ (III) (for notations, see remarks to Table 2.4). Pattern I appears to hold for Taiwan, Malaysia, Pakistan, Brazil, and Peru (1963); pattern II for India, the Philippines, Mexico (1970 and 1975), Peru (1973), and Chile. The figures for M' suggest pattern III and may better be classified as between patterns I and II, where the variance of Y/Lw within the second range is relatively large. This is seen for Malaysia, Pakistan, Brazil, and Mexico. Although the data are illustrative, the finding of these patterns is significant. Why is there such a variance in Y/Lw performance? The answer can be deduced from Japan's case because pattern I appears analogous to the 1966 case whereas pattern II is analogous to 1957. If this view is acceptable, it can be said that pattern I indicates a successful process, while pattern II shows problems involved in modern technology diffusion. This requires further support, in particular by using a decomposition procedure to arrive at a conclusive interpretation. The relevant estimated terms are summarized in Table 2.5.

Table 2.5 suggests a wide variance of the patterns of both Lw/K

---

[14] An example is drawn from M.F. Collazos, "Production Structure in the Colombian Manufacturing Industry, 1977–1986" (report submitted to IDCJ, March 1990). The indices of Y/Lw are:

	1977	1981	1986
S (1–49)	100	100	100
M (50–199)	107	108	69
L (≥200)	119	116	66

Table 2.5
Factor Input Ratio Lw/K and Output Capital Ratio Y/K: Indices of Manufacturing by Firm Scale Range, Selected Developing Economies

	Y/K	Lw/K	K/L	w	Y/K	Lw/K	K/L	w
	Taiwan, 1971				*Malaysia, 1973*			
M	86	80	138	112	77	62	197	121
M'	68	72	161	116	62	48	244	119
L	93	49	301	150	81	62	167	107
Ratio								
L/M	108	61	218	134	105	100	85	88
L/M'	137	68	187	129	131	129	69	90
	Pakistan, 1960–1970				*India, 1954*			
M	115	87	149	126	142	113	122	138
M'	78	60	200	119	153	118	142	168
L	99	70	145	101	249	218	87	138
Ratio								
L/M	86	80	97	80	175	193	71	100
L/M'	127	117	73	85	163	185	61	82
	Philippines, 1960				*Brazil, 1960*			
M	104	74	192	142	106	101	92	93
M'	90	55	281	155	117	108	89	91
L	86	70	199	150	114	103	86	89
Ratio								
L/M	83	95	104	106	108	102	93	96
L/M'	96	127	71	97	97	95	97	98
	Mexico, 1970				*Mexico, 1975*			
M	94	91	148	134	77	69	262	180
M'	93	89	174	155	66	62	339	209
L	95	93	189	180	69	63	390	243
Ratio								
L/M	101	102	128	134	90	91	149	183
L/M'	102	104	109	116	105	102	115	116
	Peru, 1963							
M	45	24	536	182				
M'	66	45	470	210				
L	79	44	544	239				
Ratio								
L/M	176	129	101	131				
L/M'	120	98	116	114				

(*continued on p. 54*)

Table 2.5 (continued)

	Y/K	Lw/K	K/L	w	Y/K	Lw/K	K/L	w
	Peru, 1973				*Chile, 1967*			
M	118	90	157	141	119	114	130	148
M'	157	112	149	168	116	106	160	169
L	116	92	152	139	56	69	328	225
Ratio								
L/M	98	102	116	99	47	61	252	152
L/M'	74	82	102	83	48	65	205	133

Source: Same as for Table 2.4.
Remarks: i) (M') is the same as in Table 2.4 to show the figures of the closest sub-range of M to L.
ii) Capital stock K is mostly physical assets, including land in some cases. These are mostly in book values.
iii) Wages w are averages (total compensation divided by the number of employees), although the coverage, etc. are not the same. Thus the indices of K/L and w used here are relative.

and Y/K, although some regularity can be determined. In applying the formula established by examining Japan's case to the cases of contemporary developing economies, the following two features are focused on: Lw/K and Y/K, respectively, in terms of the ratio between L and M (L/M in the table) and between L and M' (L/M' in the table). The relative level of Lw/K in L does not necessarily tend to be lower than expected from the original formula. Levels below unity are identified for: Taiwan and Chile (both for L/M and L/M'); Pakistan, the Philippines, and Mexico, 1975 (for L/M); Peru, 1963 and 1973; and Brazil (for L/M'). With regard to all other cases, the ratio is over unity either for both L/M and L/M' or for one of the two. However, the ratio pertaining to Y/K often tends to be higher than expected from the original formula. Values over unity are found for: Taiwan, Malaysia, India, and Mexico, 1970, and Peru, 1963 (both for L/M and L/M'); Brazil (for L/M); and Pakistan and Mexico, 1975 (for L/M'). Values under unity are found for all other cases, the number of which is small.

The authors believe that these two features of Lw/K and Y/K patterns are the most influential factors in forming the Y/Lw patterns I and II (and III) identified above. To illustrate this with examples, Taiwan's high value of Y/Lw (pattern I) is typically produced by a very low value of Lw/K with a very high value of Y/K, while India's low value of Y/Lw (pattern II) is produced by a very high value of

Lw/K with a very high value of Y/K. Malaysia's case (pattern III) does not show much variance between the value of Lw/K and that of Y/K, while Chile's case shows low values of both Lw/K and Y/K, indicating pattern II with a very low value of Y/Lw.

These examples are suggestive, but it is desirable to examine further the performance of the term of the factor input ratio (Lw/K) and output effects (Y/K), respectively. To begin with the former, imported technology is usually more capital-intensive than domestic technology. This pertains to the level difference of K/L between M (M′) and L, according to the assumption initially introduced for firms in range L to explain how imported technology is absorbed into the domestic technology system when the magnitude of Lw/K can be smaller for L as compared to that of M (M′). However, in Table 2.5 this requirement is met not in general but only to a limited extent. The important point is in the relation of variance of wages w and capital intensity K/L seen between M (M′) and L. According to the proposition drawn from Japan's case, the degree of increase in w should be smaller than that in K/L as seen from M (M′) to L. This requirement is met in only a few cases: Taiwan, Chile, and Peru, 1973 (for both L/M and L/M′), and Pakistan (for L/M). In all others, an unexpected reverse is witnessed.

Why does such a reversal occur? In estimates of K/L and w, distortions in comparing the levels of firm scale range averages (with the qualifications in the remarks to the table) are mainly due to the actual pattern of wages: the level of w in L is comparatively higher than that of M (M′) in these cases. It is a widely known fact that wage levels are often very high in large-sized firms, in particular in public enterprises. Essentially, this is due to the limited supply of technically trained persons and skilled workers. If the required K/L for imported technology is combined with such higher wage levels, the magnitude of Lw/K cannot be smaller in L as compared to M (M′). In this sense wage levels are a crucial factor related to the level of human capability HC, as discussed in chapter 3. Although wage differential analysis from this point of view is beyond the scope of the present treatment, it can be suggested that if the level of HC is improved, the magnitude of Lw/K can move toward a lower level, contributing to formation of a normal pattern of Y/Lw.

The variance in Y/K cannot be explained simply. It is impossible to grasp it in physical terms in sector aggregate observation. It varies with the output prices of M and L due to differing subsector composition. However, a type of regularity is noted in that the variance of Y/K often tends to be positively associated with the variance of wages relative to K/L. A Y/K value ratio higher than unity, associated with a high ratio of wages relative to that of K/L, is witnessed for Malaysia, India, and Mexico, 1970 (for both L/M and L/M'); Brazil and Peru, 1963 (for L/M); and Pakistan and Mexico, 1975 (for L/M'). The factors responsible for such associations may not be uniform, but a major factor may be that higher output prices make it possible to pay higher wages insofar as the domestic market is concerned. To that extent, the possible distortion of the Y/Lw pattern is diluted, but no direct contribution is expected to the international diffusion of technology.

International diffusion of modern technology is a complex process in terms of a number of factors. Usually analysis of the imported technology diffusion process tends to show only the positive side, depending upon the *ex post* data from successful cases. The attempt here is to elucidate the negative side as well by treating the process as a difficult problem that many developing economies must overcome. The distorted pattern of Y/Lw found for data from early years in certain nations might improve during subsequent years of development. If a time dimension could be introduced, the usefulness of the present simple formula would be augmented.[15]

Annex: Further Scrutiny

Further scrutiny of patterns I, II, and III, as demarcated in the main text, is aimed at I and III so far as the relevant data are available for our purpose; for pattern II no further data can be obtained.

With respect to pattern I, Taiwan, 1971, and Peru, 1963, distinctly show the inequality L > M, but Y/K of the former appears exceptionally high and Peru shows the reverse pattern M > L in 1973. Therefore, the case of Korea is examined to search for a more "normal" pattern I. M' is used to demarcate pattern III because the inequality judgment is sensitive, and thus further scrutiny is desirable. Using the case of Malaysia, Table 2A.1 presents the relevant data.

To begin with Korea, the expected normal performance of pattern I is seen. Lw/K tends to decrease distinctly from S to L, whereas Y/K tends to decrease moderately except for S (this can be con-

---

[15] In some cases the level of K/L of L appears to be lower than that of M (M'). The reason cannot be clarified readily. It may be the result of a scale effect in terms of the number of employees instead of capital. Some distortions should therefore be allowed in view of the varied combination of capital scale and labor scale among subsector industries. In the original data for Japan's case, 1957, the responsible subsector is chemicals and petrochemicals. This may help in understanding pattern II of Y/Lw performance.

Table 2A.1
Key Terms for Total Manufacturing: Korea, 1983, and Malaysia, 1974

Korea

	S	M	M'	L	L/M	L/M'
Y/Lw	2.47	3.33	4.00	4.55		
(index)	100	135	162	184	1.37	1.14
Lw/K	0.43	0.34	0.25	0.19		
(index)	100	79	58	44	0.56	0.75
Y/K	1.06	1.13	1.02	0.87		
(index)	106	107	96	82	0.77	0.85
K/L	4.60	7.50	10.23	15.67		
(index)	100	163	222	341	2.09	1.53
w	1.95	2.42	2.59	2.93		
(index)	100	124	133	150	1.21	1.13

Malaysia

	S	M	M'	L	L/M	L/M'
Y/Lw	3.02	4.12	3.85	3.73		
(index)	100	136	127	124	0.98	0.98
Lw/K	0.35	0.23	0.20	0.20		
(index)	100	66	57	57	0.86	1.00
Y/K	1.13	0.93	0.77	0.63		
(index)	100	82	68	56	0.68	0.82
K/L	6.27	12.27	14.99	15.20		
(index)	100	196	239	242	1.24	1.01
w	2.15	2.72	2.93	3.09		
(index)	100	127	136	144	1.13	1.06

Sources: Korea, National Bureau of Statistics, Economic Planning, *Report on Industrial Census 1983*, Vol. I, 1985.

Malaysia, Department of Statistics, *Survey of Manufacturing Industries, 1974*, Vol. I, 1979.

Remarks: i) The scale classification M, M', L is the same as for Table 2.4. S is 20–49 workers. This scale is taken to equal 100 to be comparable with the figures in Tables 2.4 and 2.5.

ii) For K and w, see remarks to Table 3.8 (Korea) and Table 3.9 (Malaysia).

iii) For Malaysia, data for the top scale of ≥1,000 are available but not used in the table because it is not possible to include them in L. The values of the key terms in the top scale appear exceptionally low, and their exclusion does not necessarily distort the present results.

ceived as normal). These two result in a steady increase in Y/Lw. The ratio L/M' (1.37) appears acceptable in light of pattern I shown in Table 2.4, and L/M' is above unity (1.14). In addition, K/L shows a sharp increase, but w tends to increase at a moderate rate. As clarified in chapter 7, Korea shifted to a secondary phase in the 1970s. Its normal pattern I identified for 1983 confirms this shift through the pattern of technology diffusion. In the case of Malaysia, further scrutiny confirms its pattern III, where Y/Lw tends to decrease slowly. This is due to the slow decrease in Lw/K, while Y/K shows a normal tendency to decrease. It should be noted that ratios L/M and L/M' show no difference, with both slightly under unity, indicating no vigorous pattern of technology diffusion at the top. In 1974, Malaysia was still in the primary phase, which appears consistent with the above findings.

In developing countries, the IOR pattern realized during the secondary phase is rarely observed. The case of Korea is therefore significant. If its normal pattern were decomposed into subsectors of manufacturing, this would aid in the present analysis. Sectoral observation is a major theme in chapter 3, but a more general treatment of representative subsectors from Korean data is the aim of decomposition analysis here. Data on which decomposition analysis is based are given in Table 2A.2, where S is excluded for simplicity.

The data in Table 2A.2 do not cover all subsectors but are classified broadly for five representative groups. These essentially characterize the normal pattern composed of all major subsectors. In particular, machinery, textiles, and wood exhibit a pattern broadly analogous to that of total manufacturing. As expected, basic metals and chemicals appear to create certain distortions, although the effects are limited. Those are obvious from the figures in the table,

Table 2A.2
Decomposition of Key Terms into Five Manufacturing Subsectors, Korea, 1983

1) Basic metals

	M	M'	L	L/M	L/M'
Y/Lw	3.51	5.00	7.14	2.03	1.43
Lw/K	2.68	0.15	0.05	0.19	0.33
Y/K	0.92	0.76	0.37	0.40	0.49
K/L	13.68	23.35	72.68	5.31	3.11
w	3.12	3.62	3.57	1.14	0.99

Table 2A.2 (continued)

2) Chemicals

	M	M'	L	L/M	L/M'
Y/Lw	3.73	5.26	5.88	1.58	1.12
Lw/K	2.50	2.28	0.19	0.76	0.68
Y/K	1.13	1.44	1.15	1.02	0.80
K/L	16.35	11.64	13.86	0.85	1.17
w	3.15	3.30	2.59	0.82	0.78

3) Machinery

	M	M'	L	L/M	L/M'
Y/Lw	2.86	2.94	3.70	1.29	1.26
Lw/K	0.47	0.39	0.24	0.51	0.82
Y/K	1.34	1.14	0.89	0.66	0.78
K/L	15.50	6.55	14.12	2.57	2.16
w	2.56	2.56	3.41	1.33	1.33

4) Textiles

	M	M'	L	L/M	L/M'
Y/Lw	2.48	3.03	3.23	1.30	1.07
Lw/K	0.56	0.40	0.28	0.54	0.70
Y/K	1.28	1.21	0.90	0.70	0.74
K/L	3.82	4.94	7.26	1.90	1.47
w	1.92	1.97	2.03	1.06	1.03

5) Wood

	M	M'	L	L/M	L/M'
Y/Lw	2.48	2.63	3.03	1.22	1.15
Lw/K	0.53	0.28	0.22	0.42	0.79
Y/K	1.31	0.73	0.67	0.51	0.92
K/L	5.55	9.90	11.00	1.98	1.11
w	2.55	2.74	2.43	0.95	0.87

Source: Same as for Table 2A.1.

Remarks: i) 2) Chemicals includes petroleum, coal, rubber, and plastic products; 3) Machinery includes fabricated metal products, machinery, and equipment; 4) Textiles includes wearing apparel and leather goods; and 5) Wood includes wood products, including furniture.

ii) K, Y, and w are the same as in Table 2A.1.

in particular in the ratios L/M and L/M'. While the terms for chemicals appear exceptional, that is affected by the multiplicity of groupings in this subsector. One additional important point is the relation between machinery in the modern sector, on the one hand, and textiles and wood in the traditional sector on the other. The similar Lw/K value for the two is composed of a nearly parallel difference between K/L and w. This draws attention to the normal pattern of technology diffusion envisaged in the proposed formula.

III. Small-scale Firms in Manufacturing and Family Farms in Agriculture

In small-scale firms in manufacturing the first rang S is the most important from the viewpoint of employment, even though manufacturing realizes the pattern I technology diffusion process as illustrated by Japan. In addition, without elucidating the performance of the first range, technology diffusion is not completely explained because S pertains to what is called "traditional" technology organization that is indigenous to each nation and changes in the relationship between the traditional and modern sectors form an important dimension of the domestic process of technology assimilation.

Process of Replacement and Resistance
In conventional analysis the simple assumption is often made that through the industrialization process traditional firms tend to be replaced by modern ones due to efficiency competition. Historical observation shows that this replacement effect is seen in many industries and regarded as the normal course. However, a straightforward replacement process appears too simplistic a notion. Small-scale firms often survive and even upgrade their productivity over the long term and forces of resistance against replacement by modern elements operate to a considerable extent. Thus a more realistic approach is to observe the process in any nation as formulated by the interaction of replacing and resistance forces.

Two examples illustrate such interactions: Japan and Colombia. As mentioned previously, the percentage distribution of employees by firm scale in manufacturing did not change continuously in the historical records of Japan. For simplicity, only that of S is shown by percentage distribution.[16] In the prewar period, it decreased from

---

[16] Ohkawa and Tajima, *op. cit.*, S (1–49), M (50–999), and L (≥1,000).

45.7 (1909) to 34.0 (1919) during the primary phase of industrialization, but in the subsequent phase it changed little: from 37.6 (1931) to 36.4 (1940). In the postwar period through the upswing it showed a minor decrease toward the end of the secondary phase: 43.4 (1953), 43.1 (1958), 39.6 (1961), and 38.9 (1966). At this juncture, it is difficult to explain the reason why such varied patterns are seen, but it is important to identify the changes over time in the pattern of relative position of the first range during industrialization.

For Colombia, the pattern appears different from that for Japan (Table 2.6, where M is 50–199 workers and L is ≥200).

In contrast to the case of Japan's postwar industrialization, a drastic decrease in S manifests during 1958–1977 for Colombia, which appears similar to Japan's primary phase but much more drastic. Subsequent performance appears moderate and even reversed in the 1980s during the economic downswing. While different patterns in the percentage distribution of employed workers alone are not sufficient evidence of the varied operation of the mechanism of interaction of replacement and resistance these two cases suggest the actual process of resistance (mainly Japan) and replacement (mainly Colombia) in the postwar period.

To apply the proposed formula, a ratio procedure analogous to that for previous cases is used to determine the performance of S relative to that of M (S/M), instead of relative to that of L or to the total average to clarify the competitive situation of S. If replacement is the presumed process, a dichotomous comparison, say, S + M versus L, or S versus M + L, can be adopted. The present authors think such a procedure is not appropriate, although there are data limitations in applying the ratio procedure. Complete data for S

Table 2.6
Distribution (Percentage) of Workers by Firm Scale: Three Ranges, Total Manufacturing, Colombia

	1958	1964	1977	1981	1986
S	40.8	35.0	19.0	18.3	22.9
M	23.7	24.4	28.9	29.0	29.7
L	35.5	40.6	52.1	52.7	47.3
Total	100.0	100.0	100.0	100.0	100.0

Sources: i) 1958 and 1964 from R.R. Nelson, "International Productivity Differences," *op. cit.*, Table 4.

ii) 1977, 1981, and 1986 from M.F. Collazos, "Production Structure in the Colombian Manufacturing Industry, 1977–1986," *op. cit.*, Tables 9, 10, and 11.

are not available for international comparisons, especially for the subrange of 1–19 workers. Thus the subrange 20–49 is adopted here (additional discussion is given later with regard to the behavior of the full first range of S [1–49]). The ratio and procedure for Japan's case in 1966 is given as:

	Y/K	Lw/K	Y/Lw	K/L	w
S/M	1.26	1.43	0.88	0.56	0.85

Y/Lw is smaller than unity due to the combined result of Lw/K and Y/K. Both terms are higher than M but the ratio is lower for Y/K and higher for Lw/K, which in turn is a result of the relation between K/L and w. The level of K/L is very low but the wage level w is not as low in relation to M. Is it feasible to assume that these represent the general features of production by traditional technology? Table 2.7 summarizes the ratio figures for developing economies. The following points are noteworthy. All ratios of Y/Lw are below unity with the sole exception of Colombia, 1986, although its range of variance is fairly wide. The ratio of Lw/K, however, shows two patterns: one is above unity, similar to the case for Japan in 1966; the other is below unity for Colombia. The former implies that the ratio of wages is greater than that of K/L, and the latter, the reverse relation. No uniform pattern is witnessed with regard to the ratio of Y/K, and two general patterns can be identified: one is above unity, similar to the case for Japan in 1966, and the other below unity for Colombia. Taken together, these suggest that the relative position of small-scale firms shows regularity in terms of the present formula, but cannot be determined simply.

Interpretations may differ among observers depending upon analytical purpose. According to the basic idea here, the representative indicator is Y/Lw, and its level varies with the relation of Lw/K with Y/K. This is applied in principle to the present case dealing with small-scale firms in terms of S–M comparison, but with somewhat different implications from the previous analyses. The purpose is not to analyze the general characteristics of S itself but to determine specifically the features relevant to different patterns in the internal process of technology diffusion.

In the two representative cases of Japan and Colombia, two ratios, Y/K and Lw/K, are both above unity, with Y/K < Lw/K in Japan, but in Colombia both ratios are under unity except in 1986, although also with Y/K < Lw/K. This sharp contrast is noteworthy. It is widely true internationally that Y/K is greater for S than for M, and this is broadly confirmed by the figures in the table. The level of Lw/K is usually supposed to be higher for S than for M, as seen for Japan. Why is it below unity for Colombia? K/L > w in this case against the reverse inequality w > K/L, the widely prevailing pattern shown in the table. In general the Colombian case does not show the characteristics common to range S usually seen in international comparisons. Only in a rapid process of replacement is this conceivable.

Looking at the relevant figures in Table 2.7, two patterns can be identified: pattern A, analogous to Japan; and pattern B, analogous to Colombia. Pattern B holds for India and Peru, 1973, and Chile, in addition to Colombia, whereas all other cases appear to be in pattern A. Two alternatives are recognized among developing economies in general: resistance and replacement. However, one should be cau-

Table 2.7
Key Terms for Small-scale Firms (S) Relative to Medium-scale Firms (M):
Manufacturing, Selected Cases of Developing Economies

	Y/K	Lw/K	Y/Lw	K/L	w
Taiwan, 1971	109	116	94	75	89
Malaysia, 1968	118	163	72	49	79
Malaysia, 1973	134	160	81	57	83
Pakistan, 1964–1970	113	120	94	67	81
India, 1954	77	89	87	82	72
Philippines, 1960	101	135	75	52	70
Brazil, 1960	110	117	94	79	93
Mexico, 1970	107	110	97	68	75
Mexico, 1975	128	144	89	38	56
Peru, 1963	176	295	75	69	55
Peru, 1973	63	82	77	47	53
Chile, 1967	92	88	96	77	68
Colombia, 1960	73	92	79	79	73
Colombia, 1973	84	90	93	72	65
Colombia, 1977	90	96	94	74	71
Colombia, 1981	80	87	92	79	67
Colombia, 1986	128	88	145	75	65

Source: Same as for Table 2.5; for Colombia, same as for Table 2.6.
Remarks: i) Indices are used for S and M in simple averages of subranges when required.
ii) The indices are for the ratio S/M, taking S as 20–49 employees and M as 50–499 employees.

tious in assigning such simple groupings. It is not necessarily implied that replacement occurs exclusively in pattern B economies. Rather, the characteristics of range S can be identified by applying the present simplified formula, and this implies that the forces of replacement operate strongly, perhaps together with certain resistance forces. On the other hand, with respect to the cases in pattern A, the forces of resistance operate strongly, together with a certain amount of replacement factors. The wide range of ratios Y/K and Lw/K in pattern A cases are suggestive.

The characteristics of small-scale firms cannot be fully elucidated without analyzing the remaining subrange (1–19 workers, referred to as S* hereafter) that was excluded from the preceding discussion except for special points. The performance of S including S* must be examined to clarify its characteristics, in particular the technological aspect. It has been characterized in various ways such as 1) underemployment, which means labor earnings lower than the prevailing wages assumed to approximate labor's marginal product; 2) an increasing curve of Y/K as an intrapattern from smaller to larger scale until the turning point between S and M, in contrast to the tendency to decrease toward the largest scale in L (the so-called inverse U-shaped Y/K curve); and 3) the peculiar performance of Lw/K, which shows no regular tendency of distinct changes through range S. The first aspect will be dealt with later. The second and third features were originally derived from Japan's experience, are directly relevant to the present issue, and were touched upon previously.[17]

Data from contemporary developing economies are limited. A preliminary survey was attempted on the increasing Y/K curve,[18] and the general conclusion was that the inverse U-shaped Y/K curve cannot be regularly identified for most of the 12 cases under review. A tendency for Y/K to increase in range S is seen for a number of countries but this is not necessarily combined with a regular tendency to decrease through ranges M and L. The regularity is often interrupted by a high level of L, as in Malaysia (1973), for which carefully adjusted data by C.P. Lim[19] are available. With respect to Japan, the turning point in the Y/K curve is identified at exactly the same subrange (30–49 employees) in 1957 and 1966. Therefore, the term most relevant to the operation of resistance

[17] With regard to 2), the original idea was developed in Ohkawa and Tajima, *op. cit.*, and 1) was dealt with in detail in Motai and Ohkawa, *op. cit.*

[18] Ohkawa and Tajima, *op. cit.*, Appendix Tables 8 and 9.

[19] See the citation in Tajima, *op. cit.*, p. 25.

forces could be Y/K. For the case of Colombia, no readily accessible, detailed data for range S* are available, but according to the preliminary survey mentioned above, the performance of Y/K in 1966 is as follows, taking the total average of manufacturing as = 100 (number of workers in parentheses): 81.6 (1–4); 102.0 (5–19); 100.2 (20–49); 137.4 (50–99); and 94.6 (≥100). The tendency for increase in Y/K is thus over a narrow range of very small scale (1–19), suggesting a different pattern from Japan's case. Resistance forces therefore work in a very limited range.

With respect to 3), the pattern of Lw/K, differences are noted between 1957 and 1966 in Japan. In 1966 its magnitude appears to differ only slightly while in 1957 it varies more (Table 2.1). If the smallest scale were treated as atypical in 1957, the tendency to decrease would appear to be similar to that for ranges M and L. However, the present authors contend that for range S (1–49), the variance of Lw/K shows no regular tendency taking 1957 and 1966 together. This is a reconfirmation of the previous findings reported in Table 2.1. The available data for developing economies are scanty since figures for range S cannot be broken down for its subranges in most cases. When a breakdown is available, the magnitude of K is not estimated or calculated appropriately. Of the two cases (Malaysia, 1968, and Brazil, 1960) contained in the Appendix to Ohkawa and Tajima's paper, the Malaysian Lw/K is as follows in indices, taking the total average of manufacturing as = 100 and with the number of employees in parentheses: 1.73 (0–9); 1.87 (10–19); 1.93 (20–29); 1.63 (30–49); 0.89 (50–99); and 0.70 (100–199).

The difference of Lw/K within the first five scales (0–49) can be minor, showing no trend to increase or decrease, although from (0–9) to (20–29) it tends to increase. This is largely analogous to Japan's case discussed above. In sum, it can be assumed that minor changes in Lw/K in no definite direction form the most noticeable intrapattern of range S. Thus, the authors contend that a tendency for Y/K to increase takes place, perhaps associated with the peculiar performance of Lw/K. This implies that variations in capital productivity cannot be conceived in association with variations in Lw/K, resulting in a pattern different from the one identified earlier in discussing M–L comparisons. This proposition may be speculative because empirical confirmation is not sufficient. The authors believe, however, that it is important in interpreting the factors responsible for forming resistance forces in range S.

No data are available to investigate 1) underemployment. Most of the underemployed engage in household production, and the data

presented in chapter 1, section I, are derived by imputation procedures applying the prevailing wage rates. In dealing with the first
range of manufacturing firms, household production cannot be
assumed to be profit-maximizing but it affects the level of mixed income obtained. The present analysis reveals that representative
underemployment behavior can essentially be expressed in terms of
$Y/L = w$ at the margin.[20] Equilibrium between income per working
household members and prevailing wages can be assumed on the
labor market. The term π cannot be the equilibrium criterion as
stated above but the term Y/Lw can reasonably be applied to the
second and third ranges. The accounting procedure of imputation
assumes this type of conceptual equilibrium with regard to the behavior of mixed-income workers, implying that from the viewpoint
of production their marginal productivity is lower than that of ordinary workers. This does not necessarily cover a wide portion of the
first range of manufacturing but it is more significant in family farming dealt with later.

Significance of Current Inputs
In applying the IOR approach the role played by current inputs, as
distinguished from factor inputs, is important in dealing with the
characteristics of the first range. Current inputs are composed of intermediate goods such as materials and fuel and are deducted from
products to derive added value in conventional growth accounting.
Current inputs are important in analyzing agricultural production
due to the significant role played by the so-called modern inputs
such as fertilizers and pesticides. They are less significant in manufacturing due to the dominance of mechanical and engineering processes. However, when discussing range S the situation differs.
Table 2.8 shows the quantitative significance, where Q stands for
the proceeds (products sold), the only direct data available for the
present purpose. It is assumed that the current inputs are largely
approximated by $Q - Y$. Its ratio to K is shown in the table; for
comparison the figures cover the full range. The tendency for Y/K
to increase for the range 1) to 3) matches the tendency for Q/K, and
the magnitude of $(Q - Y)/K$ tends to increase distinctly in this
range. Although it appears obvious that greater amounts of current
inputs explain the specific pattern of Y/K, the validity of this proposition should be examined by comparison with the performance of
ranges M and L. As is shown in Table 2.8, the associated movement

[20] For details, see Motai and Ohkawa, *op. cit.*

Table 2.8
Current Inputs Focusing on Small-scale Firms in Manufacturing, Japan, 1957

Scale of firms (number of employees)	Y/K	Q/K	(Q − Y)/K
1) 1–9	2.70	7.81	5.11
2) 10–29	3.70	11.63	7.93
3) 30–49	3.83	12.50	8.67
4) 50–99	3.51	11.63	8.12
5) 100–199	2.97	9.35	6.38
6) 200–299	2.70	8.20	6.40
7) 300–499	2.25	8.76	5.50
8) 500–999	1.91	5.71	6.50
9) 1,000–1,999	1.57	4.90	3.31
10) 2,000–4,999	1.50	4.08	2.58
11) 5,000–9,999	1.39	5.88	4.51
12) ⩾10,000	1.38	5.63	4.25
Total average	1.79	5.40	3.61

Source: Economic Research Institute, EPA, *Shihon kozo to kigyokan kakusa* (Capital structure and enterprise differentials by firm size), *op. cit.*, Appendix Table A II, 1960.

of Q/K and Y/K is apparent to a certain extent in the tendency to decrease for range M. However, the magnitude of (Q − Y)/K is considerably smaller and it does not reveal a regular tendency. With regard to range L, its magnitude is much smaller and shows no associated movement between Y/K and Q/K. In light of these findings the relation of Y/K with Q/K is specific to range S.[21]

The significance of this phenomenon can be interpreted from two mutually interrelated aspects: one pertains to technology and the

[21] It may be asked whether this phenomenon varies due to differences in subsector composition in manufacturing. This deserves attention in view of the varied technological property of subsectors. Broadly speaking, it tends to manifest in a stronger shape for traditional subsectors and in a weaker shape for modern subsectors. The simple indicator is the average magnitude of (Q − Y)/K of each subsector. Its variance is wide: it is large for such industries as clothing, wood, furniture, leather, and metals, and small for such industries as chemicals, petrochemicals, pulp-paper, and textiles. All others are in between. It cannot be demarcated simply by a dichotomy such as light versus heavy industry. It is broadly recognized that corresponding to these differences in the average indicator, the specific pattern of range S is witnessed for the entire coverage.

other to the relevant organization. Technological efficiency is essentially determined by the rate of utilization of capital stock—use of more current inputs per unit of capital, often by enlarging the scale of firms within this range. Not only the amount but also quality improvement, as reflected in higher payments, may contribute to increasing Y/K. This may not be a phenomenon exclusive to range S. It may operate to a certain extent also for range M, but is dominant in ranges S. Why is enlargement of firm scale within this range associated with increasing Y/K? No direct evidence is available to answer this question, but larger scale may imply a higher level of capability, both technical and financial.

This is relevant to the aspect of organization. As symbolically represented by the well-known subcontracting systems, firms in range S are connected with the firms in ranges L and M through organizational arrangements in the generally prevailing market mechanism. To the extent that such arrangements operate, the rate of capital utilization will be augmented technically and financially. In 1957, the earlier year on which present data depend, the subcontracting system was not as intensively developed as compared with the 1970s and 1980s in Japan. The effects of such organizational arrangements cannot be excluded when discussing factors responsible for supporting resistance forces in smaller-sized firms, however.

Although data are not readily available for developing economies, the forces of resistance against replacement must operate in a similar way with varied degree and scope. To that extent, the technology diffusion process may have an effect on augmenting the current inputs, in amount and quality, in range S.[22] The difference between patterns A and B that is shown in Table 2.7 is not solely caused by varied operation of current inputs, but this aspect deserves more attention than usually given in the conventional discussion of the technology diffusion process. In general, the spillover effects of modern technology on S and M as well on the internal process are more apparent in the channel supplying improved current inputs, although the operation of this function appears to vary among nations. Upgrading current inputs is thus an important theme in shifting each nation's system of technology to a higher level.

A discussion of agriculture is relevant here because it composes the

---

[22] The effects on range M are discussed in Ohkawa and Kohama, *op. cit.*, pp. 146–151, dealing with Japan's recent phenomena. This pertains to the later process of internal diffusion, which emerges following pattern I dealt with earlier in discussion of the 1966 data, and is beyond the scope of the present treatment.

major part of the traditional sector in most developing economies. In modern agriculture the requirement for increased K/Lw is the same as in industry. However, as touched upon earlier, the role played by current inputs is significant in traditional agriculture. Agricultural technology is basically different from that in industry, as discussed in detail in chapter 5. Despite this difference, common characteristics of current inputs in small-scale firms in manufacturing and in agriculture are identified and this finding plays an important part in testing the present model. With respect to the performance of replacement versus resistance in agriculture, the interpretation is as follows. The international diffusion of technology is basically carried out based on high-yielding varieties (HYVs). Due to the scale-neutral property of agriculture, production scale organization has largely remained unchanged in the process of technology diffusion. The resistance pattern thus dominates performance in most developing economies, particularly in the case of family farming.

The significance of the contribution of current inputs should be quantitatively clarified, although internationally comparable data are limited. Table 2.9 may be useful in spite of being limited to East Asian agriculture. In panel A, the share of current input ($\alpha 1$) is of considerable magnitude, being much greater than that of fixed capital input ($\alpha 2$). In this regard the case of Taiwan is most impressive. Over time $\alpha 1$ generally tends to increase, with a slight exception for postwar Korea. This presents a noticeable pattern in comparison with that of $\alpha 2$. In the case of fixed capital input no distinct tendency is seen. It appears to increase in Japan from period 2 to 4 and in Taiwan from period 1 to 3. However, in Korea it tends to decrease. These phenomena take place with a moderate pace of share changes over time with regard to the two basic inputs, labor and land. Panel B attempts to show the dynamic significance of these changes over time. As is illustrated by the growth rate of output (GY), a comparison of the three contemporary developing economies with the historical records of Japan identifies a "telescoping effect" in agricultural development. Japan's prewar GY records have never been repeated in postwar developing economies, where GY is always greater than in Japan's case. The figures of $\alpha 1GK1$ in the table give supporting evidence that increased current inputs contribute to augmenting telescoping effects. $\alpha 1GK1$ is greater than $\alpha 2GK2$ in all cases including Japan, which is a notable characteristic of agricultural development. But beyond that the inequality appears to widen in postwar East Asian development. This is obvious in the case of Taiwan, but somehow blurred in the case of Korea. For the Philip-

Table 2.9
Shares and Weighted Growth Rates of Current Inputs in Comparison
with Those of Other Inputs in East Asian Agriculture

(A) Shares of Inputs (%)

	Current Inputs	Fixed Capital Inputs	Labor	Land	Total
Japan					
1. 1880–1900	8.0	10.5	51.3	30.2	100.0
2. 1900–1920	9.5	9.9	50.4	30.2	100.0
3. 1920–1935	11.9	10.8	51.7	25.6	100.0
4. 1955–1965	15.2	11.8	50.9	23.1	100.0
Taiwan					
1. 1913–1923	8.6	3.9	52.4	35.1	100.0
2. 1923–1937	17.2	6.0	41.5	35.3	100.0
3. 1951–1960	19.6	7.4	43.2	29.3	100.0
4. 1960–1970	23.1	6.7	39.5	30.7	100.0
Korea, Rep. of					
1. 1920–1930	4.7	12.0	35.2	48.1	100.0
2. 1930–1939	12.8	11.6	31.6	44.0	100.0
3. 1953–1969	12.0	9.5	34.2	44.3	100.0
Philippines					
1. 1950–1959	4.0	4.0	53.0	39.0	100.0
2. 1959–1967					

(B) Weighted Growth Rates of Inputs (Average annual rates)

	Current Inputs (1GK1)	Fixed Capital Inputs (2GK2)	Land (GB)	Growth Rates of Output (GY)
Japan				
1. 1880–1900	0.14	0.10	0.15	1.6
2. 1900–1920	0.45	0.13	0.21	2.0
3. 1920–1935	0.38	0.11	0.03	0.9
4. 1955–1965	1.29	0.92	0.12	3.6
Taiwan				
1. 1913–1923	1.08	0.30	0.34	2.8
2. 1923–1937	1.04	0.30	0.28	4.1
3. 1951–1960	1.67	0.18	0.00	4.7
4. 1960–1970	2.40	0.32	0.12	4.2

Table 2.9 (continued)

(B) Weighted Growth Rates of Inputs (Average annual rates)

	Current Inputs (1GK1)	Fixed Capital Inputs (2GK2)	Land (GB)	Growth Rates of Output (GY)
Korea, Rep. of				
1. 1920–1930	0.52	0.13	0.03	0.5
2. 1930–1939	1.51	0.24	0.06	2.9
3. 1953–1969	0.79	0.17	0.46	4.3
Philippines				
1. 1950–1959	0.41	0.28	1.34	4.1
2. 1959–1967	0.36	0.26	0.74	3.8

Source: Kazushi Ohkawa, "Total Factor Productivity Measurement of Agriculture: International Comparison of East Asian Countries." In Yujiro Hayami, Vernon W. Ruttan, and H.M. Southworth, eds., *Agricultural Growth in Japan, Taiwan, Korea and the Philippines* (Honolulu: East-West Center, University of Hawaii, 1979).

pines the magnitude of γGB is still high and the situation differs, yet $\alpha 1GK1$ is definitely greater than $\alpha 2GK2$.

Having elucidated the significance of current inputs, the possibility of applying the simplified formula for technology diffusion to agriculture should be examined. The pattern of input-output relation is derived from the simple relation $Y/Lw = (Lw/K) \cdot (K/Y)$, although this is not conventional in treating agriculture. Table 2.10 is arranged to correspond to the case of manufacturing, although the scale in this case is in terms of the size of farming operation. The pattern shown through increasing farm scale is a distinct tendency to raise the level of Y/Lw (except in 1). This is a result of a distinct tendency for Y/K to increase with a very moderate change in Lw/K (except for a decrease in scales 1–2). The regularity of the pattern can thus be identified for the major range of all farms. This is broadly analogous to the previous case of small-scale manufacturing. The capital-widening phenomenon in the sense used here essentially prevails in agriculture: the leveling up of Y/Lw does not depend on a decline in Lw/K. This follows the characterization of the significance of current inputs identified earlier. Additional explanation is given below.

As is shown in Table 2.10, output per land Y/B has a tendency to rise as farm scale decreases. This has conventionally been explained by farmers' self-evaluation behavior in terms of land versus labor

Table 2.10
Patterns of Key Terms by Farm Scale: Agriculture, Japan, 1964

				Per land unit (0.1 ha.)	
Scale (ha.)	Y/Lw	Y/K	Lw/K	Y/B (hundred yen)	K/B
1. ≤0.5	3.78	1.21	0.32	510	420
2. 0.5–1.0	2.13	0.56	0.26	479	854
3. 1.0–1.5	2.60	0.60	0.23	421	702
4. 1.5–2.0	2.96	0.64	0.22	378	591
5. 2.0–2.5	3.36	0.75	0.22	344	460
6. 2.5–3.0	3.82	0.82	0.21	343	419
7. ≥3.0	4.70	0.95	0.20	345	345
Average	2.73	0.64	0.23	402	639

Source: Kazushi Ohkawa, "Agricultural Development in Sectoral Interdependence: Views Derived from Japan's Experience." In *Proceedings of the Conference on Agricultural Development in China, Japan and Korea*, December 1980 (Taipei: Institute of Economics, Academia Sinica), Table 4.

Remarks: i) Originally based on the *Farm Households Economy Survey*, Vol. 8, Ministry of Agriculture and Forestry, Japan, 1966, excluding part-time farmers.

ii) Y is net capital depreciation.

iii) Data on wages (w) were originally from the same source but used in Kazushi Ohkawa, "Kajo Shugyo: Sairon (Over-occupied: revisited)," chapter 9 in Kazushi Ohkawa and Ryoshin Minami, eds., *Kindai Nihon no Keizai Hatten* (Economic development of modern Japan) (Tokyo: Toyokeizai Shimposha, 1975), Table 9.3.

(higher for the former versus lower for the latter) compared to the factor evaluation by the market. Present findings do not contradict this common interpretation, as illustrated by the tendency for capital stock per land K/B to rise as farm scale decreases (except for the smallest). The constancy of Y/B for a range of scale 5–7 along with the tendency for K/B to decline composes a substantial part of the rise in Y/K. This is interpreted as a recent phenomenon showing heightened response to market evaluation.

As the result of postwar land reform, Japanese agriculture became essentially composed of family farms, and the effects of landlordism were eliminated. To what extent is this pattern indicative of the actual situation of agriculture in developing economies? One is reluctant to answer in the affirmative. The single-crop plantation system, wider distribution of farming scale, and varied agrarian land-ownership structures limit the possibility of sweeping application. Family farms make up the prevalent pattern, however, and to that extent capital widening in agriculture can be visualized in developing nations.[23]

The rapid productivity growth in agriculture for 1960–1980 was the result of rapid advances in biochemical (BC) technology in developing nations. This type of technology is characterized by its scale-neutral as against the scale-dependent property of technology of M (mechanical) type. If the pattern of family farms illustrated above by Japan's case can be widely applied to contemporary developing economies, it should be said that it is also scale-neutral in terms of labor-capital combinations pointed out earlier for small-scale manufacturing. It is well known that the development of BC technology requires capital formation for infrastructure improvement. However, compared with the rate of increase in Lw the rate of increase in K tends not to be greater in agriculture in the major development phases, with the exception of modern farming.

Despite the analogous pattern of the technology diffusion process in agriculture and manufacturing, agriculture has another aspect that differs distinctly from manufacturing. This is a problem that has been called the technological requirement for absorbing advanced foreign knowledge. Technology of the BC type, particularly HYVs, is introduced from abroad, which pertains to the international diffusion process. However, in this case the specific quantitative relationship between Lw/K and Y/K identified previously for modern manufacturing is not required to achieve technology absorption. What is essential in agriculture is the HYV, the carrier of advanced technology, which provides the possibility of augmenting modern current inputs such as chemical fertilizers. In most cases in agriculture, the HYV diffusion process is carried out by the public sector, and its combined use with the increase in current inputs is carried out by private farms. As is suggested by the figures shown in Table 2.10, the role played by Lw/K is much less significant. In most cases in manufacturing, the diffusion process is carried out by top-level private firms, as discussed in chapter 2. Thus in general sectoral comparisons a decisive dissimilarity in the process of technology diffusion in manufacturing and agriculture appears. The present authors hold that the analogous aspect of the two sectors in terms of

---

[23] Although limited to Asia, a detailed survey was carried out on this subject by Masakatsu Akino, Kazushi Ohkawa, and Saburo Yamada, "Family Farms in Rural Development: A Comparative Study of Japan and Developing Countries in Asia," *IDCJ Working Paper Series No. A-04,* March 1977.

small-scale production activities is nevertheless significant and that ignoring this aspect may lead to conclusions far from the reality.

The analogous aspect identified through the internal effects of domestic technology diffusion in family farming in agriculture raises the issue of spillover effects in a broad sense. The significant role played by current input improvement is dependent on domestic technological advances in manufacturing, since cheaper prices and/or better quality of fertilizers, insecticides, etc., are the products of technological advances in manufacturing, apart from the issue raised by increased imports of such products. Although beyond the present scope of analysis, more broad-based investigation of the interrelation between agriculture and industry is needed.

3

Output-Labor Input Ratio in the Industrial Sector: Domestic and International Aspects

Following the overview and analysis given in chapters 1 and 2, this chapter aims at further, in-depth scrutiny of the technology diffusion process and pattern. The conventional neoclassical framework has often been criticized for its treatment of technology diffusion because it ignores the important problems emanating from the domestic (internal) process. This is especially true when a common production function is assumed internationally. Our original hypothesis on developing economies assigned a dominant role to technological knowledge absorbed from predecessors. Therefore the international (external) aspect of technology diffusion is of primary importance, although its internal processes and patterns are also important since these are not common and uniform but vary considerably among developing economies. The real challenge for analysis is to clarify the relationship between the internal and external dimensions. By applying essentially the same simplified IOR formula in this chapter, focusing on the output-labor input ratio Y/Lw, further efforts are made here to meet this challenge. The term Y/Lw can be used as a general representative indicator for analyzing the technological diffusion process in detail. Ideally analysis should begin by observing Lw/K and Y/K performance, but this is often difficult due to data limitations. When and where possible, these terms are dealt with below.

The domestic aspect from the historical approach is presented in section I and the international aspect in section II. Finally, the concluding remarks attempt to examine the relationship between the two. The first section covers two major topics. One is the specific character of technology advance in the traditional sector in the dualistic structure of the present model. In applying the simplified formula to this sector an important modification is required with respect to the operation of the term K/Lw. In chapter 2, section III, this topic was dealt with by revealing the resistance and replacement patterns. The second topic concerns sectorwise performance of manufacturing, as representating the modern sector, based upon Japan's experience. First, the relative stability of Y/Lw in the sector is disaggregated into subsectoral components, with distinction between innovative and noninnovative industry made in the time dimension for illustration. It is suggested that international technology diffusion has important impacts on sectoral patterns of development in the domestic economy. Second, the machinery (or engineering) industry in particular will be taken up in comparison with the other major sectors of light and heavy industry in an attempt to elucidate in more detail the performance of this specific industry. Efforts are made to clarify the relationship between technology introduced externally and traditional technology using a three-range approach. This is closely related to the analysis of producer durables in chapter 4. The pattern of "scale effects" is discussed.

In section II, after domestic manufacturing analysis for some developing economies links the discussion with section I, the possibility of borrowing foreign technological knowledge in relation to the domestic potential of each nation is discussed empirically. This is an extremely difficult task. Wage evaluations are necessary, not in terms of market prices in developing economies but in terms of the potential of the worker activities to be realized in the process of technology diffusion. The internal use of such potential is important in successful technology absorption from economically advanced nations. Using purchasing power parity (ppp) data, Y/Lw and relevant terms are decomposed into "quantitative" and price-wage elements to clarify the implications of the proposed formula for analyzing the technology diffusion process. "Equivalent" wages representing worker potential are indispensable estimates in the analysis, and differentials among developing nations are particularly important. In the Annex supplementary treatment by subgroup is presented.

I. Domestic Overview: Japan

Hitherto enterprise behavior at the micro level has been assessed by applying the simplified IOR formula in terms of firm scale and sector. Efforts were made in previous chapters to elucidate the mechanism of technology diffusion process using Y/Lw by observing K/Lw and Y/K. This section covers different aspects that pertain directly to the patterns of Y/Lw. First, its changes over time are discussed in terms of Japan's experience, and then its disaggregation with the three-range structure is attempted to prove that the level of Y/Lw is a useful indicator of innovative process and hence competitive power.

Changes Over Time

To illustrate the problem at issue, it should be noted that Y/Lw in current prices does not necessarily tend to increase over time but often decreases. For example, in the familiar comparison between 1957 and 1966 in Japan, its level increases from 4.87 to 5.18 (petroleum), from 3.58 to 3.75 (chemicals), and from 1.81 to 2.73 (transportation machinery), whereas in the other 16 subsectors it declines and the aggregate level for total manufacturing shows a decrease from 2.91 to 2.55.[1] This does not necessarily mean that the procedure is not valid. The reason is given in the following subsector approach for analytical convenience: subsector groupings I, II, and III, breaking down III into A (heavy and chemicals) and B (machinery). The groupings III A and III B correspond, respectively, to heavy industry and machine industry, but light industry is divided between groups I and II. I excludes traditional subsectors such as leather, metal, wood and wood products, furniture, and apparel from light industry. Thus II is composed of textiles and food, with such subsectors as ceramics, printing, and rubber included. Table 3.1 presents the changes between 1957 and 1966. Aggregation is done using the employment share (v) weight Lvi/Lv (where i stands for each subsector group).

The table shows that the level of Y/Lw by group tends to decline, although not without exception: in group III B (machinery) the level increases. The percentage proportion of Lv distribution changes considerably; in groups I and III B it increases whereas in groups II and IIIA it decreases. This indicates that structural change in employment during this interval is noticeable in this specific sense. As a combined result the previous two changes, the weighted sum of Y/Lw decreases in groups, I, II, and III A, but increases distinctly in group III B. Thus aggregate decline is slight despite the considerable decrease in many subsectors.

The situation in this postwar interval in Japan must again be noted. The findings in Table 3.1, however, suggest the general pat-

[1] Kazushi Ohkawa and Hirohisa Kohama, *Lectures on Developing Economies: Japan's Experience and Its Relevance* (Tokyo: University of Tokyo Press, 1989) (*OK*), p. 98, Table 3.2a, where Y/Lw is given as the reciprocal Lw/Y.

Table 3.1
Changes in Output-Labor Input Ratio Y/Lw in Manufacturing, 1957–1966, Japan

Subsector		I	II	IIIA	IIIB	Total
Y/Lw	1957	2.67	2.32	3.47	2.31	2.91
	1966	2.35	2.06	3.17	2.36	2.55
Lvi/Lv	1957	27.7	17.6	31.6	23.1	100.0
(%)	1966	29.1	13.7	28.7	28.5	100.0
Y/Lw	1957	0.74	0.41	1.10	0.53	2.78
(weighted sum)	1966	0.68	0.28	0.91	0.67	2.54

Source: Specific estimates of L for 1957 are from Mutsuo Tajima, "Small-Medium Scale Manufacturing Industry: Further Discussion in a Comparative Study of Japan and Developing Nations," *IDCJ Working Paper Series No. A-08*, March 1978, and for 1966 from Shokichi Motai and Kazushi Ohkawa, "Small-scale Industries: A Study on Japan's 1966 Manufacturing Census," *IDCJ Working Paper Series No. 11*, December 1978. Y/L and w for 1957 and 1966 are the same as in Table 2.1.
Remarks: Some discrepancy between the original total and the sum of weighted values stems from treating "others."

tern and nature of the phenomena faced in analyzing the actual technology diffusion process in developing economies. Important aspects include the following. The aggregate level of Y/Lw may not decrease but increase depending upon the combined effects of 1) and 2) above. For example, in the phase of primary export substitution, an increase can result because group II, textiles, is a leading subsector, of which the level of Y/Lw is increasing positively with its large employment weight. Although data are not directly available, the shifts in employment structure discussed previously apply here. The employment proportion (%) of group II (textiles) is 60.8 in 1909 and 54.8 in 1919. In view of its scale shift from the pattern S > M > L to the reverse S < M < L during this interval, the level of Y/Lw of this group must have increased. The role played by textiles was doubtless analogous to the performance of machinery during the postwar interval under review. These can be called "leading industries" in this specific sense. In general a rise in Y/Lw is due to that in the leading industry and if that is influential, its aggregate value can increase. This was the actual case in the phase of primary export substitution in Japan. This raises the question of the different patterns of changes in the levels of Y/Lw seen in innovative and noninnovative industries.

In *OK*, the term Y/Lw was examined together with other relevant terms for selected representative subsectors for the interval 1971–1981. The data are comparable with those for 1957–1966, and the performance of Y/Lw over 20 years is shown in Table 3.2. The interval 1971–1981 belongs to the postdevelopment phase of the Japanese economy, and yet in a comparative sense is relevant to the present discussion. The performance over the entire interval exhibits upswings and downturns, although the order of magnitude among subsectors remains largely constant. No regularity appears discernible over time. However, a closer look identifies the following two points.

First, in the interval 1971–1981 the degree of change in Y/Lw is smaller compared with that in the interval 1957–1966. This corresponds to a shift from a more innovative path in the former to a less innovative path in the latter. It is suggested that as economies develop the magnitude of Y/Lw appears to stabilize. In order to observe longer-term change, two averages, one for the former and the other for the latter interval, are added to Table 3.2. In this comparison, a distinct decline is witnessed for textiles and food, whereas for machinery, steel, and chemicals Y/Lw increases, with the exception of electric machinery (an abnormal high in 1957 may be the cause). The authors contend that in less innovative subsectors, represented by textiles and food, Y/Lw decreases, while in those with more innovative activities it tends to increase. If the proposal of relative stability mentioned above is acceptable for aggregate Y/Lw, it can now be explained as a combined result of two counteracting forces operating positively and negatively. In view of the possible sustained increase in aggregate Y/Lw in developing economies, its stable performance may characterize the end of the long-term development path.[2]

The final illustration is of the long-term development path itself. Due to the availability of data, Japan's historical records are again used as an example of successful foreign technology absorption. A long-term trend in Y/Lw can conveniently be treated in growth terms (the average annual rate of growth) as $GY - (GL + Gw)$. In Table 3.3 the relevant data are summarized in real terms for the pri-

---

[2] A slight decrease in aggregate Y/Lw measured earlier for 1957–1966 might be affected by certain atypical factors operating in postwar Japan, because this interval was the final phase of economic development.

Table 3.2
Output-Labor Input Ratio Y/Lw of Selected Representative Subsectors of Manufacturing, 1957–1981, Japan

| | | Machinery | | | | | | |
	General	Electric	Transportation	Precision	Steel	Chemicals	Textiles	Food
1957	2.42	2.98	1.82	2.01	2.70	3.58	2.72	3.79
1966	2.22	2.69	2.73	1.98	2.00	3.75	2.27	2.98
1971	2.56	2.70	2.63	2.00	3.03	4.76	2.08	2.94
1981	2.58	2.63	2.44	2.06	2.86	4.12	2.08	3.12
Average								
1957–1966	2.32	2.84	2.28	2.00	2.35	3.67	2.50	3.39
1971–1981	2.57	2.67	2.54	2.03	2.95	4.44	2.08	3.03

Source: OK, pp. 124–135.

Table 3.3
Long-term Changes in Output-Labor Input Ratio Y/Lw, 1904–1976, Industrial Sector, Japan (average annual growth rate, %)

	GY	GL	Gw	GY − (GL + Gw)
I 1904–1919	7.3	2.4	3.0	1.9
II 1919–1938	6.2	1.9	3.6	0.7
III 1954–1965	14.6	6.3	6.5	1.8
IV 1965–1976	9.9	1.9	7.9	0.1

Source: GY and GL from Kazushi Ohkawa and Nobukiyo Takamatsu, "Capital Formation, Productivity and Employment," *IDCJ Working Paper Series No. 26*, March 1983. Gw from *Prices, Long-Term Economic Statistics (LTES)* Vol. 8, Table 35 and others.

Remarks: i) These are at 1934–1936 prices for prewar and at 1965 prices for postwar years.

ii) The estimates of Gw and GY for IV are from other supplementary sources.

vate industrial sector, including nonmanufactures since its exclusion is impossible. Therefore this treatment is not completely comparable to preceding figures, although the broad picture is legitimately shown. The level of Y/Lw did change historically but its tempo of increase varied: during periods II and IV its range of variation is rather limited, remaining relatively stable at the smallest possible rate of increase, while more rapid change occurs in periods I and III.

Two comments should be made. First, technically the results of this growth approach in real terms is essentially comparable with those of the preceding analyses based on Y/Lw measures in current prices. The reason is that the ratio in current prices should be exactly the same as the ratio in constant prices so far as output prices are used for deflating wages. As proposed elsewhere, this is intended to represent the standpoint of entrepreneurial behavior, instead of indicating the conventional real wages of workers as consumers. This approach is reasonable here for the discussion of level changes in Y/Lw so far as the domestic economy is concerned. Second, substantively the variation of the rate of changes in Y/Lw appears to correspond roughly to the long-term swings of economic growth and to that extent may be relevant to the preceding proposal that the distinction between innovative versus noninnovative industry is an aggregate measure of Y/Lw change. This includes a suggestion for the stable performance of period V shown in Table 3.3 because it is closer to the developed state.

Three Subsectors with Three-Range Structure

Technology diffusion as seen in total manufacturing is composed of the different patterns of many subsectors, and thus clarification of those subsectors is desirable. However, the numerous subsectors cannot be dealt with here due to the analytical necessity of linkages with the three-range approach by firm scale. Three major subsectors are analyzed: light industry, heavy industry, and engineering (machine) industry, generally following the previous approach. This is believed adequate for the present purpose of elucidating the pattern and process of the third subsector in comparison with those of the first and second. Observations first focus on the familiar comparison between 1957 and 1966. Table 3.4 summarizes the relevant data.

The historical characteristics of "simultaneous infusion" in this period were described in chapter 2, section I. The term Y/Lw presents different patterns between 1957 and 1966 with respect to the comparison of M and L (the second and the third range): $L > M$ in 1966, but $M > L$ in 1957. This provides background knowledge for examining its patterns in developing economies. The three-subsector approach makes it clear that the 1957 pattern was the result of heavy industry performance. In 1966, it showed the pattern $L > M$, but for light industry, the pattern change from 1957 to 1966 was reversed: from $L > M$ to $M > L$. Although the pattern of total manufacturing is less affected by the latter's smaller weight, these may illustrate that an important process of change is involved in this particular period. This can be observed more systematically in detail. As mentioned previously, the interval 1957–1966 was crucial for the development of the machine industry since it shifted from long-term import substitution to export substitution. More rapid internal absorption of advanced foreign technology was indispensable for large-scale firms (L). To achieve this, the superior competitive power of this industry must be realized by a shift in the domestic market from the second range (M) to large-scale firms (L). How was such a drastic change possible?

To begin the discussion with S' (30–49 workers, specifically distinguished from S) for machinery versus light industry in 1957, it shows essentially the same features as identified earlier in chapter 2, section III, for the smaller scale (1–9 workers): all terms, Lw/K, Y/K, and Y/Lw (and π as well), are greater for machinery than for

Table 3.4
Changes in Representative Terms: Manufacturing Subsectors, Japan, 1957 and 1966

	Scale	1957				1966			
		Lw/K	Y/K	Y/Lw	(π)	Lw/K	Y/K	Y/Lw	(π)
Machine industry	S'	2.61	5.75	2.21	3.14	1.00	1.98	1.98	0.98
	M	0.97	2.16	2.24	1.19	0.82	1.90	2.31	1.08
	L	0.68	1.67	2.47	0.99	0.58	1.73	3.00	1.15
	Average	1.08	2.62	2.44	1.55	0.70	1.75	2.50	1.05
Light industry	S'	1.25	1.85	1.49	0.60	0.77	1.88	2.44	1.11
	M	0.50	1.59	3.17	1.09	0.52	1.59	3.06	1.04
	L	0.32	1.04	3.24	0.92	0.43	1.04	2.45	0.61
	Average	0.66	1.39	2.02	0.70	0.54	1.39	2.60	0.85
Heavy industry	S'	1.33	3.10	2.33	1.79	0.87	1.97	2.26	1.10
	M	0.49	2.23	4.55	1.74	0.49	0.52	1.06	0.03
	L	0.37	1.15	4.46	1.28	0.22	0.73	3.31	0.51
	Average	0.38	1.60	4.21	1.22	0.27	0.69	2.55	0.42
Total manufacturing	S'	1.59	3.83	2.03	2.24	0.89	2.00	2.25	1.11
	M	0.66	2.25	3.41	1.59	0.53	1.65	3.11	1.12
	L	0.51	1.38	2.71	0.87	0.32	1.03	3.22	0.71
	Average	0.67	1.79	2.67	1.12	0.51	1.28	2.53	0.77

Notation: $\pi = Y/K - Lw/K$, added for reference. All other notations are the same as in preceding tables.

Sources: 1957 from EPA data, *op. cit.*; 1966 from Motai-Ohkawa data, *op. cit.*

Remarks: i) Scale is in terms of the number of workers: S' (small scale) is 30–49; M (medium scale) is 300–499; and L (large scale) is ≥10,000 (where L is lacking, the highest scale is taken).
ii) Machinery is general transportation, electric, and precision machinery. Light industry is represented by textiles, food, wood and wood products, and ceramics. Heavy industry is represented by chemicals, petroleum, steel, paper-pulp, and nonferrous metals. Total manufacturing covers all other industries not included in those three groups.
iii) The estimated terms in each group are simple averages. The average in the scale column in each group is the total average covering all other scales.
iv) All terms are calculated in current prices and their magnitudes are not directly comparable between 1957 and 1966.

light industry. This is important because S' demarcates the border between the first and the second range (like M' in chapter 1, section III). It is important to note that in S' in particular a greater Lw/K characterizes the machine industry and that its higher value of Y/Lw is due to its extremely high level of output effects Y/K. This characteristic of the machine industry thus identified for the first range may be extended to the second range.

Both Lw/K and Y/K are still greater for machine as compared with light industry at M, but Y/Lw becomes smaller for the former, which is more noticeable at L. Until some point between S' and M, the advantage of machinery is assumed to be maintained in terms of Y/Lw performance, but it shows only a slight increase in machinery, whereas for light industry it increases distinctly from S' to M, followed by an increase from M to L. The different patterns through the scale are significant, in addition to the fact that the average magnitude of Y/Lw itself is definitely greater for machinery in these two subsectors. The levels of Y/Lw in the machine industry thus show a very limited range of variation through scale differences, which characterizes this subsector in contrast to light and heavy industries. It is nearly scale-neutral, presuming the notion of positive and negative scale effects in terms of the level of Y/Lw. This is convenient for present analytical purposes. Table 3.4 shows positive scale effects in 1957 for light industry, whereas for heavy industry no such positive effects between M and L are recognized.

Examining the situation in 1966, the scale effects of Y/Lw show a drastic change for machinery: a distinct pattern of positive scale effects is witnessed which is greater for M and for L. This takes place despite a similar pattern of decreasing Lw/K. The change is due to a drastic change in Y/K: in 1957 there was a sharp decrease from S' to L, but in 1966 the decrease becomes minor. Despite capital intensification (smaller value of Lw/K), the output-capital ratio remains nearly unchanged through all scales. In contrast, the scale performance of Y/K in light industry remains almost constant through 1957 and 1966, on the one hand, while on the other the rate of decrease in Lw/K slows. Thus the level of Y/Lw becomes almost equal between S' and L, marking a drastic change from 1957 to 1966. Comparison of the two subsectors shows that competitive power undergoes a change. In 1966 machinery becomes inferior for S' but superior for L. In other words, the scale effect is positive, whereas in light industry it is positive from S' to M but negative from M to L, which is a major change from the 1957 performance. With respect to heavy industry, a remarkable decline in the level of Y/Lw from 1957 to 1966 is witnessed for M and L, with little change for S'. To this, a drastic decline in Y/K, particularly for M, makes an important contribution. Thus its superior competitive power in 1957 drops to the lowest positions in 1966 for M and L.[3]

Why did such a change in the scale effects indicated by Y/Lw occur? In order to answer this question following the hypothesis stated in chapter 1, it is argued that the pattern of scale effects in the machine industry is composed of the combined effects of domestic and international elements that operate in the process of techno-logical-organizational advance. In forming the scale pattern of the machine industry in 1957, domestic elements still played an important role, whereas toward 1966 international elements began to play a dominant role through assimilation of foreign technological knowledge. However, the latter does not replace the former completely as has often been assumed by the theoretical diffusion model, but the former becomes integrated into the advanced system with modifications. Organizational change (subcontracting system, etc.) is involved as an important ingredient here.

The scale effect of light industry in 1957 shows a progressive pattern similar to that of machinery in 1966, whereas in 1966 it becomes mixed: Y/Lw is largest in M, with the values in S' and L almost equal. This indicates that the effects of absorbed foreign advanced technology ceased to operate. With regard to heavy industry, a mixed pattern is witnessed in 1957, which changed to a new pattern in 1966, where L is largest and M smallest. At the top level, tech-nological advance appears to proceed.

An additional observation relative to total manufacturing is useful. Characteristic of the machine industry is maintenance of a linear, continuous pattern of scale effects identified in both 1957 and

---

[3] The mixed pattern of Y/Lw for heavy industry is affected by petroleum subsectors. The values excluding this subsector are as follows:

	Lw/K	Y/K	Y/Lw
S'	0.93	1.93	2.08
M	0.59	0.96	1.64
L	0.22	0.71	3.23

Table 3.5
Scale Effects of Y/Lw Relative to the Group Average, 1957 and 1966

		Machine Industry	Light Industry	Heavy Industry	Total Manufacturing
1957	S'	90.6	73.8	55.3	76.0
	M	91.8	156.9	108.1	125.8
	L	101.2	160.4	105.9	101.5
1966	S'	79.2	93.9	85.6	85.6
	M	92.4	117.7	41.6	122.9
	L	120.0	94.2	129.8	127.3

Source: Same as for Table 2.1.
Remarks: i) The group average covers all scales, including the smallest.
  ii) Total manufacturing includes all other industries not covered by the three groups specified.

1966 for Y/Lw.[4] This is significant in light of the present hypothesis since the combined effects of national and international elements are taken into account. In order to reconfirm this, Table 3.5 expresses Y/Lw relative to the group average with an estimate for total manufacturing added for reference. The relative level of Y/Lw of machinery shows the least variance in 1957 and a continuous increase in 1966 although with a sharper slope. For light industry an analogous pattern is witnessed in 1957 but in 1966 no linearity is seen for its scale effects since its magnitude tends to decrease from M to L. Heavy industry reveals a kink from M to L in 1957 but the pattern changes in 1966 and a downward kink is witnessed from S to M. As is indicated by the column for total manufacturing in 1957,

---

[4] The performance of metal manufacturing appears similar to that of machinery. This could be included in machinery but was not. The relevant terms are as follows:

1957	Lw/K	Y/K	Y/Lw	1966	Lw/K	Y/K	Y/Lw
S'	2.33	6.76	2.90		0.90	1.88	2.09
M	0.45	1.58	3.51		0.64	1.63	2.56
L	0.60	2.83	4.72		0.46	1.37	2.97
Average	1.50	4.02	2.68		0.71	1.70	2.38

(In 1957, L is for the scale of 1,000–9,999 workers.)
  The pattern in 1966 is very similar to that of machinery, but the pattern in 1957 is not: the scale effects increase sharply toward larger-scale firms and appear similar to that of light industry.

top-level firms were still behind M in augmenting the level of Y/Lw. Even in light industry and machinery the level difference between M and L was minor. However, in 1966 the level of Y/Lw in L exceeds that in M in total manufacturing; a pattern similar to that for machinery contains the deviation of L in light industry and of M in heavy industry. These patterns of scale effects may be significant viewed from the aggregate pattern of manufacturing.

Before we end the discussion on the Y/Lw pattern, the performance of the term π, added as a reference in Table 2.6, should be investigated. As discussed in chapter 2, section II, this conventional term behaves broadly similar to term Y/Lw in scale variation. However, a distinct difference is witnessed between the two with respect to the performance of L, where π often shows a significant decline. In machinery in 1966 it increases from M to L, but not as sharply as does Y/Lw. For this and other reasons π cannot be used as a primary indicator for present analytical purposes.

The discussion of Lw/K does not focus on the reasons for changes in Lw/K of total manufacturing, but on its relative changes by industry group following the procedure used for Y/Lw. The level of Lw/K in machinery is generally higher than its average in total manufacturing, whereas that of heavy and light industries is generally lower. Such generalizations, however, may conceal the points illustrated in Table 3.6.

The higher level of Lw/K of machinery is essentially sustained in

Table 3.6
Relative Magnitude of Factor Input Ratio Lw/K by Group and Firm Scale, 1957 and 1966

		Machine Industry	Light Industry	Heavy Industry
1957	S'	1.64	0.79	0.84
	M	1.47	0.76	0.74
	L	1.33	0.63	0.73
	Average	1.61	0.79	0.57
1966	S'	1.12	0.87	0.98
	M	1.55	0.98	0.92
	L	1.81	1.34	0.69
	Average	1.37	1.06	0.53

Source: Same as for Table 2.1.
Remarks: All values of Lw/K for each group are expressed relative to the corresponding scale value for total manufacturing.

1966 for M and L despite the remarkable changes from 1957. This is highlighted in comparison with heavy industry for L. Between 1957 and 1966 the former increases remarkably from 1.33 to 1.81, while the latter decreases from 0.73 to 0.69. Although in M the relative level of Lw/K increases similarly in both industries, changes in the opposite direction in large-scale firms are important in understanding the absorption process of advanced technology. Machine industry technology was absorbed keeping its property intact. In light industry a similar pattern is witnessed, in which the relative level of Lw/K in L increases remarkably from 0.63 to 1.34 between 1957 and 1966 but with different implications.

For small-scale firms, the same approach reveals that in 1966 machinery maintained its greater relative magnitude of Lw/K but the degree of difference between other industries narrowed as compared with the situation in 1957. The characteristics of the machine industry tend to weaken toward 1966. Thus, taken together with M and L, the order of relative magnitude of Lw/K is reversed between 1957 and 1966: from $S > M > L$ to $S < M < L$. While its absolute order of magnitude is sustained ($S > M > L$), in 1966 for total manufacturing the range of scale effects narrows, resulting in a noticeable pattern change for machinery.

In chapter 2, section I the general interpretation of simultaneous infusion was that domestic elements operated intensively in 1957 due to Japan's long-term isolation from international contact. During the prolonged phase of secondary import substitution, foreign advanced technological knowledge was absorbed. However, in the wartime interval of isolation certain domestic technological advances occurred. Data from those intervals can be used for analytical purposes in applying the present hypothesis. In the long-term process of technology diffusion the effects of imported foreign technology tended to be incorporated into the process of improving the domestic technology system. Domestic elements operated in the initial postwar period in this sense. This interpretation can be amplified by further observation of total performance toward the 1980s, because innovation in the machine industry continued.

In *OK*, Manufacturing Survey data for 1971 and 1981 were used to examine manufacturing behavior in some detail. In order to link those results with the present findings, the discussion below focuses on the machine industry. The level of Lw/K in 1966 had a predictable tendency to decline as the scale became larger. A noticeable change manifests itself in the 1970s, as typified in general machinery. In 1971, the same pattern remained as in 1966, but change

Table 3.7
Machinery, 1971 and 1981

		Lw/K	Y/K	Y/Lw		Lw/K	Y/K	Y/Lw
1971	S'	1.09	1.97	1.81	1981	1.20	2.20	1.83
	M	0.76	1.73	2.28		1.18	2.11	1.79
	L	0.68	1.89	2.78		1.04	2.16	2.08

Source: *OK*, Table 4.5.

was flat through the three scale groups S, M, and L. Simple averages of Lw/K and relevant terms for machinery are shown in Table 3.7.[5] The scale difference of Lw/K is still noted in 1981, particularly between M and L averages, even though it is much smaller. This is mostly affected by transportation machinery, the Lw/K of which is S 0.75, M 0.69, and L 0.44 for 1981. Corresponding changes are noted in Y/K. In a typical case of general machinery, Y/K is S 2.00, M 2.10, and L 2.24 in 1981, a reversal of the familiar pattern of decline from S to L. In four types of machinery, the usual pattern was already blurred in 1971 and in 1981 appears nearly flat, although the magnitude of S appears to remain larger. In this regard, the effects of precision machinery are substantial as this subsector continues the familiar pattern. Finally, the scale performance of Y/Lw sustains the familiar pattern of increase from S to L in 1971 and 1981, although the level of M appears slightly smaller than that of S'. What is important is that despite notable changes in the scale pattern of Lw/K, the familiar pattern of scale effects of Y/Lw essentially remains unchanged, although its range narrows.[6]

It is clear that over the entire interval 1957–1981 the Japanese machine industry presents a successful pattern of combined operation of domestic and international elements in the technology diffusion process. Substantially, this means a tendency for differences in technology type as well as in technology level to narrow over firm scale. It is important to note that the path was not linear but an inverse U-shape. This can be confirmed in terms of Y/Lw. In 1957 its level in S' and L (2.21:2.47) was similar; it was widened to 1.98 (S')

[5] Lw/K and Y/K are calculated from *OK*, Table 4.5. The scale classification is not the same as before (S, 30–199; M, 200–999; and L, ≥1,000), but this does not create serious discrepancies.

[6] Even in the "typical" case of general machinery in 1981, Y/Lw increases by scale (S', 2.33; M, 2.47; and L, 2.66). This implies that with unchanged Lw/K, Y/K tends to increase with scale. Further scrutiny is needed.

versus 3.10 (L) in 1966 (Table 3.4). Until 1971 this pattern broadly prevailed (S', 1.81 versus L, 2.78 in 1971). However, it narrowed again and in 1981 its level was nearly the same in S' and M (1.83 and 1.79), although it remained higher in L (2.08), similar to the pattern prevailing in 1957. During the former segment, advanced technology was absorbed by top-level firms, but internal diffusion from L to M and from M to S' was limited. Even so, internal diffusion was realized to a limited extent through organizational devices such as the subcontracting system. During the latter segment, the pace of foreign advanced technology introduction slowed. To what extent the effects of organizational innovation contributed to forming this pattern is an interesting theme for further study.[7]

How did the pattern of Y/Lw change in the other two industry groups? Both light and heavy industry differ from the machine industry, underlining the characteristics of machinery presented previously. Although the pattern S' < M < L for light industry held in 1957, in 1966 it changed to S' < M > L, that is, a decline in L emerged which was sustained up to 1971.[8] The 1981 data for textiles are questionable, but the same pattern may be sustained. For heavy industry the initial pattern S' < M > L, with minor difference between M and L, continued in 1966 with a wider difference between M and L. It is interesting that through 1971 and 1981 the same pattern appears to be sustained using the average of steel and chemicals as a proxy:[9]

	S'	M	L
1971	3.08	3.71	3.46
1981	3.13	3.54	3.25

Heavy industry sustains the pattern S < M > L throughout the entire interval under review. The same scale pattern holds for the other two industry groups, which distinctly differ from the U-shape of the machine industry.

---

[7] In *OK*, based on the research results of Konosuke Odaka and Susumu Hondai, a brief description was presented focusing on the problem of technology diffusion and organizational innovation.

[8] Y/Lw is S' 2.18, M 2.94, and L 2.45 in 1971 (average of textiles and food in *OK*, Table 4.5).

[9] Excluding petroleum, Y/Lw of heavy industry in 1971 is S 2.38, M 3.06, and L 2.32.

Two mutually related points amplify the implications of the shape difference. First, innovative process in absorbing advanced technology occurs most vigorously in machinery, whereas in heavy industry it is less intense and is the least intensive in light industry. Second, the greater magnitude of Lw/K is sustained even in top-level firms. In 1981, it is 0.97 for machinery, three times higher than the 0.35 for steel and chemicals. Within the machine industry itself the differential is considerable, e.g., for L in 1981: 1.61 (precision), 0.95 (electric), 0.86 (general), and 0.44 (transportation). Most representative is electric machinery, while transportation machinery seems to contain more factors common to heavy industry. Note that the level of Y/Lw at the top is greater for the former than for the latter, implying that a more vigorous innovative path appears to be realized in this subsector, which has the potential for more efficient utilization of human resources, as suggested by the level of Lw/K.

Japan's case pertains to the final interval of secondary export substitution in the postwar period. In this sense particular attention is paid to the pattern of machinery as compared to heavy industry performance. The significance of scale effects is emphasized; they are more influential in the former than in the latter in terms of Y/Lw. This indicates the superior competitive power realized in machinery compared to heavy industry. During the phase of secondary import substitution, the relative position of the two subsectors might differ, although no reliable data are available to confirm this possibility. We do not mean to state that the present hypothesis is exclusively applicable to engineering industry. It may also be applied to other industries to a limited extent. But the dominant role played by modern elements tends to be stronger in engineering. The technological property resulting in the difference stems essentially from the magnitude of Lw/K, but the divisibility of the products and process in machinery production confirms its technical nature. This technical feature of engineering is widely known and no doubt contributes to forming the scale characteristics of the industry. Combined with the effects of organizational innovation, this technical property should be adequately evaluated in discussing the scale effects of industry.

II. Developing Economies: International Dimension

The discussion in section I was dominantly concerned with domestic dimension and did not treat the international aspect explicitly. The relation between domestic and international elements focusing on the case of the machinery industry concerned the internal process of technology diffusion based on *ex post* data. By depending upon borrowed technology, Japan succeeded in realizing its national potential. This section examines the process in developing countries where the international dimension is the dominant aspect, aiming at elucidating the national potential for absorbing advanced technology. Although ideally the domestic dimension should first be elucidated in detail, that is beyond the reach of this volume. This omission is partially compensated for by analyzing the cases of a few selected countries in a general way, in addition to the earlier discussion in chapter 2, section II.

Brief Overview of Domestic Manufacturing
The pattern of Y/Lw has been examined in detail for Japan. With the background knowledge thus obtained, the performance of Y/Lw with respect to contemporary developing economies is elucidated here. However, it is difficult to carry out comparative analysis between Japan and many developing economies using the same framework due to the limited data available for the latter. Tables 3.8, 3.9, and 3.10 present data in compact form for major subsectors.

The Korean figures are based on manufacturing census data for selected years (Table 3.8, panel A) and show changes in Y/Lw in manufacturing subsectors between 1973 and 1983. In the early 1970s, Korea was at the beginning of the secondary phase of economic development and industrialization accelerated remarkably in that decade. The level of Y/Lw in total manufacturing decreased from 4.50 to 3.88 between 1973 and 1983, similar to the case of Japan from 1957 to 1966. The different changes among various representative subsectors are interesting: textiles, chemicals, and basic metals show a rather large decline in Y/Lw, while food and paper (not listed in the table) show an increase from 1973 to 1983, and the Y/Lw value of machinery is nearly unchanged between the two years. Textiles, as representative of light industry, reflect labor-intensive technologies, in contrast to such capital-intensive heavy industries as chemicals and basic metals. The capital intensity indicated by K/L was not as high in food and paper but machinery is between the other two groups. These manufacturing industries seem to have played a significant role in the development of the Korean industrial sector in the 1970s and 1980s while achieving remarkable technology innovation. Productivity of capital and labor rose significantly in these industries during the observation periods. The effect

Table 3.8

Key Terms in the IOR Formula: Korea, 1973 and 1983

(A): By Sector

		K/L	w	Lw/K	Y/K	Y/Lw
Textiles	1973	1.30	0.23	0.17	0.59	3.47
	1983	4.74	1.91	0.40	1.08	2.70
Machinery	1973	2.65	0.28	0.11	0.37	3.36
	1983	9.02	2.84	0.31	1.02	3.29
Chemicals	1973	2.00	0.33	0.17	0.99	5.82
	1983	12.35	2.71	0.22	1.11	5.05
Basic metals	1973	4.89	0.38	0.08	0.57	7.13
	1983	40.55	3.20	0.08	0.44	5.50
Total manufacturing	1973	1.89	0.27	0.14	0.63	4.50
	1983	9.78	2.48	0.25	0.97	3.88

(B): By Scale, 1983

		K/L	w	Lw/K	Y/K	Y/Lw
Textiles	S	2.97	1.76	0.59	1.30	2.20
	M	3.71	1.93	0.52	1.27	2.44
	L	7.26	2.03	0.28	0.90	3.21
Machinery	S	3.79	2.20	0.58	1.40	2.41
	M	5.64	2.65	0.47	1.43	3.04
	L	14.12	3.41	0.24	0.89	3.71
Chemicals	S	6.18	2.41	0.40	1.20	3.00
	M	23.43	3.40	0.14	0.86	6.14
	L	13.86	2.59	0.19	1.15	6.05
Basic metals	S	6.15	2.44	0.40	1.01	2.53
	M	13.46	3.21	0.24	0.92	3.83
	L	72.68	3.57	0.05	0.37	7.40
Total manufacturing	S	4.40	2.04	0.46	1.16	2.52
	M	8.11	2.49	0.31	1.15	3.71
	L	15.67	2.93	0.19	0.87	4.58

Sources: Bureau of Statistics, Economic Planning Board, *Report on Mining and Manufacturing Census*, Series I and II, 1975. National Bureau of Statistics, Economic Planning Board, *Report on Industrial Census*, Vol. I, 1985.

Remarks: i) K: Value of tangible fixed assets in million won (land is not excluded for 1983). L: number of workers. w: (employees' remuneration)/(number of workers). Y: value added in million won.

ii) Scale is representative in terms of the number of workers: S (small-scale) is 20–49; M (medium-scale) is 200–299; and L (large-scale) is ≥500.

iii) Textiles: textiles, wearing apparel, and leather. Machinery: manufacture of fabricated metal products, machinery, and equipment. Chemicals: manufacture of chemicals and of chemical, petroleum, coal, rubber, and plastic products. Basic metals: basic metal industries.

Table 3.9
Key Terms in the IOR Formula: Malaysia, 1974

(A): By sector

	K/L	w	Lw/K	Y/K	Y/Lw
Textiles	10.93	1.79	0.16	0.37	2.31
Machinery	9.40	3.44	0.37	1.00	2.70
Chemicals	13.00	2.88	0.22	1.08	4.91
Basic metals	21.25	3.57	0.17	0.66	3.88
Total manufacturing	10.99	2.63	0.24	0.91	3.79

(B): By scale

		K/L	w	Lw/K	Y/K	Y/Lw
Total manufacturing	S	5.31	2.07	0.39	1.19	3.05
	M	12.07	2.77	0.23	0.98	4.26
	L	15.20	3.09	0.20	0.63	3.15

Source: Department of Statistics, Survey of Manufacturing Industries, Vol. I, 1979.
Remarks: i) K: value of fixed assets, US$1,000.
L: number of paid workers.
w: (salaries and wages paid) / (number of workers).
Y: value added, US$1,000.
ii) Number of workers: S (20–29); M (100–199); L (500–999).

Table 3.10
Key Terms in the IOR Formula: India, 1970 and 1983

By sector		K/L	w	Lw/K	Y/K	Y/Lw
Textiles	1970	4.98	2.77	0.56	1.02	1.82
	1983	23.51	9.88	0.42	0.78	1.86
Machinery	1970	13.28	3.49	0.26	0.63	2.42
	1983	51.19	13.33	0.26	0.84	3.23
Chemicals	1970	52.06	3.82	0.07	0.38	5.43
	1983	135.20	12.11	0.09	0.50	5.56
Basic metals	1970	36.83	3.70	0.10	0.26	2.60
	1983	159.07	13.40	0.08	0.30	3.75
Total manufacturing	1970	23.69	2.67	0.11	0.34	3.40
	1983	64.61	8.02	0.12	0.41	3.42

Source: Department of Statistics, Ministry of Planning, Annual Survey of Industries, Vol. I.
Remarks: K: value of fixed capital, Rs1,000.
L: number of workers.
w: (wages and salaries for workers) / (number of workers).
Y: value added, Rs1,000.

of the Y/K increase mainly resulted in the favorable behavior of Y/Lw in food, paper, and machinery and strengthened the competitive power of those industries. As mentioned previously, many industries, except group III (B) (machinery), showed a decrease in Y/Lw from 1957 to 1966 in Japan. Thus it can broadly be stated that there was a similar change in sectorwise Y/Lw performance in Japan and Korea.

With regard to the detailed features of Y/Lw of manufacturing subsectors by scale, data are only available for 1983. Table 3.8, panel B shows the productivity of representative subsectors by scale, focusing on Y/Lw. The values of Y/Lw in textiles and basic metals decrease from 5–9 workers (not listed in the table) to 20–49 workers and then begin to increase toward larger scales. This U-shaped pattern of Y/Lw was also found in heavy industry in Japan in 1966, although light industry indicated an inverse U-shape, unlike the case of Korea. Y/Lw of machinery and chemicals gradually enlarges from S to M and finally to L, which is similar to the pattern of machinery in Japan. For total manufacturing, no distinct difference is observed from 5–9 to 20–49 employees, but a smooth increasing trend appears from M to L. This also resembles the pattern of Japanese manufacturing, although in Table 3.8 the pattern is shown by three selected scales.

Attention is especially drawn to the cases of machinery and chemicals. In these industries Y/K is highest in M so that an inverse U-shape is identified. Lw/K also shows an inverse U-shape from S to L, and yet its changes are rather small. The large increase in Y/K ultimately resulted in a decline in Y/Lw in machinery and chemicals under the situation of slower change of Lw/K, which indicates positive scale effects. The question is why such scale effects are present in these industries and not in others. A greater increase in Y/K suggests that technological-organizational advance occurred particularly in these industries during the 1970s and 1980s in Korea. International rather than domestic elements played a major role in enhancing technological-organizational level as Korea continued strenuous efforts to introduce and absorb advanced foreign technologies to strengthen its competitiveness in international markets in those years. In contrast, light industry as represented by textiles was no longer able to enjoy scale effects in the 1980s, as shown by nearly equivalent values of both Y/K and Lw/K through the scales. This implies that small-scale firms in light industry had developed sufficiently to compete with medium- and large-scale firms by that time due to technological advances.

The pattern of the terms under review for machinery in Korea in 1983 is fairly similar to that for machinery in Japan in 1966. When basic metals in Korea are compared with heavy industry in Japan, similar patterns are also found—that is, the U-shape of Y/Lw and the declining trend of Lw/K and Y/K from S to L. The case of light industry differs between the two countries, however. In Japan Y/Lw of light industry indicates an inverse U-shape, while Korean textiles have the opposite U-shape by scale. This difference can be explained by the different phases of development of light industry in the two countries. In Japan large-scale firms in light industry could no longer enjoy the scale effect in the mid-1960s after the rapid industrialization based chiefly on machinery and heavy industry, while large-scale firms in light industry continued to play a significant role in Korea in the early 1980s, maintaining somewhat higher levels of Y/Lw and Y/K. Favorable conditions for large-scale light industries may still exist in Korea.

Tables 3.9 and 3.10 present data for Malaysia and India, respectively. The Malaysian case is similar in some respects to that of Korea, but dissimilar in others, as shown in Table 3.9. Y/Lw is comparatively high in chemicals and basic metals in Malaysia in 1974 and in Korea in 1973. However, when compared with other industries, a different pattern is observed. Machinery in Malaysia achieves much higher values than wood and textiles, while their values were lower in Korea. Larger Y/K of paper and machinery in Malaysia could lead to larger Y/Lw in these compared with other industries (paper and wood are not listed in the table). With respect to Y/Lw of total manufacturing by scale, an inverse U-shape is found with its highest level in M. Y/K shows a U-shape with its lowest level in L. It should be noted that the largest-scale firms (>1,000 workers, not listed in the table) achieved rather high levels of Y/Lw together with higher Y/K. In addition to this, an increasing trend in Lw/K from M to L is also notable, as a result of sharp decrease in K/L. The type of technology adopted could have differed in M and L at that time. This does not necessarily mean that capital intensity is greatest in large-scale firms that achieve high Y/Lw and Y/K. Malaysia at the beginning of the 1970s was still in the primary phase and some shifts to the secondary phase are not yet identified.

In India, no obvious changes occurred in the performance of Y/Lw between 1970 and 1983 (Table 3.10). Y/Lw of total manufacturing remained at almost the same level, suggesting no substantial change in technological-organizational advancement, although an increase in Y/Lw is noted in machinery and basic metals. The level of Y/Lw is higher in chemicals and basic metals and lower in textiles, paper, and wood (not listed in the table). Machinery is in the middle. This phenomenon resembles the situation of Malaysian manufacturing in 1974. It is important to note that Y/K in many subsectors of Indian manufacturing is distinctly low during the observation periods. This may imply inefficient use of capital stock and limited advances in technological-organizational level. This is consistent with the view that India was still at the midpoint of the primary phase of development in the beginning of the 1980s.

International Aspect: Price-wage Ratio and Y/Lw Levels
As stated earlier, the primary purpose of this section is to conclude the preceding discussion in terms of the relationship between the domestic (internal) and international (external) elements in the process of technology diffusion in developing economies. In chapter 2, section III and in this chapter, varied patterns of technology diffusion were found by applying the simplified formula. Here, an amplification is attempted conceptually and empirically. Empirically, a different technical treatment is needed in order to determine international purchasing power parity (ppp). After a statistical examination, substantive problems at issue are dealt with. The conceptual aspect of the present approach is explained briefly below.

The relationship between domestic and international elements is examined not in the conventional way but in terms of the potential contained in the former. The same procedure for measuring the level of Y/Lw is applied, but the intention differs in that the Y/Lw measured by ppp is a representative indicator of the potential level of production activities. If this is higher for a nation it is supposed that its domestic elements operate more favorably than otherwise in the process of technology diffusion by assimilating international elements. This is consistent with the basic notion of national differences in social capability. In the preceding analysis of Japan's case, this was implicitly involved, although no discussion was attempted.[10] An acceptable comment is that it is easy to talk about potential but

---

[10] After examining postwar wage differentials in Japan by education (together with by sex and age) in comparison with those in Western Europe and the USA, Ohkawa and Rosovsky stated: "One thing is clear: in Japan, high-quality labor is available at relatively low prices, and this undoubtedly increases the country's capability to absorb new methods from abroad" (Kazushi Ohkawa and Henry Rosovsky, *Japanese Economic Growth: Trend Acceleration in the Twentieth Century* [Stanford University Press, 1973], chapter 3, p. 55). Here, the idea is expanded to the workers in the industrial sector in developing economies in general.

difficult to quantify it as operational in elucidating the process of technology diffusion. A special device is used to treat wages in terms of measuring human capability. The labor force in developing economies tends to have the potential to realize higher levels of activity as compared with levels indicated by wages prevailing in the domestic market. This stems from the fact that production factors other than labor, such as capital, technology, and organization, tend to be insufficient to realize labor's potential. Measurement requires bold assumptions, but this concept is essential.

Viewed from the technology diffusion process, the manufacturing sector should be analyzed, but due to data limitations the industrial sector was selected as second best. Subsector treatment is beyond the present scope. Two questions must be answered: first, does Y/Lw achieve relative stability; second, and more important, what is the decomposed pattern of price-wage ratios and the level of productivity? The following data on Y/Lw averaged by group are relevant:

Group	I	II	III	IV	V
	1.98	2.00	2.19	2.11	1.62
(Index)	122	124	135	130	100

Source: Kazushi Ohkawa, in collaboration with Katsuo Otsuka and Bernard Key, *Growth Mechanism of Developing Economies: Investment, Productivity and Employment* (Tokyo: International Development Center of Japan/International Center for Economic Growth, 1993) (*DE*), Technical Notes, Table 1.7.
Remarks: Groups are the same as in chapter 1, section I.

The data are derived from Lw/Y, labor's approximate income share in manufacturing, and can be used to give a broad picture of Y/Lw performance in current prices. A U-shaped pattern is recognized in the increase from I to III and the decrease from III to V. However, apart from group V representing developed economies, the range of Y/Lw variation is rather moderate. The shape itself is an important problem from a different viewpoint, as discussed in chapter 1, but here it can simply be said that Y/Lw is relatively stable for the entire development path, ignoring the conceptual difference between production and income distribution.

The answer to the second question requires a conceptual explanation, and it should be noted that the problem differs between domestic and international comparisons. In the case of Japan, this issue was not raised because in dealing with changes over time in Y/Lw, it was assumed that the ratio (Y/L)/w could conceptually be the same in current and constant price series as long as both output Y and wages w were deflated by the same index of output prices. This assumption fits the behavior of entrepreneurs as explained earlier. Therefore all the discussion in the preceding subsection on the current series of Y/Lw can also be applied to the constant price series. This implies that together with output the labor market commonly operates in all subsectors of domestic manufacturing activities. For the international dimension, however, the situation essentially differs because output prices and labor prices cannot be assumed to vary in parallel. Here the difference between the two presents a problem to be solved. The conventional deflation method can be applied to deal with this issue, but using a simplified formula supposing a single commodity case without the εpq formula. This is because technology diffusion is the central issue. For simplicity, suppose that advanced technology to be imported to developing economies comes from the group V nations (1), for which Y/Lw is expressed as Y_1/Lw_1. This technology is to be assimilated in the domestic system of technology-industry in developing countries (2), for which Y/Lw is Y_2/Lw_2. The difference between Y_1/Lw_1 and Y_2/Lw_2 is at issue. The ratio $(Y_2/Lw_2)/(Y_1/Lw_1)$ can be expressed as $(Q_2P_2/L_2w_2)/(Q_1P_1/L_1w_1)$ or $(Q_2/L_2)/(Q_1/L_1) \cdot (P_2/w_2)/(P_1/w_1)$, where Q and P/w stand, respectively, for the output quantity and price-wage ratio of the industry under consideration. Taking the values of a developed economy as 100, Y_2/Lw_2 can be treated as $(Q_2/L_2) \cdot (P_2/w_2)$ in index number for developing economies. For simplicity's sake, the former term can be called the "quantitative" productivity of labor and the latter term the output price-wage ratio. Y/Lw must be decomposed into these two terms. What kind of price-wage ratios should be used to do so? The answer cannot be given *a priori* and the selection of the measures of the price-wage ratio depends upon the purpose of analysis. It is a widely held view that the international price level can most systematically be measured by ppp. It is the view of the present authors that in theory the ppp approach cannot avoid the conundrum of index numbers, but its basic property is its dependence on the concept of equivalence between the commodities to be compared. This fits into the present purpose of deriving quantitative productivity comparisons using the terms Q_2 and Q_1. Its meaning is thus specified. It cannot be genuinely "quantitative" except when a single commodity is treated, but the supposed case in the above treatment is summed up and quantity weighted by the relevant price systems. However, such simplified use of Q_2 in comparison with Q_1 fits the purpose here because the new technology to be absorbed by developing economies is presumed to come from developed economies. Thus in each case the aspect of quantitative productivity is at issue, presenting the problem of technological requirements. Actual ppp data cannot be used in this procedure by commodity; the magnitude of Y/Lw deflated by ppp must be utilized instead. Nevertheless this quantitative approach is convenient (and indispensable) for the present purposes.

The ppp data do not present a direct comparison of P_1 and P_2 for manufacturing (or industrial) output, as the original design pertains to the expenditure rather than the production aspect. Rough approximates assume that "clothing and footwear" are proxies for the output of light manufacturing and "machinery," for the output of engineering and heavy industries.[11] The difficulty faced is much greater in wage comparisons. There are no available wage data that can consistently be used to measure wage-price ratios with the above formula. The only possible way to overcome this difficulty is to apply the same concept of equivalence to the price of human work, analogous to the case of commodities. To be sufficiently precise to arrive at reliable measures is difficult. Nevertheless, in *DE*, chapter 5, section III, an attempt was made to base measurements on some assumptions. The use of *we*[12] here makes the meaning of the formula consistent in concept with the procedure by which the Y/Lw comparison is decomposed into two terms: the price-wage ratio and the quantitative productivity ratio, both in ppp measures. Table 3.11 summarizes the results of approximations through columns 1–4. Wages at domestic market prices (w) are added for reference in parentheses in column 3. (Regarding the relation between *we* and w, see Technical Notes at the end of this section.)

The ratio of ppp thus estimated for the output of the industrial sector to that of GDP is 1.23 (I), 0.87 (II), 0.92 (III), 0.94 (IV), and 1.00 (V). These do not necessarily appear regular, and the figures in the table are smoothed by adjustment. This requires further scrutiny, and the output price figures in column 2 are not sufficiently re-

---

[11] For details, see *DE*, chapter 5, section III, "Domestic Price Structure of Developing Economies."

[12] "*we*" is a weighted sum of w_1 and w_2. The former is an estimate or equivalence assumption based on the case of personal services, with reference to government employees. The equivalent function of workers is assumed to be observable in this way in general. The latter is an additional estimate based on the productivity difference regarding the sectors of PDE use (for details, see Annex).

Table 3.11
Decomposition of Y/Lw: Quantitative Productivity and Price-Wage Ratios for Developing Economies in Comparison with Developed Economies, Industrial Sector

Group	(1) Quantitative Productivity (Deflated Y/Lwe)	(2) Output Prices P (ppp)	(3) Wages *we*	(w)	(4) Ratio (2)/(3) P/*we*	(5) Y/Lw
I	31.7	52.7	13.7	2.3	385	1.22
II	51.0	44.8	18.4	6.0	243	1.24
III	85.5	44.9	28.4	10.3	158	1.35
IV	89.7	63.1	49.8	24.8	127	1.30
V	100.0	100.0	100.0	100.0	100	1.00

Source: *DE, op. cit.*, (2) from Tables 5.8 and 5.10; (3) from Table 5.15, originally UN; phase IV of International Comparison Project (ICP), part two. (5) is reproduced from the averages presented at the beginning of this section.

Remark: (2) is derived from the ppp ratio L/P (L is a proxy for light manufacturing and P stands for PDE) and P/G (G is ppp of GDP). For the former, 1975 and 1980 data are averaged to smooth deviations, while for the latter 1980 data are used.

liable to permit precise analysis. The broad pattern derived tends to be relatively higher than expected for lower groups, with few differences among developing economies. The figures of *we*, column 3, show a straight line of increase through groups, starting from a very low level in group I. The price-wage ratios, column 4, thus present a nearly straight tendency to decrease from the very high level of group I to higher groups. The implication is that for the industrial sector the equivalent wage tends to be increasingly cheaper relative to output prices moving toward lower groups. The quantitative productivity in column 1 of Table 3.11 is calculated by dividing the original data on Y/Lw, evaluated in national currency described earlier (reproduced in column 5), by the price-wage ratio in column 4. Technically, this is the level of Y/Lw in ppp evaluation, but note that it is in the present specified sense, indicating "potential." Its magnitude tends to increase from lower to higher groups, but the range of difference appears narrower than is usually thought.

Y/Lw is thus decomposed into two factors: price-wage ratio and quantitative productivity. It is composed of two counteracting forces: a tendency to decrease in the former and to increase in the latter through lower to higher groups. This should be clarified substantively with regard to the relative stability of Y/Lw in the international dimension. It is implied that for developing economies the levels and differences of quantitative productivity through groups are of extreme importance and that this is relevant to wage performance in relation to output prices. For example, the recipro-cal of the price-wage ratio, column 4, is as follows:

I	II	III	IV	V
26.0	41.4	63.2	78.7	100.0

If the term "real wages" is used for entrepreneurs as touched upon earlier (wages deflated by output prices), this can be called the index of potential real wages, taking V as the standard. The per-formance of Q/L implies the difference in real wages in this sense.

All these statistical calculations are made depending upon the assumption that *we*, and hence Q/L, measure quantitatively the aver-age potential that each group of nations possesses. Actually *we* is much higher than w; the level of wages at the equivalent evaluation is much higher than actually prevailing wages on the domestic mar-ket of each developing economy. The measurement is approximate and the actual difference between *we* and w could be narrower or wider. What is important is the recognition that for the analysis of technology diffusion the concept of potential is crucial. The quan-titative productivity Q/L thus obtained is an indicator of the poten-tial level of productivity in comparison with that of group V. The conventional concept of the gap between developing and developed nations focuses on so-called technology levels. This is convenient but not appropriate in measuring technology levels and gaps quanti-tatively. The levels of Q/L indicate the varied levels of production capability conditionally, if not directly, in terms of technology level. The average measurement of *we* by group may not be sufficiently realistic since it may vary among nations belonging to the same group. This is another reason for the conditional aspect of present estimations. However, the use of equivalent estimates *we* provides knowledge about capability levels in international comparisons based on a common evaluation and standard. Levels of capital in-tensity obtained using the simple ratio K/L have often been used, although this notion is not useful for present purposes because capit-al is not combined with "labor quality" as generally evaluated inter-nationally. While technology of higher K/L level is a requirement of developing nations, sufficient labor quality is indispensable for its absorption.

Key Terms for Realizing Productivity Potential

The key terms Lw/K and Y/K, both in current and ppp measures, are investigated below to include the international dimension in the technology diffusion process. Potential can only be realized when and where the required levels of Lw/K and Y/K are within reach, although it is only possible to observe this in terms of sector aggregates (in this case, average performance of industrial sectors). Even in this scope, available data are limited and rough approximations unavoidable. Suggestions can be deduced, however; Table 3.12 summarizes the measured results of key terms.

The measurement procedure requires technical explanation before substantive observations can be made. Knowledge on productivity variance through groups of developing economies is provided by Y/L*we* in ppp measures in column 1 in Table 3.12. Its linkages

Table 3.12
Measurements of the Key Terms for Industrial Sector: Comparison of Developing and Developed Economies

Group	(A) ppp Measures			(B) National Price Evaluation		
	Y/L*we* (1)	Y/K (2)	K/L*we* (3)	Y/Lw (4)	Y/K (5)	K/Lw (6)
I	31.7	32.7	0.97	122.2	67.8	180.0
II	51.0	22.1	2.31	123.5	83.3	148.2
III	85.6	55.9	1.53	135.2	91.1	148.4
IV	89.7	73.5	1.20	130.2	89.4	145.6
V	100.0	100.0	100.0	100.0	100.0	100.0

Remarks: Y/Lw (4) is from β for manufacturing.

For panel B, Y/K (5) is estimated from $\Delta Y/\Delta K$ modified for 1960–1980, excluding the effects of the downswing in 1980–1985. Conversion from $\Delta Y/\Delta K$ to Y/K is done using data estimated in *DE*: GYi − GKi (Table A2.4) and GYi (Table 4.1). GYi/GKi is as follows: I 0.98; II 0.97; III 1.00; IV 0.86; V 0.75.

For panel A, K/L*we* (3) is specifically estimated for the sector of industry and Y/K (2) is derived by (1)/(2). Regarding the special estimate of K/L*we*, fixed K/L*we* for the aggregate economy is estimated and converted to that of sector of industry by counting the capital stock composition (producer durables versus construction), duration of lifetime, and difference in ppp measures.

with capital in terms of either Y/K or K/L*we* must be clarified. Because the identity between the three key terms in ppp measures can be used, either Y/K or K/L*we* requires direct estimates. The choice depends not upon theoretical reason but upon technical convenience. Y/K was chosen in panel B because it is relatively easier to access. As mentioned in the remarks to Table 3.12, a rough proxy of Y/K can be estimated. The estimated Y/K in national price evaluation is shown in column 5. Taken together with Y/Lw in column 4, it is possible to derive K/Lw in national price evaluation in column 6.

These three terms in columns 4, 5, and 6 taken together impart preliminary but important knowledge about key term performance. The differences between groups appear to be much narrower than usually expected. The relative stability of Y/Lw was pointed out earlier, but Y/K and hence K/Lw tend to vary to a limited extent. The following points should be noted. For the former segment of development (groups I, II, and III) Y/K shows a tendency to increase, followed by a decrease in group IV. This is analogous to the inverse U-shaped pattern of $\Delta Y/I$, noted in chapter 1 pertaining to macro growth. Despite modifications made in deriving Y/K from incremental values, the broad pattern of the output-capital ratio remains similar to that in the industrial sector. Assuming this is acceptable, K/Lw is estimated. Its level in developing economies tends to be considerably higher than that in developed economies and presents no distinct difference between groups apart from a questionable high for group I. This may not be acceptable by readers, but the authors are convinced that these estimates in combination can approximate the actual performance of key terms in the national market. Simply put, the pattern of Y/Lw is essentially determined by that of Y/K. The level of K/Lw merely reflects differences in the factor price ratio. What is important is that these cannot directly provide information on the process of technology diffusion; ppp measures can be applied to compensate.

The figures in column 3 of Table 3.12 show that levels of K/L*we*, the factor input ratio by ppp measures, are very high except for group I and tend to decrease sharply toward higher groups (from II to III and from III to IV). This pattern is significant, and exhibits a different performance from that in national price evaluation. This is the result of differences in the price ratio between capital and labor. Second, with respect to output-capital ratio Y/K in column 2, the pattern of an inverse U-shape in national prices nearly disappears. For the former segment (groups I, II), similar low levels are maintained, but followed by a considerable increase for the latter segment. These are created by differences in the price ratio between capital and output, although for the accuracy of estimates they must be taken with reservation.

When observing the total results of ppp evaluation, two periods draw particular attention. First, as compared to the pattern of productivity potential levels, Y/L*we*, the magnitude of the required factor inputs ratio K/L*we* shows a tendency to increase from higher to lower groups. For the numerical values of groups I and II, such a large variance may distort reality due to data restraints. If a simple average of the two is taken it is 164. It can be contended that K/L*we* tends to increase toward lower groups if it is exceptionally low for group I. The difficulty of realizing potential tends to be greater for lower groups. Second, the output effect per capital Y/K tends to be smaller from higher to lower groups. Again, some irregularity is found for groups I and II. A simple average of the two is 27.4. This illustrates another difficulty in realizing potential productivity in lower groups. How to combat these double pressures is a real problem.

Quantitative measurements using the present procedure can provide useful knowledge, although its substantive significance depends upon the interpretation of comparisons of national averages of the industrial sector. The interpretation and reservations pertaining to three aspects are as follows. First, the tendency for a sustained increase in the level of Y/L*we* throughout all groups provides a conditional view of international technology diffusion, although its tempo differs among nations, as will be discussed later. Second, no information is available regarding the relation between the national average and the leading range in absorbing foreign advanced technology, so it must be assumed that comparison of the average can generally represent that of the leading range. Third, the level of K/L*we* in Table 3.12, panel A, shows the sustained pattern above, and this can be generally acceptable as the group average. Different magnitudes of K/L*we* among nations indicate the appropriate levels and types of technology to be absorbed by developing economies. If too high a level is adopted, Y/K will be smaller, and if too low a level is pursued, the increase in Y/L*we* will be slowed. The quantitative levels of Y/L*we* variance imply these relationships between its components.

Finally, viewed from the standpoint of national price evaluation, due to the high price of capital included in imported technology, the value of K/L*we* appears extremely capital-intensive. This is exacerbated by the extremely low wage level (w), leading to a distorted figure far from the reality. But the figure in ppp measures indicates more moderate, acceptable differences as compared with that of group V. Taking the level of group V as 100, for example, K/L is 25.6 (I), 41.5 (II), 43.7 (III), and 61.8 (IV), respectively, as a rough measure calculated indirectly by dividing K/L*we* by *we*. These represent capital intensity, which corresponds exactly to the potential quantitative productivity measured earlier so far as the national average is concerned, with the reservation that at the top range of industry there is the possibility of introducing advanced technology of a more capital-intensive type depending upon the nation's industrial climate. Among factors in industrial climate, the importance of the possible operation of *we*, the potential indicator of human capability, is emphasized.[13] Even though direct estimates are available for K/L, their use alone cannot illustrate technology diffusion.

The problems emanating from the relationship between national and international elements have hitherto been dealt with only partially at each dimension. A more systematic treatment is attempted here, with some repetition. The central idea is that national elements operate in influential ways as represented by the level difference of Y/L*we* in ppp evaluations of quantitative productivity. Proceeding further, this can represent the variance of international competitive power of an industrial sector in terms of technological requirement. In other words, progress in meeting this requirement leads each nation to upgrade its capacity for technology diffusion. As shown in Table 3.12, column 1, its level in the lowest group (I) is 32% of the level in group V representing developed economies. The tendency to increase is straightforward from lower to higher groups, but it is noted that the rate of increase is rapid during the first segment (I–III) and slower during the second (III–V). Is there any confirmation that such patterns are realistic in light of the double pressures in the actual path of economic development? An affirmative answer is difficult because comparative advantage is not revealed by the productivity approach, but relevant phenomena can be pointed out. Table 3.13 is a simple summary of the magnitude of resource imbalance (import-export) pertaining to merchandise trade in manufactures. This can be used to illustrate the output of the industrial sector in broad long-term trends.

The magnitude of imbalance is expected to decrease as competi-

---

[13] Differentials of *we* among nations are dealt with, but data are scarce. See the Annex.

Table 3.13
Resource Imbalance (Import-Export) of Manufactures by Y/L Level: Ratio to GDP, 1980

Group	Manufactures	Machinery		Nonmachinery	
	(1)	(2)	%	(3)	%
I	10.7	5.9	(55.1)	4.8	(44.9)
II	21.6	9.8	(45.1)	11.8	(54.2)
III	10.1	6.4	(63.4)	3.7	(36.6)
IV	7.8	4.7	(69.1)	3.1	(30.9)

Source: *DE*, Table 6.12 (originally, World Bank, *World Development Report*, 1982 and 1983, Annex: indicator tables).
Remark: The figures in parentheses in columns 2 and 3 are percentages of total manufactures (column 1).

tive power in manufacturing increases, and this expectation is met except in the I–II interval in which competitive power increases but imports increase more than exports. The reason may be a faster increase in the competitiveness of nonmanufactures (primary products). The imbalance in nonmachinery increases in particular in internal I–II, but begins to decrease afterward. This is interpreted as the effect of the ongoing processes of primary import and primary export substitution. A sustained leveling-up of quantitative productivity also occurs, mainly in light manufacturing industries. In the machinery production subsector, as is widely known, secondary import substitution proceeds at a moderate pace with a trend toward secondary export substitution. Thus the slower leveling-up of quantitative productivity pointed out earlier in the latter segment can be understood in this regard.[14]

The equivalence comparison is the conceptual basis for the assertion that quantitative productivity can conditionally indicate international competitive power. In this context the relationship between national and international prices-wages will be discussed. Table 3.14 is presented as a summary of what has previously been examined partially.

Compared to the levels of national evaluation at domestic market

[14] To approximate reality, *averaged* observations are necessary. No data are available and the supposition is that the national distribution of competitive power among subsectors of industry is rather wide: even in lower groups high competitive power can be expected for certain top-level firms or subsectors. To that extent, the competitive position of other portions must be even lower than the low average.

Table 3.14
Ratios of Key Terms (ppp Measures/National Price Measures) by Group

Group	Y/Lw	K/Lw	Y/K
I	25.2	55.8	48.2
II	41.2	155.8	26.5
III	63.4	103.1	61.4
IV	69.0	82.4	88.3
V	100.0	100.0	100.0

Source: Same as for Table 3.12.
Remark: Price-wage ratios are: wages/output prices in Y/Lw; wages/capital price
(factor input price ratio) in K/Lw; and capital price/output price in Y/K. These are
estimated, respectively, from figures in preceding relevant tables.

determination, international prices measured by ppp are high for
K/L*we* with a tendency to decrease from lower to higher groups,
whereas they are low for Y/K, with a tendency to increase from
lower to higher groups, although with some irregularity for I and II.
The ratio performance of Y/L*we* is, in the opinion of the authors, a
combined result of these two reverse tendencies. Y/L*we* still shows
a distinct tendency to increase from lower to higher groups because
the former trend of K/L*we* operates more weakly than the latter
trend of Y/K. In discussions of the relationship between national
and international prices, the significance of the difference in factor
input prices is conventionally emphasized. While the difference is
also recognized as influential in the present approach, as eloquently
presented by the ratio performance of K/L*we*, it is not the entire
story. The role played by the ratio performance of Y/K should not
be ignored. If its effects were less influential, the ratio of Y/L*we*
would present a much milder trend of difference from higher to lower groups. In other words, the Y/K pattern has a major influence on
productivity potential.

Two points may require further explanation. First, why are factor
input prices not the sole element in determining the differences in
international and national evaluations? Second, why do output
prices play a considerable role in this regard? These are mutually
related questions because basically both pertain to the core idea that
quantitative productivity can represent the levels of international
competitiveness. The basic formula used in examining the process of
technology diffusion begins with the level of K/Lw as determined by
entrepreneurs who meet the technological requirement. The role

played by the difference in factor input prices appears decisive, but its determination also depends upon the expected magnitude of Y/K. Thus Y/K is inseparably linked with K/Lw, and the level of output prices in relation to the levels of factor input prices is at issue. Domestic elements are much more involved in the pattern of output prices, whereas the pattern of capital prices is determined mainly, if not exclusively, by international elements, since dependence on capital goods imports tends to be greater in developing economies.

These are the implications of the approach using Y/L*we* with respect to the role played by international price-wage differences. In *DE*, chapter 5, estimates of capital goods prices were made for investment and producer durables in macro-economic terms. The ppp data were available only for 1980, yet it was suggested that international differences in capital prices were narrower than those in output and wages with regard to the sector of industry for the period under review. Thus, a supplementary explanation of the present treatment of wages and the problems thereby raised is required. Note that *we* is the major element in forming potential in the process of technology diffusion. The availability of workers with equivalent activity cannot be assumed, and the differentials between nations are important. In subgroup observations in the Annex labor appears less expensive in E than in F. These differentials stem from various factors, but the realization of the potential depends mainly upon the effects of learning by doing and education. No systematic data are available to link those effects with the *we* approach. Potential is complex and multifactoral, and includes the industrial system as well as educational organizations in a nation. Nevertheless, realization of the potential contained in workers' production activities is one of the most crucial factors to be clarified in the process of technology diffusion.

Annex: Equivalent Wages by Subgroup Observation

The proposition derived from the analysis in the main text is not conclusive because observations depend upon the results of "average" figures of *we* by group. If the group average alone is taken, the fundamental determinant is the level difference in Y/L, which does not conform with the reality of development. It is necessary to arrange the statistical data to deal with the response differentials among nations in the same group, classified by Y/L level. Thus the subgrouping is desirable, although this will include different coverage and time intervals.

A compromise is thus unavoidable. Two steps are adopted here:

first, approximation by group observation for 1980 for which the most comprehensive ppp data are available. The patterns of *we* thus obtained are tested in comparison with those used in the main text. Second, using these results subgroup observation is attempted, although the number of countries is limited.

The level of *we* is directly assessed using the price level of "services" of individual countries selected. For details see chapter 4, Annex II, where this level is discussed in comparison with price levels of other components of expenditures. In addition to *we*, two other wage indicators are utilized: *wd* and *wp*. The former is wages evaluated in US dollars and the latter is their value deflated by the aggregate GDP price level. The results are listed in Table 3A.1.

The figures in panel A are group averages. The primary purpose

Table 3A.1
Estimates of Terms Relevant to Evaluating Wages, 1980 (US = 100)

	wd		*wp*		*we*	
A: By group						
I	1.8		3.0		20.0	
II	4.8		9.7		19.8	
III	20.3		32.7		29.0	
IV	42.5		55.4		48.5	
V	109.1		88.8		91.0	

	wd		*wp*		*we*	
	E	F	E	F	E	F
B: By subgroup						
I	1.9	1.8	3.9	2.7	15.5	24.5
II	3.9	5.6	8.4	10.8	17.1	22.5
III	23.8	18.8	33.9	32.1	25.8	30.2
IV	39.8	46.2	56.5	54.3	54.3	66.2
V	109.1	112.0	88.4	91.5	91.5	87.0

Source: *wd* is from the Y/L approach in grouping based on World Bank, *World Development Report, op. cit.*, applying β, labor's increase share in aggregate (*DE*, chapter 1, Technical Notes). For *wp* and *we*, see Remarks. For countries selected, see chapter 4, Table 4A.3, Remarks.

Remarks: i) β is estimated as follows: I 53.0, II 51.4, III 48.9, IV 51.2, and V 69.0.

ii) *wp* is *wd*/aggregate price level, since *wd* is in US dollars.

iii) *we* is estimated by averaging the price of services estimated in the Annex to chapter 6 and the estimates of "services" for 1975 by ICP. It is I 15.7, II 19.0, III 26.1, and IV 84.8 (*DE*, Table 5.9). This excludes commodity prices. Corresponding data are not available for 1980.

is to compare the values of *we* presented in the main text and those derived here. The former are the original values (shown in *DE*, Table 5.15, as w1) modified by the variance of productivity levels, so that the comparison should be made between *we* in the table and the original measures. The figures in panel A are derived by taking US = 100 and converted to those taking the level of group V as = 100. These can be compared as follows:

	I	II	III	IV	V
1) Original *we*	18.5	23.4	30.8	51.9	100.0
2) Converted *we* from panel A	22.0	21.8	31.9	53.3	100.0

The discrepancy between the two is not sizable, although the level of 2) tends to be somewhat higher than that of 1), except for group II. The approximated measures for 1980 can generally be used for investigation by subgroup. It may be desirable to discuss the performance of *wd* and *wp*. The former illustrates the enormous differences in wages between lower and higher groups. So-called cheap labor cannot be discussed in this type of economic analysis. The degree of difference becomes much smaller in the case of *wp*. This is often used as "real wages" in the international dimension. As a first approximation this appears acceptable, because the aggregate price level is the ratio of the ppp evaluation to exchange rate. However, the important but difficult condition is that the standard (US) price system prevails through all developing countries. This cannot be assumed to hold true, and *we* is estimated when discussing the operation of domestic factors.

The relation between *we* and *wp* is thus important and it changes throughout the development path. In lower groups *we* > *wp* is commonly observed, but in higher groups the inequality *we* < wp is seen narrowing the gap. In group V the two values become close. The lower level of *we* implies that the equivalent capability of workers is available at lower wages, a potential advantage for entrepreneurs.

Second, in panel B of the table, the measurement methodology is not new, except that the component is essentially applied to the relevant discussion on the development interval 1960–1980 in the main text.

Thus, as stated previously, *we* is lower in E, the subgroup with a higher rate of macro-productivity growth, than in F, the subgroup with a lower rate, without exception throughout the entire develop-ment path. For group V, the reverse relation is not statistically sig-nificant. This finding is significant in light of the present conceptual framework. Subgroup E has the advantage of higher human capabil-ity than subgroup F. Beyond the subgrouping, this suggests that wider deviations in this respect may prevail in individual countries.

4

Significance of Producer Durables in Technology Diffusion

The direct application of the proposed simplified formula to the process of technology diffusion was essentially completed in chapters 1, 2, and 3. In this chapter the approach is somewhat different in that it treats the role of capital in the process of technology diffusion. The basic objective of analysis remains unchanged: clarification of the interplay between national and international elements. The crucial role played by national elements in human capability was dealt with in chapter 3, section II. In contrast, external (international) elements play a dominant role in capital in light of the pressure of heavy import dependency for capital goods in developing economies. However, under this pressure from external elements, how do internal elements operate to combat the external pressure? The answer appears to vary among nations, but why? To respond to these questions, a device is needed in the procedure of analysis.

In the proposed simplified formula, production capacity (PC) is indicated by K/Lw, but the decomposition of capital stock K has not been discussed. Here producer durable equipment (PDE) as a specific component of K is investigated because empirical knowledge about its actual performance in developing economies is insufficient despite the fact that it plays a significant role in the process of technology diffusion.

As is clear from the preceding discussion, the significance of PDE performance is not uniform through the entire economy, but varies by sector and by scale of production. This stems from the category difference of technology and pertains directly to technology of the mechanical type (M), mainly in industry but also in agriculture, particularly in the latter segment of development. PDE is the carrier of technological knowledge in the process of international diffusion of M technology. For technology of the BC (biological-chemical) type, the carrier is HYVs (high-yielding varieties), as will be discussed in

113

chapter 5. Following the concept of technological requirement in the problem of describing technology diffusion, the performance of investment resource allocation emerges as the first issue as it is one of the crucial determinants of the speed of technology diffusion. Empirically this can be examined by observing the PDE share in domestic investment. It is influenced strongly by its price: higher prices retard the process of PDE function whereas lower prices accelerate it, other things being equal. With regard to its behavioristic mechanism, the conventional notion of substitution may be relevant, although not dominant, since it operates under the influence of technological requirement. Empirical knowledge in this study area remains insufficient. Detailed statistical treatment is thus unavoidable to arrive at valid conclusions.

In section I, discussion focuses on two separate aspects: share (allocation of capital resources) and prices (costs for share input) in developing economies. Japan's experience is used as a preliminary in order to present the analytical procedure systematically. Meeting technological requirements for diffusion of advanced technology involves a greater share of capital resources at higher cost. This is the core issue. The relation between imports and domestic production is additionally examined in terms of PDE to link the analysis with the discussion in the following subsection. Treatment of high PDE prices follows, with Japan's experience discussed to amplify the findings for developing economies.

Section II attempts historical analysis to observe a broader framework of development phases. Japan, which promoted rapid PDE import substitution, is used for illustration. What are the domestic factors and conditions necessary for latecomers to cope with the international pressure of PDE requirements? This important but difficult question is answered in terms of the "telescoping effects" in economies developing later. PDE performance in contemporary developing economies is discussed in detail in section III, with a focus on changes in import dependency. Finally, the problems are subjected to further scrutiny under two topics: the turning point in PDE import dependency and the possibility of PDE price decline.

I. Greater Share and Higher Prices of Producer Durables

Greater Share and Import Dependency of Producer Durables

The greater share of capital resource allocation and higher prices-costs required combine to characterize PDE performance in developing economies. This proposition has been made in the relevant literature but not confirmed as systematic knowledge. To begin with the capital share, Japan's historical records are presented as a prelude to tackling the main subject of developing economies. This is necessary for two reasons. First, the pattern of latecomers should be identified in presently developed nations, even though only in broad outline. Second, the technical plausibility of flow series of PDE, used as a proxy for its stock series, must be tested because stock series are not available for developing economies.

Table 4.1 summarizes the relevant figures for Japan with period demarcations comparable to subsequent tables in section II. "Gross" figures are used because they are closer to the reality of production activity but "net" figures are added for reference. In the long-term pattern the two series are broadly similar, although the PDE share is noticeably lower in net figures in the 1930s.

The sustained increase in PDE share is noticeable. The rate of increase is moderate during early periods 1)–4), but sharply accelerates toward the 1930s. During periods 9)–11), it reaches a very high level. The share remains almost unchanged in "gross" figures but decreases in "net" series during this interval. Over the entire period, however, no sizable difference is seen between the two series: 1), (3) excluding and 2), (4) including residential construction. The effects of artificial acceleration due to military mobilization in the 1930s should be noted, although the PDE share in Table 4.1 estimated for nonmilitary involvement shows no increase after period 9). PDE share reached the maximum at the beginning of the 1930s before military mobilization began in earnest.

How can such a pattern be characterized in international comparisons? No systematic data are readily available for capital stock by type in order to answer this question. A comparison with the USA may serve as supportive illustration, however. According to estimates by R.W. Goldsmith, the PDE shares (%) were 1900, 20; 1912, 23; 1929, 24; 1945, 25; and 1958, 31 in terms of net capital stock.[1] Around the turn of the century (between periods 5) and 6)), Japan reached around 20% in net capital stock. After that its accelerated pace of increase resulted in its PDE share reaching some 33% in period 8), a higher level than 31% in the USA in 1958. Differences in the ratio magnitude between the two cases are seen, and to that extent the shares of structures and nonresidential buildings in

[1] For details, see *LTES*, Vol. 3, chapter 2 (detailed citation in footnote to Table 4.1). U.S. estimates exclude perennial plant, and to that extent the PDE share is slightly higher in comparison with that in Japan.

Table 4.1
Shares of PDE in Capital Stock Accumulation, 1879–1938, Prewar Japan   (%)

| Period (overlapping decades) | (A) Capital Stock | | | | (B) Gross Domestic Investment | |
| | Gross Series | | Net Series | | | |
	Excluding Residential (1)	Including Residential (2)	Excluding Residential (3)	Including Residential (4)	(5)	(6)
1) 1879–1888	9.8	4.8	8.5	4.5	23.5	17.1
2) 1884–1893	10.7	5.1	9.1	4.8	24.5	16.5
3) 1889–1898	12.1	6.0	11.0	5.8	23.3	17.4
4) 1894–1903	14.6	7.5	14.2	7.5	24.5	19.8
5) 1899–1908	18.3	9.8	17.7	9.8	33.9	26.4
6) 1904–1913	22.4	12.6	21.4	12.5	42.5	34.8
7) 1909–1918	26.8	16.1	25.4	15.8	34.5	28.1
8) 1914–1923	33.6	21.6	32.5	21.7	25.5	21.1
9) 1919–1928	38.3	26.2	36.1	25.1	23.0	25.9
10) 1924–1933	38.7	27.3	33.2	23.6	23.4	23.4
11) 1929–1938	38.9	28.2	31.4	23.0	31.4	29.6

Sources: All capital stock data are from *Long-Term Economic Statistics (LTES)*, Vol. 3, Appendix Table 1. Data for total investment series are from *LTES*, Vol. 4, Appendix Table 1, *ibid*. Data for PDE investment are from the same source as for Table 4.7.

Remarks: Capital stock series in A are in 1934–1936 prices. Investment series (including residential buildings) in 5 are current prices, and 6 is in 1934–1936 prices. The price indices for gross domestic investment and PDE are from Table 4.10 calculated for the median years in each interval of overlapping decades so that possible distortions would be minor in long-term performance.

the USA are greater than those in Japan. It is contended that with regard to the long-term prewar period, Japan represents the pattern of latecomers, which is characterized by trend acceleration of economic growth rate.

Such bias toward PDE in capital resource allocation in terms of ratio magnitude and pattern over time must be relevant to the speed of borrowed technology diffusion in latecomers. It is desirable to elucidate this pattern in contemporary developing economies. The availability of capital stock data is limited, and thus the orthodox stock approach is precluded. The flow approach using investment data can be used as a proxy. For this, column 5 is included in Table 4.1, which is roughly comparable to the figures in column 2, including residential buildings. As expected, the PDE ratio is much higher in the investment series, mainly because its shorter service life and ratio difference tend to be greater for earlier periods due to the changes over time in the weights of capital items. The pattern over time of the two series, however, is broadly similar for the former interval, period 1) to period 6), although some discrepancy is seen in the latter interval. For the series of constant prices in column 6, as expected the pattern is much closer to that of stock series. During the former segment the PDE share increases distinctly, whereas during the latter segment the increasing trend ceases and declines occur.

The above is intended as background knowledge for observing the performance of PDE share in contemporary developing nations, for which data are limited even in flow series. To facilitate comparisons with Japan, Table 4.2 lists data for developing economies grouped by Y/L level for a single year.

The PDE share in total investment, including residential construction in column 3, is strikingly large at some 40–45%, with a tendency to increase in the former segment and to decrease to about 30% in group V. In current Japanese prices, from the former interval of the primary phase until approximately the turn of the century, the comparable share was some 23–24%, followed by an increase to over 40% at the end of the primary phase. In constant prices, it is some 17–20% during the former segment, nearly reaching the peak of 35%.

Precise comparison cannot be made between the cross-sectional and historical series. However, the following can be stated. First, in the early phase in developing economies, the PDE share is much higher than that of presently developed nations. Second, the greater share tends to be sustained during the subsequent path of develop-

Table 4.2
PDE Share in Developing Economies and Its Import Dependency, 1980

(%)

Group	I/Y (1)	PDE/Y (2)	PDE/I (3)	PDE Import Dependency (4)	PDE Import/ Total Investment (5)	(6)
I	19.7	7.8	39.5	57.7	22.8	23.6
II	24.8	9.7	39.1	59.1	23.1	33.9
III	21.8	9.8	45.1	41.0	18.5	33.5
IV	24.2	9.1	37.6	33.0	12.4	26.6
V	28.8	8.9	31.0	33.9	10.5	27.1

Source: Columns 1, 2, and 3 are from Kazushi Ohkawa, in collaboration with Katsuo Otsuka and Bernård Key, *Growth Mechanism of Developing Economies: Investment, Productivity and Employment (DE)* (Tokyo: International Development Center of Japan/International Center for Economic Growth, 1993), chapter 5, section III, Table 5.13. The original data are from the UN International Comparison Project. Columns 4 and 6 are from *DE*, chapter 6, section I, *DE*, Tables 6.5 and 6.3, respectively.

Remarks: Column 3 is derived from 2/1. In column 4 PDE is approximated by machinery. The figures for I are estimated by use of growth rates presented in *DE*, Table 6.4. Column 5 is 4/3, and column 6 is averages for 1960–1980.

ment. It begins to decrease toward higher groups, apparently corresponding to Japan's pattern in the semi-industrial phase around 1919, although this possibility requires further elucidation. The phenomenon of bias toward PDE identified earlier for Japan emerges much more strongly in contemporary developing economies. Abrupt industrialization required a larger PDE share from the start and was followed by additional increases during the subsequent phase.

This requirement is met by a far greater (twofold) PDE import-dependency ratio (compare column 4 of Table 4.2 with column 1 of Table 4.8 in section II). Together with column 5, these pertain to a single year. Although comparable data on domestic production of machinery are not available, the average amount of machinery imports can be estimated for 1960–1980 as the ratio to gross domestic capital formation I. This is shown in Table 4.2, column 6. Although the pressure of the PDE import requirement is sustained, developing economies must meet this important requirement. Therefore greater PDE share inevitably leads to its greater import dependency, raising the important issue of import substitution by promoting domestic production. The mechanism of this is discussed below, because it is relevant to PDE bias.

From the viewpoint of investment, columns 5 and 6 in Table 4.2 show the position of PDE imports in gross domestic capital formation. The two cannot be directly used to compare the rate of PDE import decrease by group because the original data differ, but a broad picture is presented. With a slow tendency to decrease, the ratio is sustained at higher levels than in historical Japan at a ratio of 5–10% (derived from column 3 in Table 4.8 and column 5 in Table 4.1). Pointing out this feature of contemporary developing economies does not necessarily imply failures of resource allocation, but is done to emphasize the significance of the difference from the historical path of presently developed economies. Amplification may be needed to clarify this point.

On the one hand, technology diffusion requires more imports of PDE, while resource restraints require promotion of domestic PDE production on the other. The two operate interactively. It is not easy to grasp how the mechanism actually works, but a simple approach is to examine the ratio in Table 4.2, column 6—PDE import to total domestic investment—and break it down into the familiar subgroups classified in terms of investment efficiency: greater A versus smaller B (chapter 1). The relevant terms are listed in

Table 4.3
PDE Import and Investment Efficiency, 1960–1980, by Subgroup: Developing Economies

(%)

	Subgroup	I	II	III	IV	V
1) Mp/I	A	24.8	33.2	32.6	23.0	21.7
	B	22.4	34.5	34.4	30.2	32.4
2) I/ΔY	A	4.7	3.2	3.0	4.2	6.4
	B	6.0	6.9	3.6	5.0	6.5
		Average of I and II				
3) GMp	A	5.9		9.0	3.5	7.8
	B	4.9		5.8	3.3	7.6
4) GDp	A	7.0		15.6	12.0	5.1
	B	7.3		8.8	9.3	2.4

Source: 1) and 2) are from *DE, op. cit.*, Table 6.3; 3) and 4) are from *DE*, Table 6.4. In these tables, the subgrouping is E versus F, but is used here as a proxy for A versus B, 1960–1980.

Remark: GMp and GDp are the average rates of growth of import and domestic production of PDE, respectively.

Table 4.3. Mp/I stands for the ratio of PDE import to investment and I/ΔY, the ICOR, is specifically adopted as a rough proxy of investment efficiency.

In Table 4.3, the ratio Mp/I is smaller in A than in B except for group I. This suggests that PDE import substitution goes on faster in A, although the difference is less distinct for lower groups. The magnitude of ICOR is definitely smaller in A than in B. The negative association between the two can be interpreted in various ways. It is possible that greater PDE import substitution is realized in economies where greater investment efficiency and higher productivity growth rates are realized. Providing evidence for and interpreting this possibility are important but difficult tasks because PDE domestic production cannot be systematically linked with the data in the table. Lines 3) and 4) are added to Table 4.3 to give relevant information in terms of growth rates of import, GMp and production, and GDp of PDE. The GDp > GMp pattern is common to both subgroups. Domestic production proceeds faster than imports and import substitution appears to be similar in subgroups A and B, although a noticeable difference occurs in magnitude. Both GMp and GDp are greater in A than in B; the more rapid increase in PDE imports appears to be associated with a much more rapid increase in PDE domestic production in subgroup comparison. This suggests that import substitution activity cannot be elucidated merely by comparing the difference or variation in the ratio of imports/domestic production. On the one hand, PDE imports tend to increase not only due to increased domestic investment demand, but also due to raised technology level. PDE domestic production activity, on the other hand, is augmented with varying degrees of correspondence by the impact of higher technology level in individual nations. This implies the dynamic aspect of import substitution activities.

The meaning of this implication can be illustrated in the technology dimension. A representative example is PDE composition change due to technological advance, e.g., a shift of requirement, say, from general machinery to electric machinery takes place in developing economies. The issue of import substitution must shift from the former to the latter. Before general machinery technology is completely absorbed import requirements for electric machinery may increase, creating a second import substitution problem. The example is simple, but suffices to indicate the sequential relationships that exist between the emergence of import requirements and the corresponding need to promote domestic production. The figures in Table

4.3 imply, among others, such a sequential path with varying speed: faster A versus slower B. To that extent, the ratio Mp/I describes the effects of technological advance: first, absorption of foreign technological knowledge through increasing PDE imports and then the subsequent path of its internal progress by promoting sequential domestic production. Since the discussion here pertains to investment, I/ΔY is used to observe whether the variance of these effects between subgroups is associated with that of investment efficiency as a rough macro measure. The answer is affirmative. Better performance of import substitution leads to higher investment efficiency, or vice versa, although no causal relationship exists between the two. Instead, the same basic factors are the common cause of variance in Mp/I and I/ΔY performance: factors relevant to variance in the level and components of social capability.

The validity of these arguments should be tested by examining changes over time in individual cases. That is beyond the present scope, but selected successful cases are briefly observed to supplement the comparison of cross-section averages. Throughout the development path, the ratio Mp/I is assumed to sustain a tendency to increase up to a certain point, from which it may begin to decrease in successful cases. The sequential path described earlier reaches its turning point when the decrease begins. Japan's case is not typical because the path of secondary import substitution during 1919–1960 was interrupted by World War II, as discussed in detail in Annex I. Table 4.4 shows changes over time in Mp/I for the Republic of Korea and Taiwan.

The turning point appears to be somewhere between periods 3) and 4) in Korea, but in Taiwan a plateau appears to be sustained. The distinct trend of Mp/I ratio increase ceases after period 3). This focus on technology-investment aspects differs from the conventional phase demarcation of secondary import substitution in terms of durable goods, although it is close to it. For reference, ratio Xp/Mp is added to the table. Exports actually began to increase considerably from period 3) onward. If the import net of exports is used the turning point is 2) Korea and 3) Taiwan, as shown by the ratios in parentheses. Secondary export substitution began there in the sense that it began to replace the export of nondurable goods. In subsequent years the end of this phase will be reached (the mid-1970s in Japan's case).

As a complementary, instead of competing, comparison with conventional phasing, another approach in terms of investment with data on domestic PDE production added is recommended. But even

Table 4.4
Changes over Time in the Ratio of PDE Import to Gross Domestic Investment: Korea and Taiwan

(%)

	Mp/I				Xp/Mp	
Period	Korea			Taiwan	Korea	Taiwan
1) 1962–1966	17.1	(16.6)	16.4	(14.8)	3.0	9.9
2) 1967–1971	28.3	(26.4)	25.9	(21.2)	6.8	18.3
3) 1972–1976	33.3	(22.6)	34.0	(21.6)	32.1	36.4
4) 1977–1981	27.1	(13.5)	34.8	(15.7)	49.5	54.8

Source: International Development Center of Japan worksheets based on International Monetary Fund data (for details, see Table 4A.2).
Notation: Mp is used, although the data pertain to PDE. Xp stands for exports.
Remarks: For Taiwan 1) 1963–1966; 4) 1977–1980. The figures in parentheses are for
net exports.

without this it would be safe to say that after passing the turning
point the PDE domestically produced tends to increase relative to
its import through a sustained path of sequential technological
advances. This provides the technological basis for the secondary
export substitution phase to proceed.

It is important to note that the greater PDE share in contemporary developing economies is due to a combined process of high
import dependency and import substitution process. Absorbing
technological knowledge at higher levels requires increased PDE
imports and thus increases the PDE share. While latecomers enjoy
the favorable effects of the telescoping process, greater PDE share
is indispensable for them because their rate of technology diffusion
must be more rapid than that of their predecessors. Contemporary
developing economies are late-latecomers as compared to Japan in
this respect, despite differences among nations. The greater PDE
share as compared with Japan is a necessary, acceptable phenomenon in association with the possibly greater telescoping effects.

Higher Prices of Producer Durables
The strong pressure of high price raises the cost of producer dur-
ables in contemporary developing economies. In chapter 3, section
II, this was examined by industrial sector by presenting levels of
Y/Lw and relevant terms in comparisons of ppp and national price

measures. However, this pertained to capital in general, not specifically to PDE. Here PDE is the main concern, although its sectoral breakdown is impossible. The present problem recognition may differ from the usual treatment because the importance of deviation in PDE prices among nations is emphasized instead of simply dealing with averages. This is basically due to the conceptual framework in which factor input prices for developing economies cannot be assumed to be "given" but to a certain extent can be understood as an independent variable depending upon national performance, as was suggested earlier in the discussion of the relation between PDE import and domestic production. The treatment of prices can be conventional and does not require a preliminary assessment, unlike shares. Below, the general situation of developing economies is explained using group averages, and then the differentials among nations are examined.

It is widely known that capital goods are extremely expensive in developing economies. In *DE*, chapter 5, section III, ppp data provided by the United Nations International Comparison Project are utilized since their significance has been clarified quantitatively. The figures for relevant terms are summarized in Table 4.5, for the single year 1980. Supplementary data are available for 1975 but not for earlier years.

The conceptual basis of ppp measures is "equivalence" of commodities as defined from expenditures, and the lower level of GDP prices in lower groups is well known, as clearly shown in column 1 of the table. Taking column 1 as the standard, the ppp of producer durables tends to be increasingly higher toward lower groups, as shown by the ratio PDE/GDP in the same column (the exceptional low for I is questionable). This is the simplest indicator of the high price pressure of PDE. Column 2 is intended to clarify this further, viewed from the expenditure-costs aspect. In national currency the ratio PDE/GDP is larger but the range of variance is limited among groups. This corresponds to the conventional term for investment proportion I/Y, the relative magnitude of which in developing economies has often been pointed out. In this case of PDE in particular, as shown by (a), the ratio of PDE/GDP is surprisingly greater for developing economies (again with questionable exception of I) as compared to that of group V representing developed economies. By ppp measure, the ratio tends to be much lower in developing economies as compared to group V (irregularity among groups requires further investigation). As discussed in chapter 3, section II, if the ppp measure is assumed to be a quantitative indicator, the ratio

Table 4.5
Prices of Producer Durables by ppp and Relevant Terms in Group Averages, 1980

Group	(1) ppp			(2) Ratio in Expenditure PDE/GDP			(3) Ratio in Expenditure Construction/GDP		
	PDE	GDP	PDE/GDP	(a) In National Currency	(b) In ppp	(a)/(b)	(a) In National Currency	(b) In ppp	(a)/(b)
I	120.3	51.4	2.34	7.76	2.69	2.89	11.90	4.14	2.87
II	176.3	53.1	3.32	9.69	4.75	2.04	15.09	7.29	2.07
III	153.1	58.2	2.63	9.82	3.72	2.64	11.94	8.65	1.38
IV	164.6	79.9	2.06	9.09	4.57	1.99	15.10	16.24	0.93
V	124.5	119.7	1.24	8.93	6.92	1.29	19.86	19.28	1.03
USA	100.0	100.0	1.00	8.33	8.33	1.00	9.84	7.84	1.00

Source: Table 5.8 for (1), Table 5.11 for (2), and Table 5.13 for (3), all from *DE, op. cit.*
Remark: Grouping is by Y/L level, but the countries are not the same as for previous cases due to data limitations.

(a)/(b) shown in the same column indicates the magnitude of the very high costs for PDE in meeting technological requirements in developing economies.

Column 3 for construction is provides additional comparisons between the two major component of gross domestic investment. The performance of construction is obvious in (a) and (b) in this column. The specific concern here is the ratio (a)/(b) in comparison with the corresponding ratio of PDE. It might be expected that the ratio would be much lower for construction and this expectation is met in most developing economies (groups III and IV, together with group V). However, the two ratios are nearly equal with regard to the lower groups I and II. Why is there such a difference between the former and the latter segment? The answer is found in the major influence of the extremely high proportion of construction expenditure in African countries. Imported construction materials may be partly responsible, although the details are not clear. At any rate, in these countries the characteristics of low prices of construction due to use of local elements nearly disappear. In the non-African countries in groups I and II, where local elements operate normally, the high PDE prices prevail, as discussed earlier.

To analyze the effects of PDE prices on its share, the share in ppp measures, PDE/I (I: PDE + construction), can be derived from the figures in Table 4.5 as follows (%):

I	II	III	IV	V
39.4	39.5	30.1	23.0	26.4

As compared with the corresponding figures in Table 4.2, the shares in the latter segments III and IV are much smaller (and somewhat smaller for V), whereas in former segments I and II no sizable difference is seen. This can be interpreted to mean that the relative highness of PDE prices are affected to a considerable extent in all developing economies, but the peculiar situation of African countries mentioned above may disrupt this general tendency.

Since the PDE import-dependency is large in developing economies, its price is not expected to differ much between individual nations. To what extent is this expectation actually met? The answer to this question is important because it provides basic information on the possibility of individual national responses to the pressure of high PDE prices. Two examination procedures are adopted. The

Table 4.6
Variation in International PDE and GDP Price Levels in ppp by Group (US = 1), 1980

A

Group	PDE			GDP			PDE/GDP
	Average	L	H	Average	L	H	Average
I (5; L3, H2)	1.348	1.270	1.465	0.515	0.466	0.630	2.62
II (7; L4, H3)	1.467	1.357	1.614	0.606	0.579	0.641	2.62
III (7; L4, H3)	1.421	1.210	1.565	6.000	0.669	0.548	2.40
IV (9; L5, H4)	1.649	1.355	2.016	0.749	0.691	0.821	2.20
V (10; L5, H5)	1.496	1.311	1.682	1.197	1.164	1.230	1.25

B

Group	PDE		GDP	
	A	B	A	B
I (A3, B2)	1.406	1.261	0.505	0.572
II (A4, B3)	1.357	1.614	0.579	0.641
III (A3, B4)	1.210	1.565	0.669	0.548
IV (A4, B5)	1.427	1.820	0.668	0.814
V (A6, B4)	1.372	1.682	1.179	1.224

Source: United Nations, *World Comparisons of Purchasing Power and Real Product for 1980*, Phase IV of the International Comparison Project, Part One, Table 9.

Remarks: i) The figures in parentheses in the group column are numbers of countries selected.
ii) Simple averages are used.
iii) Subgroups L (lower) and H (higher) are divided to make the number even by the order of magnitude of ppp of PDE in panel A.
iv) Subgroups A and B in panel B correspond with the subgrouping in chapter 1 in terms of macro investment efficiency. The original subgrouping differs for a few countries.

first establishes the variation of high (H) or low (L) PDE price itself and in relation to that of GDP. The second examines the variation using the present subgroup classification. Both remain in the framework of group Y/L levels previously used. Table 4.6 summarizes the results, in which panel A is from the first and panel B from the second procedure.

Each nation has its own domestic price system as measured by ppp of GDP. Even within the same group it varies to a considerable extent. With respect to the PDE price a similar pattern appears. As expected, however, PDE price shows fewer differences than GDP price in group average comparisons (panel A). The ratio PDE/GDP tends to be greater for lower groups almost without exception, as pointed out above. Nevertheless, within each group there is sizable variance in PDE price. The ratio (%) to the average is as follows:

	I	II	III	IV	V
L	94.2	92.5	85.2	82.2	87.6
H	108.7	110.0	110.1	148.8	112.4

The variance tends to be wider toward higher groups except for V. The wider difference between individual nations is illustrated by the largest range between Korea (93.4) versus Paraguay (203.4) in III and Brazil (119.3) versus Argentina (292.6) in IV. These variations can be explained to a certain extent by GDP price variation. This is a natural expectation. Its ratio to the group average is actually as follows:

	I	II	III	IV	V
L	90.5	95.5	111.5	92.3	97.2
H	122.3	105.8	91.3	109.6	102.8

The ratios shown above suggest a somewhat positive association between the two prices, except in group III. To that extent it is possible to say that lower (higher) PDE price levels take place in association with lower (higher) GDP price levels. For example, in group II for Pakistan, PDE is 105.5 with GDP 31.6, while for Senegal PDE is 160.0 with GDP 95.8, and in IV, for the example mentioned earlier, GDP is Brazil 61.5 versus Argentina 141.3. However, the association is not very strong. Thus, although international elements operate influentially in determining PDE prices, the operation of national elements must also be recognized to a certain extent.

In determining PDE price levels the effects of other factors are important as well, as illustrated earlier by the deviation of group III from the broad tendency. In order to examine the plausibility of this supposition, panel B in Table 4.6 is presented as a means to test the effects of other factors. It is the presumption here that the differential of PDE price levels is associated with domestic investment efficiency. In panel B, subgroups A and B are adopted to observe the differentials of PDE price levels based on this presumption. The implication is as follows. The results of analysis in chapter 1 showed that the magnitude of the factors relevant to technology diffusion is greater in subgroup A and smaller in subgroup B. The interpretation is that such a difference is indicative of level differences in social capability, which integrates basic factors pertaining to the absorption of advanced technology. The association of PDE price level with investment efficiency by subgrouping suggests the actual operation of one of these basic factors at issue.

Panel B in Table 4.6 shows that the PDE price level is definitely lower in subgroup A and higher in B for the entire range from II to V (a reverse in group I is questionable). The ratio (%) to the group average is as follows:

Subgroup	II	III	IV	V
A	92.4	85.2	82.2	91.7
B	109.9	110.1	110.4	112.4

Thus the presumption that PDE price levels are associated with domestic investment efficiency is valid. For reference, the figures for GDP prices are added to panel B. GDP prices appear generally associated in this subgrouping, although again there is the exception of group III. Statistically, the figures in panels A and B are intermingled to some extent. Focusing on the second approach, however, why are PDE price levels lower for subgroup A and higher for subgroup B? The "border price" must be the same except for transportation costs, tariffs, and customs related to PDE import. The differential must essentially be due to national elements, although this view is not endorsed sufficiently by the findings above, perhaps because "snapshot" data are limited. But beyond that, data that can be used to elucidate the ways in which national elements operate are lacking. Thus the performance of domestic supply-production of PDE is left untouched in the present discussion. Nevertheless, the strong pressure of expensive PDE prices on developing economies is not "given" as the conventional factor price thesis assumes, but to a certain extent can be mitigated. The differences between nations in the ability to do so suggests an important implication for development policy. The underlying mechanism is not completely clear and requires further investigation (see Annex II).

The preceding discussion of the PDE relationship in terms of import ratio to investment Mp/I and investment efficiency I/ΔY, referring to Tables 4.3 and 4.4, is relevant to the sequential process of import and domestic production. The hypothesis may imply more efficient import substitution in A than in B, although further examination of the performance of domestic supply-production of PDE is necessary. In order to back up this argument, Japan's historical experience is examined to determine the changes over time in the price of PDE. It is hypothesized that the relative price of PDE will show a long-term trend of decline over time in the general price level of the domestic economy in successful cases of industrialization. The reason is the shift of the supply curve to the right, mainly due to the faster rate of productivity increase in PDE production activities while its increased demand is sustained. Applying this hypothesis to the historical records of prewar Japan, changes over time in the relative price of PDE are observed from three aspects: relative to the general price in the macro economy; relative to investment goods; and relative to the general output prices of the manufacturing sector. The second represents the demand-expenditure aspect and the third the supply-production aspect, respectively. Table 4.7 presents simple averages of two years taken to represent the center of the overlapping decade chosen in Table 4.1.

The hypothesis appears generally valid for Japan's case throughout the entire period. Particularly distinct is the sharp leveling down of the ratio in the years after World War I in both series A and B. This exactly corresponds to the basic demarcation of the two major phases. The secondary phase can thus be characterized by lower PDE prices than in the primary phase. This is reasonably acceptable in view of faster PDE productivity growth in the so-called semi-industrial phase. The ratio (5)/(4) in panel B in Table 4.7 for manufacturing products shows a distinct trend of decline almost from the beginning. This pattern is also witnessed for the other ratios, although the pace of decline appears somewhat slower. Since there

Table 4.7
Relative Prices of PDE: Changes over Time in Prewar Historical Japan

(Price index, 1934–1936 = 100)

Selected Years	(A) Expenditure					(B) Manufacturing		
	General Price (1)	PDE Price (2)	Ratio (2)/(1)	Investment Goods (3)	Ratio (2)/(3)	Total Output Price (4)	Machinery Price (5)	Ratio (5)/(4)
1) 1884, 85	32.1	43.6	135.8	31.7	137.5	35.0	48.4	138.3
2) 1888, 89	31.1	52.8	169.8	35.8	148.9	36.0	57.9	160.8
3) 1893, 94	31.4	48.7	155.1	36.3	134.2	39.3	54.1	137.4
4) 1898, 99	45.2	64.7	143.1	52.3	123.7	57.5	71.9	105.0
5) 1903, 04	52.4	67.8	129.4	52.9	128.0	64.1	76.2	118.9
6) 1908, 09	58.7	70.1	122.8	59.1	122.0	78.0	77.6	102.1
7) 1913, 14	64.7	76.9	118.9	62.7	122.6	78.1	82.6	105.8
8) 1918, 19	122.2	164.6	134.7	136.2	120.9	173.9	170.2	97.8
9) 1923, 24	131.2	122.9	93.6	147.5	83.3	150.0	138.7	92.5
10) 1928, 29	117.4	102.7	87.5	115.8	88.7	101.7	106.5	87.5
11) 1933, 34	97.3	99.8	102.6	100.0	99.8	101.2	103.1	101.9
12) 1937, 38	118.2	144.7	125.6	136.2	106.2	135.9	148.8	109.5

Source: LTES, Vol. 8, "Prices" (K. Ohkawa and others), Appendix Tables.
For (A) (1), from Table 1; and (2) from Table 7. For (B), both (4) and (5) from Table 15.
Remark: PDE in (A) (2) and (3) is a sum of machinery, tools, and ships.

are no systematic data on the supply aspect for developing economies, this deserves particular attention. Although it does not necessarily coincide with the pattern of PDE import/production ratios to
be discussed later, the findings provide important information for interpreting the initiation of PDE import substitution. It was suggested previously that a certain amount of domestic PDE production can be assumed beyond the specific scope of hybrid technology.
This must be examined further, but PDE price performance appears
to confirm this assumption. The hypothesis can be applied not only
to modern but also to traditional technology advances. During the
primary phase the productivity of producing machinery can be
assumed to increase more rapidly, at least relative to that of total
manufacturing products.

It is known that the final shift to secondary export substitution in
Japan eventually became possible in the 1960s. The story of its process from the end years of the prewar period is outside the present
scope.[2] The main concern here is the significance of the "early" start
of relative decline in PDE price in the primary phase and its fuller
realization in the secondary phase in the prewar period. The sustained trend of shifting PDE supply curve is mostly due to the more
rapid rate of productivity increase in PDE production. Yet it should
be noted that the development of the domestic market and its structure played a considerable role in this process, although it was supported by the protectionist policies of the government and demand
effects of defense expenditures.

It is important to determine how and why such a domestic market
is formed and developed. Based on the conventional notion of a
uniform market, no realistic answer can be derived. One must
therefore examine the differentiated characteristics of the market,
referred to as the multirange structure of the domestic market. This
pertains to both supply and demand sides (makers and users). In the
analysis of technology diffusion in chapter 2, the three-range
approach by firm scale was adopted with regard to manufacturing.

---

[2] In *OK* (Kazushi Ohkawa and Hirohisa Kohama, *Lectures on Developing Economies: Japan's Experience and Its Relevance* [Tokyo: University of Tokyo Press,
1989]), Lecture 4, the phase of secondary export substitution is fully analyzed (pp.
118–158), focusing on the technological-organization progress of machinery industries. During the 1950s textiles still were the major export; machinery exports sur-
passed those of textiles in 1961. A decade later in 1971, machinery exports were
50% of the total exports of manufactured goods, while textiles were only 11%.
Through detailed examination it is concluded that the phase of secondary export
substitution starts at the beginning of the 1960s and ends in the mid-1970s (p. 157).

That is also relevant here, although the approach is basically concerned with the supply aspect. With respect to PDE import activities, top-level firms (L) are the major route of technology diffusion and are associated with international elements on the one hand. On the other, at the lowest level consisting of small-scale firms (S), traditional elements are more influential and PDE imports are not directly relevant to production activities. For the sake of simplicity, the intermediate range (M) can be taken to prevail, although the range of variation when S and L are combined may vary widely depending upon the subsectors concerned.[3]

Japan's protectionist policies relied mainly on tariff measures. Import control by quota was adopted only after 1937 as an emergency measure. Similar to many contemporary developing nations, prewar Japan adopted the so-called escalating tariff structure, with clear-cut distinctions between tariff rates for consumer goods (higher) and capital goods (lower). In 1913, the year immediately after tariff autonomy was fully established, the average tariff rate was 17.3% for capital goods as against 30.1% for consumer goods. In 1938, the beginning year of artificial heavy industrialization, the difference had widened to 7.3% for the former as against 63.1% for the latter.[4] Tariff measures for PDE appear to operate differently, corresponding broadly to the primary and secondary major phases. In the former, virtually no effects due to the lack of tariff autonomy are seen, while during the latter to a certain extent the PDE domestic market is protected by tariffs with only moderate effects. Most likely the Japanese government recognized the import requirement and avoided levying overly high tariff rates that would have unduly discouraged PDE imports.

---

[3] In this respect, valuable knowledge can be drawn from the detailed research by Mitsugu Sawai, "Multilayer Type Development of Machine Tool Industry in the 1920s," Chapter 9, in Ryoshin Minami and Yukihiko Kiyokawa, eds., *Japan's Industrialization and Technology Advance* (Tokyo: Toyokeizai Shimposha, 1987) (in Japanese). Viewed from the sides of both users and makers, the author presents three different markets: i) imported machine dominant, ii) domestically produced machine dominant, and iii) competitive market of imported and domestically produced elements. i) is composed of the major enterprises in the electronic machinery and aircraft industry; iii) pertains to major enterprises mostly belonging to military demand, shipbuilding, railways, and general machinery; and ii) pertains dominantly to small-scale users. The share of imported machinery in 1920–1930 was roughly 60–80% in i), 34% in iii), and almost zero in ii), whereas the share of ii) in total demand was roughly 40–45%, approximated by small-scale firms with 5–29 workers.

[4] Cf. *OK.* "External Restraint and Industrial Policy," in lecture 7, in particular Table 7.1.

A symbolic example is presented by the case of machine tools, a backward subsector for which tariff rates were kept relatively low. In 1926, however, tariffs were drastically increased, to be lowered again in the latter part of the 1930s. Import substitution and the technology requirement alternately appear stronger, representing "selective import substitution" in the context of technology diffusion. In fostering operational domestic market and production activities, flexible protection policies and measures rather than stereotyped protectionism thus appear more workable in terms of the relation between international and domestic elements.

II. Problems for Latecomers: Relevance of Japan's Historical Experience

In discussing the significance of PDE in terms of shares and prices, Japan's experience has been dealt with fairly intensively to clarify the problems of developing economies. In this section, the possible relevance of Japan's experience to contemporary developing countries is examined in two parts. First, an attempt is made to clarify the sequential relationship between the production of PDE and its import by emphasizing the significance of the competitive aspect on the domestic market. Second, the major theme of relevance is discussed mainly in terms of the characteristics of the machinery industry and the telescoping process of latecomers.

Domestic Production and Import of Producer Durables
Technology advance requires further imports of PDE on the one hand, but its import substitution by promoting its domestic production is an indispensable process of development on the other. Developing economies face a number of difficulties pertaining to secondary import substitution between the primary export substitution and the secondary export substitution stage. This is the conventional way of demarcating phases of shifting trade patterns, and while this broad framework is useful, the significance of promoting PDE domestic production should be analyzed explicitly. Secondary import substitution is not merely a step toward secondary export substitution but in itself comprises significant activities in promoting technology diffusion in the domestic economy.

It is a widely accepted view that Japan's long-term development process consisted of two major phases, the primary and secondary, demarcated by the end of World War I, which is reconfirmed in chapter 7. This phase demarcation is desirable in discussing the possible relevance of Japan's long-term performance to contemporary developing economies; without it, no legitimate comparisons can be made between Japan's case and individual developing economies. An alternative is phasing in terms of shifting trade patterns as mentioned above. Because domestic production is treated below, this alternative is not adopted, but the two phasing approaches are essentially complementary.[5] Data on changes over time in PDE import and domestic production are summarized in Table 4.8 to clarify the requirement and substitution pattern.

Japan is widely known as a country with a very slight import dependency of PDE, largely because of the ratio of PDE imports to gross domestic capital formation. Although this is the focus of subsequent discussion, another aspect pertaining to manufacturing is the focus here, to allow direct observation of the relationship of import to domestic production. The overview obtained from column 1 in Table 4.8 is that the ratio of import to domestic production does not necessarily present a smooth inverse U-shaped curve that would indicate a regular pattern consistent with the phase framework: first a tendency for ratio increase and then another tendency to decrease, with 1919 being the turning point. The first tendency of ratio increase is distinctly witnessed, followed by another tendency to decrease, but the turning point comes much earlier, and, furthermore, it increases again. The ratio in column 2 in Table 4.8 broadly presents a similar pattern. This is the problem at issue, and it needs more detailed investigation.

First, the ratio of import-production, column 1, reached its peak early in period 5) for capital goods and for PDE in period 4). Until that period the ratio tends to increase sharply and after that begins to decrease. Its rate of decline for periods 5)–8) is also rapid. This illustrates the impact of import restraints Japan faced during the World War I period. PDE domestic production was encouraged (column 3), but this topic requires separate treatment. At this juncture, the concern is with the formation of the inverse U-shape by such *ad hoc* exogenous factors. The ratio regained its normal lower

---

[5] Regarding the details of phase demarcation in terms of trade patterns, see John C.H. Fei, Kazushi Ohkawa, and Gustav Ranis, "Economic Development in Historical Perspective: Japan, Korea and Taiwan," in Kazushi Ohkawa and Gustav Ranis with Larry Meissner, eds., *Japan and the Developing Countries* (Oxford: Basil Blackwell, 1985).

Table 4.8
Imports of Producer Durables and Domestic Production: Manufacturing, Japan, 1879–1938

Periods (overlapping decades)	(1) Import/Production		(2) Ratio to Import of Manufactures		(3) Ratio to Manufacturing Production	
	PDE	Capital Goods	PDE	Capital Goods	PDE	Capital Goods
1) 1879–1888	22.8	11.1	7.5	11.0	3.9	13.1
2) 1884–1893	28.4	18.0	11.8	16.1	5.7	11.9
3) 1889–1898	35.2	20.2	15.2	20.1	6.6	12.1
4) 1894–1903	54.2	27.3	17.6	24.5	5.5	12.0
5) 1899–1908	51.5	32.3	16.6	24.8	5.2	11.5
6) 1904–1913	36.9	27.9	15.6	22.9	6.3	12.2
7) 1909–1918	19.5	17.9	11.0	20.6	9.2	15.1
8) 1914–1923	11.1	15.9	10.7	22.1	10.9	16.0
9) 1919–1928	23.7	25.1	13.5	24.9	10.2	12.6
10) 1924–1933	25.2	24.5	13.1	24.4	8.5	11.4
11) 1929–1938	14.9	14.9	15.0	24.1	8.7	13.8

Source: Yuichi Shionoya, "Structural Change in Demand for Manufacturing Products," Chapter 6, Appendix Tables 13 and 14, in Kazushi Ohkawa and Ryoshin Minami, eds., *Kindai Nihon no Keizai Hatten* (Economic development of modern Japan) (Tokyo: Toyokeizai Shimposha, 1975).

Remarks: i) Ratio percentages are calculated from the annual series in current prices.
ii) Decade averages are shown with five-year overlapping for smoothing.
iii) The difference between capital goods and PDE is virtually all due to construction materials.

level in periods 9) and 10). A sharp decline again in period 11) is caused by artificial industrialization for military mobilization.

Second, compare the ratios (columns 2 and 3, respectively) between the earlier interval until period 6) and the later interval from period 8) onward. On the one hand, the ratio of PDE import to total import of manufactures was kept at around 16–18% during the former interval, whereas it tended to decrease to some 11–13% during the latter. On the other hand, the ratio of PDE production to total manufacturing production was sustained at some 5–6% during the former interval, whereas it tended to increase distinctly to 9–10% during the latter interval. With respect to the performance of capital goods, however, such structural changes are not identified or are less distinctly witnessed from both the import and domestic production aspect. The ratio in column 2 was sustained at some 20–25% through both the former and the latter intervals, except for very early periods and during World War I. The ratio in column 3 appears to continue at 11–12% during the former interval, followed by somewhat higher levels during the latter.

The problem of phase shifts is not treated specifically here, but attention is drawn to the significance of changes in PDE performance that clearly demarcate the two intervals under consideration. A domestic shift of resources to PDE production could result in less dependence on imports of PDE, a typical pattern of import substitution. What should be explained is the discrepancy found in time dimension between the pattern of import substitution and the conventional phasing, since the former comes much earlier than expected from the latter. Is it possible to incorporate PDE performance into conventional phasing without ignoring its substantive significance? This important problem is discussed below.

Elsewhere the authors referred to this time as the "early start" of secondary import substitution (cf. *OK*, lecture 2). Here the conceptual significance is retained while a more comprehensive empirical basis is provided. To begin with the distortion in the composition of the machine industry by output share (%) in 1909,[6] the major firms were in steel shipbuilding (39.9) and mining machinery and equipment (19.8), as against less than 50% for other items. Such distortions suggest the causes of the tendency to decrease in the import-production ratio of PDE, which was witnessed earlier around the turn of the century (Table 4.8). If the early start is responsible, however, what was the PDE ratio performance of other machinery

---

[6] Data from *OK*, Table 2A.1.

and equipment? Is it also responsible for the early start of PDE import-substitution?

The data for 1909 referred to earlier are not available for earlier years. An illustrative estimate utilizes the dichotomy of PDE into shipbuilding versus nonshipbuilding (no data are available for mining). Table 4.9 summarizes the relevant data. The share of ships in PDE production in column 1 shows a sharp rise around the turn of the century in period 4). After that the high share was maintained, although with a slight tendency to decrease. Thus between the former and the latter interval, that is, before and after period 4) (1899–1903), the composition of PDE changed drastically. The import-production ratio of ships in a) of column 2 shows a remarkable increase in the former interval, followed by a drastic decrease in the latter interval. The exact correspondence is identified in terms of import substitution between the two ratios in columns 1 and 2 a). The authors share the view that the early start of secondary import substitution occurred due to the effects of such biased development of specific industries. The role played by the government in initiating the early start is often pointed out, illustrated by the building of steel mills. Development of steel-shipbuilding was pursued by private enterprises, as discussed in chapter 2, but support rendered by the government made a major contribution. To that extent, the industrialization strategy of the government was influential.

The pattern of other PDE is shown by the figures in column 2 b). The pattern of the import-production ratio of nonships is distinct: during the former interval it tends to increase broadly, although somewhat slowly in early years, but peaks sharply in period 4) at 88%, and then begins to show a tendency to decrease during the latter interval. This is the same import-substitution pattern, although with differing magnitude and time dimension, as for the case of shipbuilding. The reason is as follows. The early start of PDE import substitution is a general phenomenon identified in the private sector in historical Japan, although the promoting effects of strategic distortions should also be recognized.

While available data are not sufficient for earlier years, the activities of the private sector can be characterized by a combined pattern of two features: one is a sustained increase in the import-dependency of PDE, mostly seen in cotton textiles, and the other is import substitution by domestic technological devices, typically seen in the raw silk industry. With respect to the former, Otsuka specified the year in which the import curve and domestic production curve crossed for three types of machinery: 1) 1915 for power weav-

Table 4.9
Shipbuilding Share in PDE, Import Production Ratio and the Total Ratio of PDE, Japan 1884–1918

(%)

Period (5-year averages)	(1) Production Share of Ships in PDE	(2) Import Production Ratio		(3) PDE Total
		(a) Ships	(b) Nonships	
1) 1884–1888	12.9	65.9	29.4	32.3
2) 1889–1893	12.0	48.5	21.1	24.4
3) 1894–1898	14.5	1115.1	34.2	45.9
4) 1899–1903	33.2	11.2	87.9	62.4
5) 1904–1908	23.1	9.6	52.5	40.6
6) 1909–1913	19.4	5.1	40.0	33.2
7) 1914–1918	30.3	Δ13.2	20.9	5.8

Sources: 1) and 2): S. Ishiwata data in Table 18, p. 190 and Table 21, p. 195, *LTES*, Vol. 3, *Capital Stock, op. cit.*; 3) from Kazushi Ohkawa and Nobukiyo Takamatsu, "Capital Formation, Productivity and Employment." *IDCJ Working Paper No. 26*, March 1983.

Remarks: In column 2 import is net of export. Δ means export > import. Column 2 (b) is simply calculated by use of the weight of PDE production on the period average.

ing machines; 2) 1925 for automatic weaving machines; and 3) 1930 for spinning machines. These are measured by incremental changes in the number of machines at work. The peak year of the import curve is around 1912 in 1), around 1923 in 2), and around 1927 in 3).[7] These represent the PDE performance pertaining to textiles, the major industry in the private sector. One receives the impression that machinery imports began to decrease from the beginning of the secondary major phase, although with regard to power weaving machines the early start element should be noted.

With respect to the latter, Minami and Makino's research is noteworthy.[8] It distinctly clarifies the significance of the so-called intermediate technology represented by wood-steel mixed spinning machines developed in the raw silk industry. During 1904–1914, the share of mixed machines increased, while that of wooden and steel machines decreased. Such intermediate or hybrid technology is highly significant in technology diffusion. However, it is desirable to evaluate it in terms of its contribution to the early start of PDE import substitution by promoting domestic machine production. The figures in Table 4.9 imply that the share of nonships in PDE products was rather high at 70–80% except in period 7). The effects of distortions may be underestimated and yet it is believed that machinery production in the private sector prevailed to a considerable extent, including activities of small-scale firms.[9] This important point will be returned to, but for the time being it should simply be pointed out that during the primary phase, in particular in its latter

---

[7] Keijiro Otsuka, "Development of Cotton Industry and Technological Innovations," chapter 6, in Ryoshin Minami and Yukihiko Kiyokawa, eds., *Nihon no Kogyoka to Gijutsu Hatten* (Industrialization and technological progress in Japan) (Tokyo: Toyokeizai Shimposha, 1987). He concluded that PDE imports are greatly determined by the domestic technological innovations so long as the capital formation is concerned.

[8] Ryoshin Minami and Fumio Makino, "Technology Choice in [the] Raw Silk Industry," chapter 3, in Ryoshin Minami and Yukihiko Kiyokawa, eds., *op. cit.*

[9] Detailed research results are presented by Tadashige Ishii, "Development of Production Technology of Power Weaving Machine," Chapter 7, in Ryoshin Minami and Yukihiko Kiyokawa, eds., *op. cit.* The following are particularly noteworthy: 1) Weaving machine production was carried out by small-scale firms: over half had fewer than five workers in the primary phase though it decreased sharply toward 1920. 2) The production of general machinery and equipment was jointly pursued to a considerable extent. A tendency to modernize weaving machine firms implies a possibility of developing general machine production. 3) During the primary phase the difference in demand for apparel (narrow breadth domestically versus wide internationally) played an influential role in development of power weaving machines of the traditional type, which were much cheaper than imported ones.

interval, machine production capability developed to a considerable extent, and this formed the basis for devising technology of the hybrid type. If this supposition is accurate, the early start is even more significant.

Finally, while the conventional approach views PDE import in terms of domestic capital formation, the authors retain the concept that PDE imported to latecomers from economically advanced countries is the *carrier* of technological knowledge. Qualification is needed on two points. First, this is not the same as the concept of "capital embodiment." In latecomers the import of capital goods and its domestic use for achieving the technological purpose are not the same. In order to treat it as "embodied" it must be assumed that equivalent capability exists in both latecomers and advanced countries, which is not the case. Second, PDE import is no doubt the major route of technology diffusion, but other routes operate as well. Technological knowledge and/or know-how can be transferred separately from capital goods import through technology contracts between enterprises, receiving of technical experts, etc. Currently the official development assistance route is an important addition.

The preceding discussion emphasized the importance of the technology aspect in dealing with the IOR formula due to the recognition that output effects of technology are realized by using capital stock K. Here, imported PDE is interpreted as its incremental increase ΔK. Data for specifying this relation are not available, but Table 4.10 shows data in terms of capital formation as proxies. Excluding ships, columns 1 and 3 show the PDE import-investment ratio. Column 3 is added to show the case including shipbuilding. These figures pertain to the macro level, not only the manufacturing sector. The magnitude of the ratio naturally differs. A different standpoint for deriving the ratio of investment to production is also used. This difference is important because with investment the problem concerns the resource allocation of investment funds. Specifically, the issue is how and to what extent investment resources are allocated for import of PDE and/or the use of domestically produced PDE. Two aspects can be considered separately. Assuming a certain total amount of PDE investment, the issue of resource allocation is that of domestically produced versus imported. From the macro viewpoint, the allocation issue is between PDE and non-PDE investment. Table 4.10 covers the former aspect. No exact comparison can be made between the relevant ratios in this table and in preceding tables. For example, column 3 in Table 4.10 pertains to the import net of exports, which was of considerable magni-

Table 4.10
PDE Import and Domestic Capital Formation: Import-Investment Ratios,
Prewar Japan

(%)

Period (overlapping decades)	General Machinery (1)	General Machinery, Including Others (2)	Total PDE, Ships Included (3)
1) 1879–1888	12.9	18.7	24.7
2) 1884–1893	15.2	22.0	26.4
3) 1889–1898	20.2	26.3	32.5
4) 1894–1903	22.2	29.2	35.0
5) 1899–1908	20.2	27.8	28.7
6) 1904–1913	15.7	20.0	21.3
7) 1909–1918	11.3	14.1	14.7
8) 1914–1923	15.1	13.2	16.6
9) 1919–1928	19.9	20.2	23.9
10) 1924–1933	16.6	22.6	22.1
11) 1929–1938	11.6	15.7	15.3

Sources: Ishiwata data, *LTES*, Vol. 3, *op. cit.*: 1 and 2 from Table 22 for imports and from Tables 18 and 19 for gross domestic investment; 3 from Tables 18 and 19 for both net international balance and gross domestic investment.
Remarks: i) 1 and 2 show amounts of import, but 3 shows net international balance.
ii) The others in 2 are rolling stock, tools, fixtures, and automobiles and other vehicles.
iii) All ratios are calculated from the series in current prices.
iv) The figures are in ten-year averages, five-year overlapping.

tude toward the 1930s, particularly to Asian countries. Yet, the long-term pattern appears broadly similar from both the production and investment approach in two points: clear identification of the early start and a considerable magnitude of the import ratio of capital goods is still recognized for the period after 1919.

The early start and its mechanism were points of primary phase analysis. Analysis of the secondary phase is concerned with elucidating the operation of a competitive market in the domestic economy to explain the development of the machine industry. During the primary phase competition operates, but mainly between agriculture and industry, as stated clearly by the term "primary export substitution." In the secondary phase competition within the realm of industry is the issue. Competition between textiles, the major export sector, and machinery, the newly developing sector, occurs through what is called a "simultaneous process." In order to deal with it simply and briefly, discussion focuses on the performance of wages in relation to output prices and productivity.

As clarified in chapter 3, the machine industry is characterized by its greater input of qualified labor as indicated by its higher wages. When compared with the textile industry, the leading subsector, in terms of K/Lw, the level of K/L, or capital intensity in the usual sense, does not differ much between these two subsectors of manufacturing. However, wages w are noticeably higher for machinery beyond the sex differential (female workers are dominant in textiles). This raises the problem of entrepreneur response to changes in wages in relation to changes in output prices and productivity.

To begin with, simple figures of the relevant terms for machinery industry, taking textiles = 100, are as follows for the beginning and the end years of the prewar semi-industrialized phase:[10]

	Wages	Value Productivity	Productivity in Real Terms*
1919	254	172	262
1938	286	273	207

* In 1934–1936 prices.

The relative wage was very high in 1919, but it increased further in 1938. One could expect a corresponding rise in productivity, but in real terms it drops. The expectation is met by a distinct rise in value productivity. The rise in relative output price seems to absorb the rise in relative level of wages. The range of variation of output prices was wide, so that a single-year comparison may not be sufficient. The broad picture of the competitive position of machinery versus textiles can be seen, however, which is important in indicating the difficulty faced by the newly developing machinery industry in increasing its competitive power in the domestic market to the level of that in textiles, the internationally competitive sector.

Data on wages are given in Table 4.11. First, with respect to the differential of nominal wages between the two subsectors in A, it is wider through all years except 1939, which is affected by military mobilization. In four-year averages for 1900–1915 and 1920–1935, textiles is 54.0 and machinery 142.4 for the former interval taking the manufacturing total as 100. The corresponding index for the lat-

---

[10] From *OK*, lecture 2, Table 2.1, p. 53. More detailed treatment is given there.

Table 4.11
Wages in Total Manufacturing Compared with Machinery and Textiles: Changes over Time in Prewar Historical Japan

	(A) Manufacturing Wages (per day, Sen)			(B) Wage Indices Deflated by Relevant Price Indices (1934–1936 = 100)			
	Total (Male) (1)	Machinery (Male) (2)	Textiles (Male, Female) (3)	(1)	(2)	(3)	(3′)
1900	38	55	19	61.9	77.6	31.2	56.5
1905	41	57	20	72.4	84.7	29.4	52.6
1910	48	64	27	75.0	76.3	40.0	67.7
1915	55	75	29	80.6	100.6	46.9	72.0
1920	181	224	92	195.2	159.9	49.3	92.2
1925	203	256	97	147.7	114.1	66.4	106.4
1930	205	249	79	91.8	93.3	112.9	109.2
1935	196	239	69	98.7	98.1	101.3	99.5
1939	232	245	85	167.0	148.8	80.9	101.5

Source: (A) from *LTES*, Vol. 8, "Prices," Appendix Table 27, *op. cit.* Price deflators for (B) from *DE*, *op cit.*, Tables A2.4, A2.5, except for (3) and (3′) from Tables A2 and A15.

Remarks: Wages in (A) are simply converted to indices, taking the 1934–1936 average = 100 and used for (B), where the price deflator is

(1) output prices of total manufacturing;
(2) output prices of machinery;
(3) ouput prices of textiles; and
(3′) general consumer prices.

ter interval is textiles 42.9 and machinery 122.7, when the differential narrowed slightly between machinery and total manufacturing. However, it widened between machinery and textiles. Assuming simply that the wages of textiles can represent the performance of wages of "unskilled" workers, we can say that the differential between "unskilled" and "skilled" as represented by machinery wages was widened between the two intervals under consideration.

Second, using the figures presented in B apart from (3′), the effects of wage changes on entrepreneur accounting can be assessed. The standard term Y/Lw is converted to QP/Lw (Q and P stand for output quantity and prices, respectively) where the reciprocal of ratio w/P changes over time. The values of the ratio taking 1934–1936 = 100 show wide variation in particular during the latter interval. Simple four-year averages for the former and latter interval are as follows:

	1900–1915	1920–1935
Textiles	36.9	82.0
Machinery	84.8	116.4
Total manufacturing	72.5	133.4

During the former interval, development of the textile industry depended heavily upon the use of cheap labor, as expected, while with respect to the machinery subsector the pressure of higher wages was notable. In the latter interval the situation changed greatly: the difference between textiles and machinery becomes much narrower. While the wage cost pressure increased in both subsectors, its degree was greater for textiles. In the case of machinery the ratio becomes even smaller than that in total manufacturing. Thus the real wage pressure became relatively weaker for the machinery subsector in a comparative sense. This is due mainly to the effect of changes in output prices. The ratio of output prices (machinery/textiles) changed in selected years as follows (from *OK*, Table 2.3):

1907–1916	1917–1926	1927–1936	1936–1939
87.1	70.3	90.3	105.3

The ratio tends to be favorable to machinery toward the end of the 1930s, with its base level in the years immediately after World War I.

Third, column B (3') is the conventional index of real wages in the textile industry deflated by the consumer price index. During the earlier interval, 1900–1915, not much change is seen compared to the latter interval. The model of unlimited supply of unskilled labor has often been applied to the primary phase, including Japan's case. Due to the scarcity of data the possibility of unchanged real wage levels for earlier years, before 1900, cannot be confirmed, although this interval is characterized by flexible supply of unskilled labor at cheap wages. Of more concern here is the difference between columns (3') and (3): the wage level is much lower in (3) than in (3'). Entrepreneurs in the textile industry could rely upon extremely cheap labor costs due to the favorable situation of output prices. Conceptually, it is not simply another version of flexible supply of labor because it pertains to the demand rather than the supply aspect, but substantively it can represent the performance of "real wages" for the present analytical purpose. In comparison with this specified unskilled labor wage level, skilled labor wage level as represented by that in the machinery subsector is noticeably high during the former interval. Since real wage levels during the latter interval, 1925–1935, are on average close to the 1934–1936 base of 100, the wage performance of the machine industry in the former interval can be characterized by a relatively high level with a tendency to increase.

The interpretation is as follows. In the years 1934–1936 the output prices of machinery industry dropped considerably. Taking this situation as the standard, the high wage pressure on this subsector was relatively weaker in the former interval but became stronger toward the beginning of the latter interval. This presents a pattern of change over time broadly similar to that of textiles. In other words, in terms of subsector comparison, machinery started with much stronger wage pressure as compared to textiles, and this was sustained during the former interval. Furthermore, this situation was aggravated toward the beginning of the latter interval. In Japan's case this took place in a situation of widening nominal wage differentials. If the differentials had been wider, the wage pressure on the machine subsector would have been stronger and the development of machine production would have been even more difficult. The problem of the supply price of skilled labor is thus important in developing economies.

Three points should be commented on. First, in terms of wage performance of unskilled labor the turning point between the primary and the secondary phase is around 1919–1920 by the conventional phasing framework. The performance of textile wages described above appears consistent with this. If the significance of this turning point is emphasized, specific attention should be paid to the effects of wage hikes in PDE industry. The hikes are greater in machinery than in textiles due to the greater magnitude of machinery Lw/K than that of textiles. The impact of wage hikes cannot be dealt with in the same way as for other industries producing durable goods, since it must be stronger.

Second, this applies to not only modern but also traditional elements in technology diffusion. In discussing the competitiveness of industry, wages usually are treated in addition to productivity, by pointing out that cheaper wages tend to strengthen the international competitiveness of developing economies. In PDE industry this view is also appropriate, but the difficulty of increasing competitiveness in the domestic market should also be emphasized, focusing on the relation between wage and output prices. This is particularly important due to the multirange market structure of PDE industry.

Third, machine production is sensitive to demand, and the rate of output growth measured in constant prices varies widely, so that stable performance of productivity growth is difficult to measure. The drop in relative productivity mentioned at the outset needs careful consideration in this respect. Yet the contribution of a rise in relative productivity to increasing competitiveness power is indispensable. However, this appears rather limited in machinery compared to textiles so far as top-level enterprises are concerned.

Price Decline of Producer Durables in Latecomers: Early Start and Multirange Structure

The difficulty involved in developing PDE industry in the phase of secondary import substitution, clarified in the preceding discussion, requires further analysis because Japan eventually overcame it in the postwar period. The interest here is in clarifying the historical factors relevant to this problem in the long-term dimension, rather than the factors that developed during and after the war. Two aspects are examined: the early start and multirange structure.

The major topic concerns the possibility of realizing a relative decline in PDE prices in the domestic market of latecomers. This is one of the most important factors in inducing technology diffusion, granting that the PDE share bias is inevitable. The conditions for realizing it are outlined below, although they remain speculative since fact-finding research with regard to developing economies has been limited. Throughout the subsequent discussion the characteristics of machinery production clarified in chapter 3 form the conceptual basis.

The conventional framework for major phases is sufficient for the present discussion, with the addition of two phases referred to as the "preprimary" subphase and the "secondary export substitution" subphase. The reason for the former is simple: Japan had no historical experience.[11] With regard to the latter, Japan's experience in the 1960s might better be treated systematically to clarify the shift from secondary import substitution to secondary export substitution, which took place at the beginning of the 1960s. The performance of the domestic market in the prewar semi-industrial phase is relevant

---

[11] For details, see chapter 5, section II.

to most of contemporary developing nations. In applying the phase pattern of predecessors to latecomers, dealing with the effects of the telescoping process is an important problem that is related to the time dimension of phase shifts. In principle, the required time duration can be compressed in latecomers, mainly because latecomers have the advantage of using technological knowledge supplied by predecessors. The notion itself is generally accurate; the problem is the variation of its effects among latecomers. No attempt is made to discuss this issue here systematically,[12] but it should be noted when applying the phasing framework to the present analysis. The central point is how PDE performance functions in realizing telescoping effects in developing economies.

Japan was a latecomer to industrialization. Its early start in PDE production during the primary phase can be interpreted as a strategy of realizing the positive effects of the telescoping process, rather than as catching up. The concept of catching up is widely cited, often without specifying what it means in the performance of latecomers. From the aspect of economic analysis, the early start contributes to realizing the positive effects of the telescoping process in the long term.

Among the findings in section II, the most important in confirming the telescoping process are the PDE share bias and the tendency for its price to decline. It is hypothesized that without making an early start in the primary phase, these could not be realized effectively in an intensified manner in the secondary phase. The hypothesis stems from the general recognition that the establishment of the machine industry requires accumulated efforts in upgrading both the production capacity and social capability components pertaining to this subsector. As is illustrated by the textile industry, technological progress is focused on output production depending upon PDE imports required during the primary phase. This is illustrated by the PDE price behavior in the manufacturing context (Table 4.7, column B). The output price ratio of machinery/ total manufacturing output distinctly declines during most of the primary phase. The authors assert that this provided the basis for its further decline during the secondary phase. Despite its rise relative to that of textiles, the internationally competitive sector, in the long-term perspective, this tendency of price decline is essentially

---

[12] In *OK*, lecture 2, "Semi-industrialization," the telescoping process is dealt with in the concluding remarks. Illustrative comparison of Taiwan and Korea with Japan regarding secondary import substitution is particularly illuminating.

due to a sustained shift of its supply curve to the right in the total manufacturing context.

These tendencies can be extrapolated to latecomers in general, including contemporary developing economies. The positive effects of the telescoping process basically depend upon PDE performance: a trend of decline in its relative price is a symbolic indicator of a favorable response, while an unfavorable response is indicated by the lack of such price performance. No data are available for changes over time. The cross-sectional data presented in section I, however, allow speculation. Higher PDE price pressure prevails in contemporary developing economies. Table 4.5, column 2, shows that the PDE price level relative to that of GDP is extremely high in developing economies in national currency account. Taking the price ratio of group V as 100, it is: I, 224; II, 158; III, 205; and IV, 154 (smoothed: I–II, 191; II–III, 182; and III–IV, 180).

It is expected that the ratio would decrease toward higher groups. Irregularity may stem from the limited number of selected countries and the single year 1980. Some information on the order of the ratio of magnitude can be obtained by comparing the ratios with Japan's historical case. The corresponding ratios are given in Table 4.7, column A. The averaged ratios are: 1)–5), 147; 6)–8), 126; and 9)–12), 105.

An exact comparison is not possible between cross-sectional and over-time series, but for developing economies the smoothed series in parentheses indicate a slow tendency to decline from lower toward higher groups while maintaining a very high ratio level, while in Japan's case a long-term trend of decrease in the ratio level is seen. Although no data are available for comparison at the manufacturing production dimension, it can be contended that a shift in the PDE supply curve can be seen, albeit with wide variance among developing economies. Some are successful in realizing PDE price decline, while others tend to increase it, with a variety of intermediate cases in between. The slow overall pace is a combined outcome of these.

The sizable variation in PDE price found within each group in Table 4.6, column A is further analyzed (column B) to determine the relationship between PDE price levels and subgroups A (higher $\Delta Y/I$) and B (lower $\Delta Y/I$). The subgroup approach clarifies the operation of national elements, which are mainly responsible for the variation in PDE prices, while international elements operate rather uniformly. There are no data on changes over time in the nations belonging to subgroup A, yet, it is conceivable for them to sustain operation of the forces that cause PDE price levels to decline. Although the statistical association between higher $\Delta Y/I$ and lower PDE price level should be investigated further, it is known that the rate of macro residual growth is greater for A than for B and this inequality can represent the inequality of the pace of technological-organizational progress. In this broader setting, the lower PDE price level operates in association with promotion of the pace of technology diffusion, as derived from the comparison between Japan and subgroup A nations.

How and why can the PDE price level be lowered? The conventional answer is given by the rapid supply curve shift to the right in the machinery industry. This is amplified below in the context of the relevance of Japan's historical experience. In chapter 3, section I, the characteristics of the machinery industry were analyzed in some depth, and it was noted that the machinery industry in Japan presents a successful pattern of combined operation of domestic and international elements in the diffusion process of advanced technology. The conventional model of technology diffusion assumes a homogenous structure underlying the replacement process in the domestic market, as discussed in chapter 2, section III. In Japan's case the structure of both demand for and supply of machinery has been sustained in what is called a multirange market. A three-range (S, M, and L) approach was adopted to represent the differentiated structure. At the top level, modern technology diffusion occurs as described above, and no further elaboration is needed except for domestic elements. Available data for domestic element operation are taken from a 1957 survey and presented in Table 4.12 to clarify in detail the characteristics of machinery production in the bottom range. It is assumed that supply is represented by machinery and the other industries represent the demand side in the traditional economy. In panel A the familiar terms used in the present analysis are listed, and in panel B the conventional original terms are added. One feature of machine production as compared with other traditional industry is that a much greater output-capital ratio Y/K is the result of a larger magnitude of Lw/K, which is a combination of the lower level of K/L and the distinctly higher level of wages (indicator of higher level of worker quality).

During the prewar period, the weight within both groups was somewhat different. For example, the share of nonelectric machinery was greater in the machine group and factor combination differed to a certain extent, i.e., Lw/K might be greater for textiles, etc. Yet the order of magnitude of differences shown in Table 4.12

Table 4.12
Machinery Industry in Comparison with Other Industries in Small-scale
Firms (1–9 Workers), 1957: Japan

	(A): Basic Terms (Ratios)		(B): Relevant Terms (Thousand Yen per Person)			
	Lw/K	Y/K	Y/Lw	Y/L	K/L	w
Machinery (average)	1.90	4.22	2.22	235	57	145
Nonelectric	1.61	3.58	2.22	246	69	143
Electric	2.37	5.26	2.22	262	50	149
Transportation	1.58	3.68	2.33	223	61	143
Precision	2.00	4.35	2.18	208	48	144
Selected others (average)	0.72	2.05	2.85	177	87	108
Textiles	0.57	1.78	3.12	151	85	92
Food	0.54	1.92	3.56	206	107	103
Wood & wood prod.	0.89	2.34	2.63	199	87	117
Ceramics	0.90	2.15	2.39	153	71	121
Total manufacturing	0.95	2.70	2.84	186	69	114

Source: Economic Research Institute, EPA, Study Series No. 6, *Shihon kozo to kigyokan kakusa* (Capital structure and differentials among enterprises), II. Estimated data from the Basic Survey of Medium-Small-Scale Enterprises.

is clear enough to support the assumption that a similar feature was present during the semi-industrial phase. Machine production in the bottom range operated and developed with this characteristic to supply PDE for use in traditional production. An important implication is that such a supply of PDE formed the basis of technology advance in the traditional sector of the economy, and to that extent this range was least dependent on the effects of international elements.

Although systematic knowledge on the technological property that must have been the major cause of this feature of machinery production is lacking, relying upon the detailed historical research conducted by Odaka,[13] the following can be stated. For small-scale firms involved in machine production and metal processing, traditional technology played an important role during the primary phase

[13] Konosuke Odaka, "The Role Played by Artisans in the Industrialization Process," chapter 11 in Ryoshin Minami and Yukihiko Kiyokawa, eds., *op. cit.* Odaka treats metal processing and machine production together. According to the 1957 data used earlier, metal processing has a similar feature to machines. Y/K is 3.58, Lw/K is 1.83 in the 1–9 scale. This subsector is excluded in the "Others" column in Table 4.12.

and depended upon the capability of *shokunin* (artisans). The property of this technology pertains historically to domestic output of the traditional type, but it might have been influenced by newly introduced foreign technological knowledge, although that influence was probably least in the bottom range. Yet its contribution to the domestic market during the semi-industrialization phase was sustained in the process of foreign technology diffusion in more modernized firms of larger scale.

With regard to the possible relevance of Japan's experience to contemporary developing economies, little can be said so far as empirical analysis is concerned. Nevertheless, the present authors believe that the conceptual framework of the differentiated process of technology diffusion through the multirange structure derived from Japan's experience can and should be applied to the telescoping process of developing nations. More realistically, two mutually interrelated points should be amplified. First, the economic characteristics of machine production are essentially common to all developing economies: factor inputs with greater magnitude of Lw/K can produce output with greater magnitude of Y/K. The technical feature of the divisibility of product and process in machine production backs up this characteristic with possible organizational innovations. The possibility of achieving a tendency for PDE price decline is determined by the possibility of superior competitiveness within the differentiated range of the domestic market. A shift in the supply curve can be conceived through the relation between changes in Lw/K and changes in Y/K conditioned by the character of this subsector. Instead of following the conventional suggestion of increasing capital intensity, it is suggested that the possibility of upgrading worker capability is the key issue. In this connection the scale effects discussed in chapter 2, section II, are relevant. Through the differentiated ranges, positive effects of small scale (S') are found. The range treated earlier is toward the bottom and the effects may thus be diluted. At least, however, no negative effects operate in that range; in other words, in the bottom range in developing economies possible shifts in the supply curve of PDE production can be expected.[14]

[14] In the telescoping process the situation may be altered. For example, the requirement of the high skill levels for workers in the machinery industry will be weakened by technology modernization. Substitution by semiskilled and even unskilled female workers may become possible, particularly in electric machinery. To that extent, the function of traditional artisans becomes less important. This new phenomenon would contribute toward increasing the possibility of decline in PDE prices. This requires further investigation.

By way of conclusion, the significance of the role played by producer durables in the technology diffusion process should be noted. The conventional approach based on secondary import substitution requires amplification, in particular from the time dimension, price performance, and market structure. Differences among nations are noticeable in responses to these requirements.

The early start of PDE production was dealt with primarily pertaining to import substitution in section I. The problem of PDE production in the domestic market in general was also discussed. Since the concept of multirange structure was proposed, it is desirable to explain the relationship between the early start and this differentiated structure. The early start with the purpose of import substitution of a specific product (a typical case is steel shipbuilding in Japan) actually pertains to the top-level range of the multirange structure. Steel shipbuilding replaced the traditional production of wooden ships and to that extent it affects the traditional range. This is a problem of replacement effects. Not only in the primary phase but in the secondary phase in general PDE import substitution leads toward eventual export of the product concerned. This essentially relates to top-level firms (a typical example is machinery for textiles in Japan). Therefore, if domestic PDE production in developing economies is discussed merely in relation to import substitution, the observations will be biased and even misleading. On the other side of the multirange structure, there is the problem of how to promote production of PDE of the traditional type in the bottom range, where there is no internal aspect of import substitution leading toward export. In the intermediate range, international and traditional elements are mixed in a variety of combinations, as is illustrated by the case of machine tools described above.

The relation between PDE import substitution activity and the domestic PDE production process is dynamic. Increased PDE import contributes to technological progress, and its limitation under protectionist policies discourages the operation of this positive effect. However, without promoting domestic PDE production, the internal process of technology diffusion cannot be realized. In a long-term perspective, appropriate realization of a dynamic sequence in responding to these two requirements appears to be the solution. In this context, the significance of "spillover" effects of the international elements of technology diffusion need emphasis. Achievements by top-level firms can create domestic effects spreading throughout the multirange structure. Viewed from the national import strategy and policy for long-term development, this aspect presents the problem of options in both negative and positive dimensions.

In making an early start in specific PDE production, negative selection is required with respect to the import of PDE specified. Usually this dimension is considered alone. However, there is an additional, positive dimension as well. It is positive because under a policy of sustaining an increase in the import of certain kinds of PDE, the issue is how to select or specify such PDE items. Generally this is done through an escalating tariff system; a typical example is machine tools in Japan. In the negative option, what are termed replacement effects are at issue because success in import substitution results in replacement of traditional production activities in the domestic market. During the primary phase in particular, developing economies cannot overcome these effects since it is difficult to direct the operation of forces. As clarified previously, counterforces that can work to sustain and even develop traditional production activities must be taken into account.

It is important to recognize the specific character of PDE production and technological progress. It is characterized by a relatively lower level of capital intensity as a result of a higher level of worker capability. In this sense, it is sharply distinguished from heavy industry. The conventional phasing framework does not make such a distinction, but demarcates too broadly in terms of nondurables versus durables among both producers and consumers. The technological requirements should be more clearly defined, particularly for analyzing contemporary developing economies. The authors propose that the specified orientation of PDE production-import performance be incorporated into the conventional phasing framework. At least for the primary phase the early start should be specified, and for the secondary phase the turning point in terms of import ratio to investment. In the primary phase the turning point is identified in terms of the ratio of PDE import to total domestic investment. In view of the great pressure of PDE requirement in terms of shares and prices explained in the preceding discussion, all developing economies make efforts to alleviate this pressure through a sequential process of PDE import increase and domestic PDE production promotion. The former predominates over the latter in the early path, after a certain point the two become equal, and subsequently the latter surpasses the former. At the point of equality the ratio changes from an increasing to a decreasing trend. Further examination is needed of this topic (see Annex I).

The phase demarcation essentially relates to individual countries;

analysis based on averages obscures the factual problems. It is important to consider the deviations of individual cases regarding the performance of an early start. This is an important challenge for strategy makers, particularly because an early start alone cannot necessarily guarantee favorable long-term performance of PDE prices. As illustrated by Japan's case in the preceding subsection, domestic competition is severe even in the secondary phase. The early start may create more difficulties, leading to higher PDE prices. Much depends upon the selection of appropriate subsectors.[15]

Annex: PDE Performance in the Development Path

Further examination is made here to amplify the contents of the preceding discussion, focusing on two aspects that may emerge in the development path. One is the pattern of PDE import dependency and the long-term decreasing trend; the other is the possibility of PDE price decline as seen by item comparison in the price system of developing economies.

I. PDE Import Dependency: Turning Point, Gross and Net of Imports

In *DE*, chapter 6, the PDE import requirement was dealt with conceptually and in previous discussion in this chapter the results of empirical studies, particularly on Japan's historical experience, were presented in detail. The issue examined here is confirmation of the turning point in the ratio of imported PDE/domestic investment. While a trend of increase in this ratio can be identified during the earlier interval of development, at a certain point in time it begins to decrease due to the growth in domestic production of PDE. This point E is significant in interpreting the development path. PDE is the carrier of borrowed technological knowledge, and the achievement of technological progress is pursued through domestic capital formation. Thus, point E can indicate basic change in the technology structure in terms of the relation between international and domestic elements. From the viewpoint of domestic expenditure and foreign payments, this basic change is also important.

The meaning of this approach should first be clarified in relation

---

[15] See the paper by De Long and Summars, "Equipment Investment and Economic Growth," in *The Quarterly Journal of Economics*, May 1991. This paper encourages research in the present study area aimed at clarifying the significance of the role played by producer durables, although the methodology differs from the present approach.

to the conventional approach in terms of import and export substitution. The performance of producer durables in terms of the relation between import and domestic production is included in the concept of secondary import substitution, but the shift from primary to secondary import substitution is not. Likewise, in the case of export substitution, primary means replacing traditional goods export with nondurable manufactures and secondary means replacing nondurables with durables. The concern here is the change in the technology expenditure aspect of domestic capital formation pertaining specifically to PDE. Its export is discussed later in addition to its import, the major topic here. The consistency and utility of the trade pattern approach are recognized, while the present approach is considered indispensable in interpreting development performance from the standpoint of domestic capital formation.

The cases of Korea and Taiwan presented in Table 4.4 illustrate the actual pattern and issues involved in identifying point E. To reconfirm the difference between "gross" and "net" export series, point E for the former is identified in period 3) for Korea and period 4) for Taiwan, but for the latter it is in period 2) for Korea and period 3) for Taiwan. It is important to identify the existence of the turning point in both cases of Asian NIEs with such time lags. In applying the conventional approach, the "phase of secondary import substitution in Taiwan and Korea can be identified after the beginning of the 1970s, but it is still too early to demarcate the dates of a shift to the secondary export substitution."[16] Regarding secondary export substitution, further points are discussed below but here it can be pointed out that after passing through point E the economy is mainly in the phase of secondary import substitution. However, the present approach implies an additional aspect: PDE export is treated "concurrently" with its import. In Table 4.4 the ratio Xp/Mp tends to increase at a rapid pace from a very small percentage in period 1) to almost 50% in period 4) in both cases. The sustained trend of this pattern leads the economy to the phase of secondary export substitution. Concurrency is an important aspect in the present approach, and its significance is clarified further in examining the case of Japan.

Based on the historical records of Japan in Table 4.10, point E can be identified for three kinds of PDE series: total PDE including

---

[16] John C.H. Fei, Kazushi Ohkawa, and Gustav Ranis, "Economic Development in Historical Perspective: Japan, Korea and Taiwan," in Kazushi Ohkawa and Gustav Ranis, eds., *op. cit.*

ships (column 3), general machinery including others (column 2), and general machinery (column 1). These series present the same general pattern of changes over time in the ratio to domestic investment, and the turning point is identified at period 4), 1894–1903. Toward that point E, a trend of increase is definite, whereas after passing that point a declining tendency is realized although with considerable fluctuations. Note that these are calculated from the original data of "net," that is, import minus export. In this regard, Japan's case requires special consideration of the effects of colonial trade. During the earlier interval PDE export was minor. For example, the ratio (%) Xp/Mp is 0.6 in 1884, 1.0 in 1894, and 0.5 in 1904. Therefore "gross or net" is not an issue in demarcating point E. However, for the latter interval the issue matters a great deal, as illustrated by the following figures for selected years (%):

	1914	1924	1934	1938
Xp/Mp	16.9	13.8	123.2	139.6
Ratio in colonial trade	44.1	58.2	30.5	46.1

(*Source*: Same as for Table 4.10.)

In short, the concurrent process of Mp and Xp increase occurred, not only internationally but with expanding colonial trade in the yen terms.

The general significance of the concurrent process should not be underestimated because of this particular circumstance. For machinery, the major item of PDE, the ratio (%) Xp/Mp is as follows for selected years:[17]

1913	1919	1931	1936
13.0	39.8	74.1	184.1

In the early 1930s Japan reached the point of Mp = Xp, including colonial trade. If colonial trade is excluded, that point might have been reached by the late 1930s. Following the conventional notion of trade pattern phases, a shift from secondary import substitution to the secondary export substitution took place in Japan in the

---

[17] *OK*, Table 2.4, based on Yamazawa-Yamamoto data in *LTES*, Vol. 14.

postwar years, around the beginning of the 1960s. To avoid possible inconsistency that may arise between the two approaches, the realistic effects of prewar military expansion under colonialism and the postwar process of recovery from war damage must be taken into account. Although those effects may render the historical records of Japan "atypical" for the present analytical purposes, useful suggestions can nonetheless be derived if they are interpreted adequately.

In particular, the significance of an early start and multirange market structure is emphasized. To amplify this assertion, the previous identification of point E in the interval 1894–1903 is statistical confirmation of the early start of domestic PDE production in the conventional phasing framework. The declining trend in the ratio Mp/I definitely began earlier than the interval 1904–1919, demarcating the beginning of the secondary phase. In other words, the ratio of imported PDE to domestic capital formation tended to decrease during the primary phase. As illustrated by the case of steel shipbuilding discussed in chapter 2, the contribution of government was sizable in achieving a subsequent decline in the ratio following the early start. The basic operation of market mechanisms in absorbing foreign advanced technologies through the activities of private enterprises also contributed, yet without the role of government, formation of such a pattern would have been impossible. The ratio decrease was sharp: from 35.0 at point E to 14.7–16.6 during and immediately after the World War I years (Table 4.10, column 3). It is commonly recognized that isolation from international trade forced Japan to carry out PDE import substitution during this interval. What the authors want to argue is that the PDE production capability developed by the early start made it possible to achieve such import substitution. The ratio began to increase again in subsequent years, around the 1930s, in a normalizing process which was interrupted again by a sharp drop due to military mobilization.

Due to the effects of such *ad hoc* forces it is not easy to draw upon Japan's case to interpret the development path in general. In this regard the multirange structure of the PDE market, particularly in relation to PDE export activities, is noteworthy since the differentiated market can be thought of not only domestically but also for export. It is often pointed out that PDE of relatively lower quality can be exported if foreign demand exists; an example is colonial trade. PDE exports to Korea and Taiwan should be investigated in more detail by item for this purpose, together with exports to other Asian countries. These are beyond the present scope of analysis, but it can be argued that the expansion of PDE export to colonies implies an enlargement of the multirange PDE domestic market without altering its basic property. Illustration is given for the relatively normalized year 1924. Original data are for four major items of PDE: general machinery (34.1); rolling stock (19.7); tools, fixtures, and others (17.5); and automobiles and other vehicles (28.7) (the figures in parentheses are percentages of each item in total PDE export). The percentage exports to Korea and Taiwan in the total export of each item is 71.1, 100.0, 17.5, and 28.7, respectively. Although there is considerable variation among those major items, the following two points generally apply: first, PDE export goes on concurrently with its import for all major items; and second, the colonial trade plays a sizable role in this process for all major items. The concurrent process evolved in a sustained multirange market structure in the interval under consideration, although the rank of each item in terms of higher, intermediate, and lower range regarding exports cannot be specified. In this process colonial trade played a significant role, in particular for PDE items that are less competitive internationally in terms of quality level and price. To this extent, domestic PDE production expanded in Japan proper and PDE market differentials widened.

The pattern of PDE import dependency in contemporary developing economies is amplified here in light of the previous discussion. Table 4A.1 lists available data.

First, the group average, taking both the 1960–1980 average and 1980 figures, shows a regular pattern in the gross-term series through the major segment of the development path II–IV: from II to III the change in the ratio is either very minor or zero, whereas from III to IV a decline occurs. In the change from I to II the two series are not consistent for reasons that are not clear. The data may be less reliable for group I.

The overall pattern of increase in the 1960–1980 average and 1980 may be emerging in lower groups. Regarding the change from IV to V, a change to increase, instead of a sustained decrease, is witnessed against expectations. The most important problem is how to identify the turning point. The observation of net (excluding export) term series may be useful. Apart from the questionable figure for group I, the ratio tends to decline from II because the PDE export percentage of investment (approximated by the "gross-net" column in the table) increases from II to III onward. The percentage change itself is small but greatly affects the ratio comparisons between groups. From III to IV it becomes more substantial. Regrettably, corresponding data are not available for the 1960–1980 aver-

Table 4A.1
PDE Import Dependency in Gross Domestic Capital Formation, Developing Economies in 1960–1980 and 1980

(%)

Group	1960–1980 Average	1980 (Gross)	1980 (Net)	Gross – Net
I Average	23.6	45.8	43.7	2.1
II Average	33.9	36.6	34.6	2.0
E	33.2	33.6	30.8	2.8
F	34.5	39.6	39.3	1.3
III Average	33.5	36.6	31.6	5.0
E	32.6	34.6	26.1	8.5
F	34.4	38.5	37.1	1.4
IV Average	26.6	34.2	23.4	11.8
E	23.0	23.3	11.7	12.6
F	30.2	45.0	35.1	9.9
V Average	27.1	34.6	−8.5	43.1
E	21.7	26.4	−17.3	43.7
F	32.4	42.8	0.3	42.6

Sources: For 1960–1980 in gross terms, the same as for Tables 3.2 and 3.3. For 1980, World Bank, *World Development Report*, 1982, Appendix tables on structure of merchandise exports and imports (Table 11) together with Table 5 on structure of demand.

Remarks: i) The item "machinery and transportation equipment" is used as a proxy for product durables.

ii) The difference between imports and exports (gross versus net) is approximated by the figures of resource balance for adjustment, first in percentage of GDP and second converted to that of gross domestic investment.

age, so the net term in the full sense cannot be used. One viewpoint is that the turning point may broadly be identified between groups II and III, but is this appropriate?

Second, can further useful suggestions be obtained using the subgroup approach? The answer is affirmative, particularly with regard to two points. One point is that in the ratio in gross series either of 1960–1980 averages or in the single year 1980, the magnitude is smaller, instead of greater, in subgroup E than in subgroup F. The difference is not necessarily great, especially for lower groups. Yet the inequality is perfectly regular without exception. The second point pertains to export activity. The magnitude of "gross-net" is definitely greater in E than in F without exception. These points taken together appear to suggest that countries realizing faster rates of macro productivity increase (E) achieve decreased PDE import dependency with concomitant faster export ratio rates. The countries with slower rates of macro productivity growth (F) fall behind in this respect. This interpretation is generally acceptable so far as comparisons of subgroup averages are concerned due to the basic contribution of productivity advances. However, the effects of import substitution policy vary among nations. In general, the sequential process of PDE import substitution is composed of productivity growth in domestic industry and import requirement augmentation resulting from further technological progress. The combined results of these cause variations in the performance of import substitution. This aspect can only be clarified by the study of individual countries. The cases of selected countries are examined in Table 4A.2 to supplement those of Korea and Taiwan (Table 4.4).

The relevant findings from Table 4A.2 are as follows. First, the turning point E is identified only for Brazil (in 1972–1976). Taken together with Korea and Taiwan, the attainment of this point characterizes the pattern of nations that reach the secondary major phase. Second, for all other countries (most in the primary major phase), the capital goods import dependency ratio tends to increase toward recent years. The turning point is reached in the three cases above in 1972–1976, toward the end of the primary phase. Third, however, for all other countries a tendency of decline in the ratio is witnessed, except for Thailand, which instead presents a tendency of continuous increase.

Although the number of selected countries is limited, these long-term patterns help in forming speculative interpretations of the patterns previously shown by cross-sectional analysis. The near constancy of the import dependency ratio found in II–III has to do with point E; one nation increases the ratio, another decreases it, and near constancy is maintained by a third. The combined results of these may appear as a near-zero change for II–III. Such multiplicity must be recognized, the reasons for which were mentioned previously.

The effects of import substitution policy and telescoping effects are also relevant. The former tends to bring about a ratio decrease, whereas the latter tends to increase the ratio due to the greater technological requirement, for example, as compared to Japan's case. Import substitution measures often lead to the high cost of capital goods, but this is not necessarily valid in all cases. Thus the importance of an early start is emphasized. The later date of point E attainment in the three cases above is related to telescoping effects:

Table 4A.2
Changes over Time in the Ratio of PDE Import to Gross Domestic Investment: Selected Countries

(%)

	Brazil			Argentina		
	Gross	Net	G − N	Gross	Net	G − N
1) 1962–1966	5.7	5.2	0.5	12.0	11.6	0.4
2) 1967–1971	8.5	7.8	0.7	9.4	8.4	1.0
3) 1972–1976	11.9	10.5	1.4	5.7	4.0	1.7
4) 1977–1981	8.3	5.0	3.3	9.5	7.6	1.9
5) 1982–1986	6.6	1.5	5.1	12.2	8.5	3.7
6) 1987–1990	5.6	1.3	4.3	16.2	11.2	5.0

	Thailand			India		
	Gross	Net	G − N	Gross	Net	G − N
1) 1962–1966	20.5	20.0	0.5	8.6	8.5	0.1
2) 1967–1971	20.0	19.7	0.3	7.4	6.8	0.6
3) 1972–1976	21.7	20.9	0.8	5.7	4.6	1.1
4) 1977–1981	21.3	18.1	3.2	5.6	4.1	1.5
5) 1982–1986	23.3	16.9	6.4	7.7	6.6	1.1
6) 1987–1990	34.8	22.0	12.8	6.1	4.7	1.4

	Indonesia			China		
	Gross	Net	G − N	Gross	Net	G − N
3) 1972–1976	22.1	21.8	0.3			
4) 1977–1981	16.0	15.3	0.7			
5) 1982–1986	17.1	17.0	0.1	1.0	0.9	0.1
6) 1987–1990	17.5	17.1	0.4	14.4	11.0	3.4

Sources: United Nations, *International Trade Statistics Yearbook* (database). International Monetary Fund, *International Statistics Yearbook*, 1992.
Remarks: i) Periods are demarcated to be comparable to Table 4.4.
   ii) 6) is 1987–1989 for Brazil and Argentina; 1987–1988 for Thailand and India. 5) is the single year 1985 for China; 3) lacks 1973 for Indonesia.
iii) Net means "Gross" − Export, so that G − N, Gross − New Shares export (X).

the requirement of PDE import is heavier for latecomers. In addition, a contributing element to the distinct increase in the ratio in recent years for a number of other countries may have been "direct investment" from developed countries. Identifying the turning point in such cases is a problem for future research.

In summary, an early start and multirange market are relevant to contemporary developing economies. First, the phenomenon of the early start is clearly recognized, and the tendency for PDE import dependency to decline starts earlier than the beginning of the secondary phase in a number of countries. The figures in the 1980 column (net) in Table 4A.2 can be referred to in particular. The ratio of subgroup E tends to decrease (30.8 (II)–26.1 (III)–11.7 (IV)), and this is confirmed by changes over time in selected cases.

Second, data on the multi-range market structure are not directly available. Based on export performance, however, PDE export occurs even early in the development path, followed by a considerable increase later. As indicated by the figures in the last column in the table, a shift to higher PDE export activity is achieved between IV and V in terms of the group average. Before that point PDE export activity proceeds gradually due to its differentiated quality level. This may be possible because of the growth in domestic production of these PDE items. Note that such a pattern is assumed to be formulated more vigorously in subgroup E than in F, although confirmation by examining the pattern of selected countries as in Table 4A.2, G – N is not sufficient.

II. Possibility of Lower PDE Price

The second topic concerns the possibility of decreasing the level of PDE prices along the development path. How and to what extent can the sustained pressure of high PDE prices be mitigated in developing economies? To deal with this problem comprehensively, a systematic investigation of possible changes in price systems would be required above and beyond treating PDE prices. In *DE*, chapter 5, the results of empirical studies on domestic output prices in major sectors of developing countries were discussed. For the present purposes, this production aspect approach should be extended to the expenditure aspect approach.

An "illustrative" approach by selecting representative items, commodities, and services generally reveals the performance of PDE prices in relation to the changes in the entire price system. The relevant aspects pertain to at least three dimensions: first, national versus international (or tradables versus nontradables); second, output price changes in major production sectors; and third, factor input price differentials (capital versus labor). The illustrative approach simplifies the mutual relationships between these dimensions.

The actual procedure is as follows. Basically ppp estimates are relied upon with certain assumptions. The notion of "price level" applied to individual countries can be defined as the ratio ppp/ actual exchange rate with regard to GDP, and this notion can also be applied to its components. This notion is convenient for the present purpose, since price data in national currency evaluations are not systematically available for individual components. The ppp estimates pertain to expenditures, and "consumption" is used as a proxy for wage goods expenditures. Approximations are unavoidable for output prices by production sector. Finally, with regard to wages, the specific assumption is applied to estimated *we*, the equivalent wage level, discussed in the Annex to chapter 3.

Two steps are taken as methods to observe the development path. First, the patterns of prices are examined using cross-sectional data through groups by Y/L level to discover any regularity in the average tendency. Second, possible deviations from that pattern are scrutinized. This is particularly important in answering the question raised at the outset of this section. While subgroup observation is a familiar procedure in such analysis, the number of countries for which the relevant data are available is limited in this case. Nevertheless, approximation is attempted using the E and F subgrouping clarified in terms of macro productivity growth rates.

In Table 4A.3 the results of the first step are shown. The selected items (columns 1, 2, and 3) represent PDE (1), light manufactured goods (2), and agricultural products (3), respectively; services (column 4) are a simple average of "medical care" and "recreation and education" ICP components. Consumption (column 5), GDP (column 6), and the "price level" are all taken from ICP data; figures in parentheses in groups are the numbers of countries selected.

Despite the limited number of selected countries, a general regularity can be seen through group average observation. In particular, the machinery price is highest by any comparison throughout the entire development path. This fact was clarified earlier but its relative place in comparison with other items is the focus here. Its highest level tends to increase (with a dip at III) and decrease until group V, where for the first time its level becomes lower than that of manufactures of light industries. Its price tends to increase distinctly toward group V. This is expected in light of primary export substitution for lower groups but the sharper increase toward IV and V is to be noted. Food is not necessarily adequate for indicating prices of agricultural products and is affected by variance in natural resource endowments. Its tendency to increase moderately, except from IV to V, appears acceptable, however.

The price of "services" is extremely low in lower groups. It in-

Table 4A.3
PPP of Selected Items: Averages by Y/L Level Group, 1980

Group	Machinery (1)	Clothing & Footwear (2)	Food (3)	Services (4)	Consumption (5)	GDP (6)	Overall Price Level (7)
(A) Average							
I (4)	1.280	0.871	0.661	0.243	0.499	0.762	0.573
II (6)	1.438	0.661	0.607	0.216	0.487	0.527	0.493
III (7)	1.386	0.662	0.831	0.319	0.587	0.541	0.620
IV (7)	1.565	0.934	0.963	0.528	0.783	0.763	0.767
V (8)	1.507	1.586	1.425	0.971	1.253	1.232	1.230
(B) Changes (lower group = 100)							
I–II	112.3	75.9	91.8	88.9	97.6	69.2	83.0
II–III	96.4	100.2	136.9	147.7	120.9	102.7	131.1
III–IV	112.9	141.1	115.9	165.5	132.9	141.0	123.7
IV–V	96.3	169.8	148.0	183.9	134.5	161.5	160.4

Source: All ppp data (columns 1–6) are from the International Comparison Project, phase IV, part two, Table 9. Column 7 is from part one, Table 1, GDP in national currency and international dollars.

Remarks: i) The components of producer durables in ICP are machinery, electric machinery, and transportation equipment. Machinery is selected because its coverage is largest and deviates least among countries including lower groups.
ii) "Services" include certain goods expenditures and may not necessarily be fully adequate for the present purpose. Unlike 1975, specific estimates for services are not available for 1980.
iii) The price level is originally measured in terms of expenditure per capita GDP by the ratio ppp/exchange rate per US dollar.
Countries selected for this observation are as follows (E and F are subgroups to be discussed in the second step). The requirements for selection are two: one is to fit into the framework of grouping set since *DE* and the other is data availability of ppp estimates for all selected items in the International Comparison Project (the one exception is Bolivia in the former and Yugoslavia in the latter, for which producer durables are used due to the lack of machinery data).
I E–India, Malawi; F–Ethiopia, Madagascar
II E–Pakistan, Philippines, Kenya; F–Sri Lanka, Senegal, Bolivia
III E–Rep. of Korea, Tunisia; F–Colombia, Morocco, Paraguay, El Salvador, Honduras
IV E–Brazil, the Dominican Republic, Greece, Yugoslavia; F–Argentina, Peru, Costa Rica
V E–Japan, France, Germany, Belgium, Denmark; F–United Kingdom, Netherlands, Norway

creases toward higher groups; the rate of change from IV to V is particularly noticeable. But even in group V it continues to be much lower than the price of any other item. There is no suitable indicator for the price of wage goods, and thus the price of consumption is assumed as a rough proxy. The level of service prices appears to suggest a certain associated movement with that of consumption in the tendency to increase toward higher groups, but it cannot be assumed that the former is explained by the latter: as shown in Table 4A.3, panel B, the price of services tends to increase distinctly between III and V, whereas the prices of wage goods appear to increase much more moderately.

The first step is a preliminary approach to the development path. The results of the second step, determining deviations from the development pattern in individual countries' price performance, are derived from subgroup data presented in Table 4A.4.

The degree of deviation in each item is simply indicated by the ratio E/F. In group V, representing developed countries, it is most homogenous through all items, as generally expected. In comparison, the degree of deviation in developing countries is greater. The crucial item in the analysis, machinery price, shows considerable difference between E and F, among others. It is thus necessary to determine the factors responsible for such deviations.

As suggested earlier, the common-sense expectation is to explain deviations in the development pattern by differences in macro price levels. However, this is not borne out by the estimated figures. Between the items of machinery and GDP no precise general association is seen, and a reverse relation is noted for group III. An important finding is that the lower (higher) level of machinery price corresponds exactly to the higher (lower) rate of macro productivity growth in subgroup E (subgroup F). This seems to fit into the general hypothesis that the supply price of commodities is basically determined by the rate of productivity increase in the long term. However, this is not necessarily witnessed for other goods. The ratio E/F often appears to be above unity in Table 4A.4, columns 2 and 3, proxies of output prices in light manufacturing and agriculture. In other words, the hypothesis does not appear valid for these items, due to shifting trade patterns. For example, primary export substitution takes place earlier in E, II and later in F, III. If the possible effects of price rise in this item were due to increased tertiary activities for the subsequent path, it could be explained. However, such scrutiny is beyond the present scope. Examination of the prices of other items which show possible association with the machinery

Table 4A.4
Price Levels of Selected Items by Subgroup, 1980

		Machinery (1)	Clothing & Footwear (2)	Food (3)	Services (4)	Consumption (5)	GDP (6)	Price Level (7)
I	E (2)	1.227	0.890	0.550	0.190	0.459	0.702	0.480
	F (2)	1.333	0.852	0.771	0.296	0.589	0.821	0.665
	E/F	92.0	104.5	71.3	64.2	77.9	85.5	72.2
II	E (3)	1.145	0.436	0.607	0.186	0.432	0.468	0.467
	F (3)	1.731	0.885	0.607	0.245	0.541	0.586	0.520
	E/F	66.1	49.3	100.0	75.9	79.9	79.9	89.8
III	E (2)	1.080	0.845	0.870	0.285	0.682	0.638	0.706
	F (5)	1.509	0.589	0.816	0.333	0.552	0.503	0.586
	E/F	71.6	143.5	106.6	85.6	123.6	126.8	120.5
IV	E (4)	1.308	0.962	0.892	0.433	0.678	0.705	0.705
	F (3)	1.907	0.897	1.058	0.655	0.923	0.843	0.850
	E/F	68.6	107.2	84.3	66.1	73.5	83.6	82.9
V	E (5)	1.442	1.606	1.444	0.978	1.260	1.241	1.234
	F (3)	1.616	1.533	1.201	0.928	1.224	1.217	1.223
	E/F	89.2	104.8	119.3	105.4	102.9	102.0	100.9

Source: Same as for Table 4A.3.
Remark: The simple ratio (%) E/F is added for reference, taking F = 100.

Table 4A.5
Comparisons of Machinery and Services in ppp

		I	II	III	IV	V
Machinery	E	1.23	1.15	1.08	1.31	1.44
	F	1.33	1.73	1.51	1.91	1.62
	Average	1.28	1.44	1.39	1.57	1.51
Services	E	0.19	0.19	0.29	0.43	0.98
	F	0.30	0.25	0.33	0.66	0.96
	Average	0.24	0.22	0.32	0.53	0.97

price pattern focuses on the pattern of services shown in column 4. Its ratio E/F manifests distinctly lower prices in E than in F without exception apart from group V. To distinguish the pattern of each subgroup from that of group averages in comparison of machinery and services, the original figures in rounded numbers are reproduced in Table 4A.5.

The former segment (I, II) and the latter segment (III, IV, V) should be separated in dealing with cross-sectional data. For the former segment, the number of selected countries is limited, particularly for group I. It might be better to examine the former segment broadly by taking I and II together, although the changes from I to II would be significant if examined using more reliable data. Yet from I to II the machinery price increase is mainly seen in F, whereas in E it tends to decrease. The deviation thus witnessed is further sustained in group III, the early·path of the latter segment: lower machinery prices in E versus higher prices in F. This pattern appears to be positively associated with the price level of services: lower in E versus higher in F, the pattern sustained from the former segment. This pattern of services is further maintained in group IV, but the machinery price tends to increase again in group average and both E and F contribute to forming this pattern. For group V the deviation by subgroup is minor, but with regard to the latter segment between III and IV, two factors appear to operate in combination. The positively associated patterns of machinery and services are similar for both groups, but a dissimilar factor works on the group average: in III it decreases machinery prices but increases its level. The high level of machinery prices in F for groups II and IV is notable.

These phenomena suggest that the argument for associated patterns of deviations between machinery prices and service prices requires some reservations if applied to the entire path of development. The associated patterns found earlier between the machinery price and the rate of macro productivity growth can better be understood in association with the pattern of service prices, however. Machinery represents producer durables, but what is implied by the pattern of services? The answer is found in its relevance to the wages of equivalence *we*, which were incorporated in the international measurements of potential productivity levels in chapter 3, section II. In the Annex, a conceptual and technical explanation was given of how to use the price of services to measure *we*. Comparing service prices with prices of other items endorses the view that the level of *we* is lower in E than in F. However, in light of the present investigation, it is desirable to explain the contents of such "endorsement."

If the price of consumption represents the price of wage goods as a proxy, the level of wages, which is determined by the price of wage goods, can be deduced. In other words, the cost of employing labor is assumed to depend upon the worker expenditures on consumption as measured by internationally equivalents. Such hypothetical wage levels are expressed by *We*. The pattern of *We* is given by that of "consumption (5)" in Table 4A.3. As compared with "services (4)," the broad pattern appears similar, although the level of *We* is distinctly higher than that of services and the difference between the two tends to widen toward lower groups. The price of services is a direct measure of human work on the equivalence assumption although it pertains to specific activities. It was assumed in *DE*, chapter 5, that this (*we*) can be used as a proxy of the price of human work in general.[18] The problem is how to explain such different performances between the two kinds of wages.

The answer is found by characterizing *we* as representing the operation of domestic elements viewed from the human capability aspect. The measured figure of *We* and *we* show that the former is more relevant and the latter less relevant to the analysis of the growth mechanism in the development path. No systematic methods exist to support this, but subgroup observation illustrates its validity. The value of the ratio E/F is smaller for services than for consumption through all groups of developing economies without exception, apart from V. This implies that the capability difference represented by *we* is associated more closely with the rate of macro produc-

---

[18] Actually, *we* is calculated by adjustment using 1975 data on services proper, but this does not change the essential nature of *we*.

tivity growth than is *We*, which shows a reverse pattern in group observation.

In light of our discussion above, the implications of the data in Table 4A.4 become more substantive. The price level of machinery can be lowered by shifting the supply curve more rapidly in relation to that of other goods. The importance of human capability and its possible contribution to realization of lower machinery prices through the process of technology diffusion cannot be overemphasized.

5

Productivity Growth and Residual Growth: Comparison and Integration

Analysis of the technology diffusion process was virtually completed in the preceding chapters. The present chapter integrates those results with residual growth analysis. Comparison and integration of the two are aimed at, in the recognition that these are complementary, instead of competing, methods in elucidating the pattern and mechanism of the development path.

Productivity growth pertaining to labor input is a simple, first-hand *ex post facto* indicator of the results of technological advance, to which both the IOR and residual measurement pertain. Why is productivity growth instead of technological progress the focus? The technology diffusion process was the central topic of the preceding chapters, and the results must be seen from the standpoint of technological progress. However, its effects cannot be separated from those due to productivity growth, and are simultaneously incorporated in productivity growth. Can the effects of technology advance be distinguished by measuring residual growth or TFP? Often an affirmative answer is given, the authors hesitate since the contribution of nonconventional factors includes the effects of organizational-institutional innovations beyond technological progress, and quantitative decomposition of these is impossible. This does not mean that measurement of residual growth is not useful; it is indispensable for the present purpose. In this introductory explanation, the relation between productivity growth and residual growth is stated simply. To borrow a simplified neoclassical formula, productivity growth (Gy) with respect to labor is decomposed into residual growth (GR) and capital-intensity growth (Gk) as follows, where α is the output elasticity of capital:

$$Gy = GR + \alpha Gk, \qquad (1)$$

where the effects of technological progress are incorporated in GR since they are separate from the effects of increasing capital intensification. Productivity growth with respect to capital is as follows, where β is the output elasticity of labor:

$$GY - GK = GR - \beta(Gk). \qquad (2)$$

Capital productivity is a specific term from the viewpoint of capital accumulation. Gy is used here instead of $GY - GK$ because labor productivity can be linked directly with the Y/Lw used hitherto. In these formulae, GR can be used as a representative indicator or conditional proxy quantifying the effects of technological progress. The condition implies that nontechnology factors, particularly organizational progress, occurs in parallel with technological progress, although this assumption does not usually conform with reality.

The model described in chapter 1 assumes Gk = Gw for traditional technology and Gk > Gw for modern technology. For the former Formula (1) becomes $Gy - Gw = GR - \beta Gk$, while for the latter it is $Gy - Gw = GR - \beta Gk + \delta(\delta = Gk - Gw)$. In both cases Gy − Gw represents the growth performance of Y/Lw. In a comparison of the two, not only the pattern difference of capital intensification but also the magnitude difference of residual growth is the issue. It cannot be assumed *a priori* that a greater rate of capital intensification in modern technology diffusion will accompany a greater rate of residual growth than is the case in traditional technological progress. The reverse pattern is possible and the actual process must be examined.

In section I, the outcome of the IOR formula (represented by Gy − Gw) and that of the conventional residual approach are compared first in group aggregate and subgroup terms. Returning to the dualistic model proposed in chapter 1, the dimension is extended to traditional versus modern. In section II, using the conventional sector classification, the relation between Gy and GR is investigated in detail to enable fully understanding of the contents of section I. Finally, section III discusses the characteristics of development paths to clarify the basic changes in the sectoral structure from a phase demarcation approach.

I. Input-Output Ratio Formula and Residual Measurement

To begin with the macro patterns based on the data listed in Table 1.1, the relevant terms contained in the two equations

$Gy = GR + \alpha Gk$ and $Gy - Gw = GR - \beta Gk + (Gk - Gw)$ are given numerical values by group average in Table 5.1. In panel A the conventional formula in its application to the data is presented to clarify the changes in the two terms in the form of contribution to the productivity growth: residual growth and capital-intensity increase. Panel B is specifically designed to fit into the IOR formula, presenting the three key terms Y/Lw, K/Lw, and Y/K in explicit growth forms.

The ratio GR/Gy shown in panel A appears to suggest that residual growth contributes to nearly two-thirds of productivity growth in all groups with the exception of group IV. GR measurements are examined further in section II, but if this contribution is accepted as accurate, the greater role played by residual growth (or the lesser role played by capital intensity increase) appears to be a general phenomenon regardless of the varied levels of Y/L, the different degrees of development, in group averages. The interpretation focuses on two questions: first, why is such a similar pattern seen despite differences in Y/L level; and second, why is group IV an exception? The different patterns of component terms must be examined to arrivate at an acceptable interpretation.

The rate of productivity growth Gy shows a distinct trend of acceleration through the former segment, I, II, and III, but at III it begins to decelerate toward the latter segment, IV and V, although it increases again near V. The rate of residual growth GR shows an even more distinct trend of acceleration during the former segment and clearly begins to decelerate toward the latter segment, although again with a certain increase in group V. Therefore, the ratio GR/Gy can be expected to show a pattern of increase during the former segment. Actually, its numerical values in panel A of Table 5.1 present a slight increase. It is important to recognize the factors that operate to augment the contribution of residual growth in the development path of nations located in the former segment. Toward the latter segment, however, such factors cease to operate; the low ratio of GR/Gy for group IV is not an exception but evidence of a crucial mechanism of change toward the latter segment.

Why does the ratio increase again in group V? The answer can be found in the characteristics of developed economies in comparison with group IV. Both feature a distinct leveling up of the rate of capital intensity increase: the technology diffusion requirement changes from the former to the latter segment. In this situation, a clear difference is found between IV and V. The numerical values of GR and αGk differ between the two; in V the former is greater and

Table 5.1
Residual Growth versus Key Terms in the IOR Approach by Group

(A)	Gy	GR	Gk	GR/Gy	(B)	Gy – Gw	Gk – Gw'	GY – GK	GR – Gk
I	0.8	0.40	0.7	0.50		0.3	0.2	0.0	0.0
II	1.6	1.08	1.1	0.68		0.8	0.3	0.5	0.0
III	2.4	1.65	1.5	0.69		1.1	0.2	0.9	1.2
IV	2.1	0.92	2.4	0.44		0.3	0.6	-0.3	-1.3
V	2.4	1.51	2.9	0.63		0.3	0.7	-0.5	-1.4

the latter smaller. In short, the capability for absorbing technology diffusion differs between the two groups.

So far the discussion has proceeded along the lines of the conventional formula $Gy = GR + \alpha Gk$, which is acceptable in terms of the residual approach. However, real pattern recognition and its interpretation are possible based on the figures listed in Table 5.1, panel B. As stated in chapter 1, referring to Table 1.1, the behavior of $Gk - Gw$ (K/Lw in the growth term) is clearly distinguished between the former and latter segment. During the former it is extremely small, while toward the latter it becomes sizable. The significance of the distinct difference should be recognized in group averages, without specifying the exception for group IV.

As shown in Table 5.1, panel A, the rate of capital intensification differs between the two segments. A distinct demarcation of the capital widening versus capital deepening pattern is seen in the two intervals, signifying on the one hand an important change in the factor inputs combination emanating from the technology diffusion requirement. On the other hand, the output effect (Y/K) on growth is shown by $GY - GK$ in panel B of Table 5.1. Its numerical values present an inverse U-shaped curve: during the former segment it is positive but becomes negative toward the latter segment. In the former segment the positive value tends to increase, whereas toward the latter its negative value tends to increase. Note that no exception is witnessed for IV. The identification of such a pattern of the output-capital ratio is simple but important, along with that of the K/Lw pattern.

The performance of $Gy - Gw$ (Y/Lw in the growth term) is simply the combined results of $GK - (GL + Gw)$ and $GY - GK$. Actually, the different patterns of $Gy - Gw$ between the former and the latter segment are combined results. The actual value of $Gy - Gw$ shown in panel B of the table forms an inverse U-shaped curve with a sharp decline from III to IV. In the former segment it tends to accelerate, while toward the latter segment it begins to decelerate. The identification of this pattern is noteworthy because the turning point is much more clearly presented at group III by the IOR formula compared to the other terms in panel A when the conventional formula is applied. The major reason for the difference between the two approaches is the performance of the latter segment. During the former segment, the performance of $GY - GK$ is influential in forming the trend of acceleration of $Gy - Gw$, while $Gk - Gw$ changes little. In the latter segment the rate of increase in the capital-output ratio $(GY < GK)$ occurs in positive association with the rate of capital deepening (Gk > Gw) in the present sense for groups IV and V. This implies that the property and mechanism of technology diffusion change between the former and the latter segment.

Additional information is given in panel B of Table 5.1 on the relation between Gy – Gw and GR by listing the numerical value of the term GR – βGk. This should be equal to that of GY – GK (the slight difference between the two stems from rounding off in actual computation), and nothing substantial is implied by it. However, it is convenient to use it to discuss the conceptual difference between the two approaches. In the conventional neoclassical approach the use of output elasticities (α and β) is indispensable to measure the contribution of the conventional factors and hence the residual growth as the result of nonconventional factors. This property is given simply by GR = α(GY – GK) + β(GY – GL). Thus, GR measures cannot deal explicitly with the behavior of GY – GK and GK – GL, although it is incorporated implicitly. This is inconvenient in attempts to clarify the changes in the patterns of development, but application of IOR formula can supplement the conventional approach without depending upon the use of output elasticities of production factors.

No knowledge is available on the actual growth path of individual nations which underlies the group average observation presented above using cross-sectional data. Estimated figures are listed in Table 5.2 in order to compare subgroups A and B by applying the same approaches as in the case of group averages. For the sake of

Table 5.2
Residual Approach versus Key Terms in the IOR Formula by Subgroup

	(A)	Gy	GR	GR/Gy	(B)	Gy – Gw	Gk – Gw	GY – GK
I	A	1.4	0.94	0.67		0.4	0.4	0.0
	B	0.2	−0.21	−1.05		0.0	0.1	−0.1
II	A	2.4	1.72	0.72		1.2	0.2	1.0
	B	0.9	0.44	0.49		0.5	0.5	0.0
III	A	3.5	2.77	0.79		1.7	−0.4	2.1
	B	1.3	0.39	0.30		0.6	1.1	−0.5
IV	A	2.6	1.05	0.40		0.4	1.0	−0.6
	B	1.6	0.74	0.46		0.3	0.5	−0.2
V	A	2.9	1.99	0.69		0.3	2.1	−2.4
	B	2.0	1.06	0.59		0.3	1.4	−1.0

Remark: All the figures are not necessarily consistent on average with those in Table 5.1 due to data adjustments.

convenience, the relevant terms are reproduced from Table 1.1. Gw is simply assumed to vary in association with Gy, because no data are available.

Applying the conventional formula, shown in panel A of Table 5.2, both Gy and GR are distinctly greater in A than in B through all groups without exception. The conventional ratio GR/Gy is thus larger for A and smaller for B, with a slight exception for group IV. It is reconfirmed that what are referred to here as nonassociated factors (other than Y/L level) operate strongly in A, resulting in greater residual growth. The most impressive case is group III. The remarkable difference in Gy between A and B stems from the largest difference of the ratio GR/Gy (A 0.8 versus B 0.3). The reason for this was given previously in terms of the balance or imbalance between SC (social capability) and PC (production capacity). The IOR formula appears to yield an acceptable interpretation. As is shown in panel B, the values of Gy − Gw present a more impressive pattern of subgroup difference (greater in A, smaller in B) which is decisive since there is no exception in all the groups. This is the combined result of the patterns of terms Gk − Gw and GY − GK. However, it must be noted that their subgroup difference tends not to present the expected pattern of being greater in A versus smaller in B. In the case of Gk − Gw for groups III and V, the reverse is witnessed, and in the case of GY − GK, the reverse is seen for group IV. In group III the remarkable difference in output-capital ratios overwhelms the countereffects of factor inputs. In group IV the opposite difference in the two terms tends to be in favor of a regular pattern of Gy − Gw.

Finally, in group V the greater Gk − Gw of B exerts unfavorable effects on GY − GK, similar to the case of group III. These three cases appear complex, but an inverse relation is generally found between the greater rate of K/Lw increase and its unfavorable effects on Y/K performance. This relation is particularly noticeable in groups III, IV, and V. This is a possible pattern involved in the IOR formula. Simply stated, capital intensification does not necessarily increase the output effects. The magnitude of GY − GK is often larger in the case of smaller values of Gk − Gw. The criterion for the subgrouping of A and B is investment efficiency $\Delta Y/I$, estimated on average for 1960–1985. Using other criteria would have different results. In the operation of nonassociated factors this formula appears to indicate the effects of adopting different patterns of technology. This supports the view that in terms of subgroup differences what is important is not the difference in PC but the difference in SC, which is balanced in A and imbalanced in B.

The sectoral dimension, envisaged by the dualistic structure model proposed in chapter 1 can be elucidated by applying the IOR formula centering on Gy − Gw to cross-sectional data by group average. Using the conventional formula it is possible to attempt a sectoral approach to the role of residual growth. Section II describes a number of notable phenomena in this regard. For example, the growth rate of the residual in agriculture GRa, both simple and weighted, presents a pattern analogous to that of the aggregate Gy − Gw described above. However, this approach is not compared with the IOR approach due to data limitations. Therefore, it is attempted to test quantitatively the simple model assumed at the outset of chapter 1 in relation to the proposed hypothesis concerning the dualistic composition of the modern (M) and traditional (T) sectors.

The main procedure is to disaggregate the macro pattern of Gy − Gw. From the preceding discussion, it is expected that the contribution of the two sectors M and T to the aggregate should vary distinctly between the former and latter segments demarcated by the turning point at group III. This pattern must be quantified using only limited data. For this purpose, disaggregation of Gw is reproduced from the preceding treatment (Technical Notes in chapter 1), while that of Gy is specifically derived from what is called the difference indicator in *DE* (Table 4.10).[1] This is sectoral Gy, measured as the disaggregated value of macro Gy. The estimated results are summarized in Table 5.3 (where m and t stand for the modern and traditional sector, respectively).

Although the estimation procedure is rough, the results derived by this disaggregation broadly indicate an important characteristic of sectoral patterns of Gy − Gw through the former and latter segments of the entire range. In the traditional sector the magnitude of Gyt − Gwt tends to be near zero (actually slightly negative in groups I and II) but makes a drastic surge to its highest positive magnitude at III. Toward the latter segment, in IV and V, it tends to be somewhat smaller. With respect to the modern sector, the positive magnitude

---

[1] Kazushi Ohkawa, in collaboration with Katsuo Otsuka and Bernard Key, *Growth Mechanism of Developing Economies: Investment, Productivity and Employment* (Tokyo: International Development Center of Japan/International Center for Economic Growth, 1993).

Table 5.3
Disaggregation of Gy − Gw, 1960–1980

(%)

	I	II	III	IV	V
(A) Weighted sectoral magnitude					
Gyt	−0.23	0.34	1.29	1.01	0.90
Gwt	0.44	0.39	0.31	0.25	0.12
Gyt − Gwt	−0.67	−0.05	0.98	0.76	0.78
Gym	0.58	2.16	2.46	2.08	2.19
Gwm	0.20	0.50	0.97	1.51	2.06
Gym − Gwm	0.38	1.66	1.49	0.57	0.13
(B) Aggregate					
Gy	0.4	2.5	3.8	3.1	3.1
Gw	0.6	0.8	1.3	1.8	2.2
Gy − Gw	−0.1	1.7	2.5	1.3	0.9

Remarks: i) The weighted Gyt, productivity growth of the traditional sector, is from Da and Ds, difference indicators of agriculture and services. The weighted Gym, productivity growth of the modern sector, is from Di, the difference indicator of industry and Ds. Regarding the difference indicator, see section III.

ii) For estimating Gwt, the rate of wage increase in the traditional sector, and Gwm, that of the modern sector, Gw in Table 1.1 is used.

iii) Allocation of the service sector to T and M is by the same procedure as mentioned in Technical Notes, chapter 1.

iv) Some inconsistency between the sum of sectoral difference indicators Da, Di, and Ds (*DE*, Table 4.10) and aggregate Gy (*DE*, Table 4.1) is adjusted to the latter's magnitude by assuming proportional discrepancies among sectors except in group I. Ds for this group is from specifically adjusted data, but reliability is limited.

v) This is for the 1960–1980 interval, while Table 1.1 and the preceding macro treatment is for 1960–1985. This is due to the difficulty in obtaining reliable sectoral data for 1980–1985.

of Gym − Gwm is smaller for group I, but tends to increase considerably in the former segment and to decrease rapidly in the latter segment. As a whole, it can be concluded that the formation of the aggregate pattern of sustained increase in Gy − Gw during the former segment the effect of the traditional sector is dominant, whereas in the latter segment its tendency to decline is dominated by the modern sector. At the turning point identified earlier, the basic structural change in the relation between productivity growth and wage performance is recognized.

With regard to the wage performance, the estimates depend upon the imputation procedure for the traditional sector, as shown in section I. This results in a higher magnitude of Gwt than would otherwise be the case, contributing to negative values of Gyt − Gwt in the former segment. However, the more influential factor in this regard is on the productivity side. Sectoral productivity performance is examined by introducing the concept of the "sectoral turning point" in section III.

In concluding this section, it is argued that the dualistic approach is indispensable to grasp the pattern and mechanism of development. Application of the IOR formula is useful and appropriate for this analytical purpose. The macro pattern of Gy − Gw is distinctly characterized by the inverse U-shape, and it has been clarified that the shape of the former segment is dominantly influenced by the traditional sector, and that of the latter segment, by the modern sector. The data are cross-sectional, but it is conditionally suggested that demarcation of development phases characterizes the two segments: the former segment by the primary phase and the latter segment by the secondary phase in light of the change from the traditional to the modern sector. Phases concerned with over-time series from individual nations and the present model cannot be used to determine these. The subgroup approach may illustrate this aspect, as discussed in section III. Nevertheless, the turning point at III in the macro approach is relevant to demarcating the development path into the primary and secondary phase.

II. Productivity Growth and Residual Growth in Major Sectors

In the preceding section, overviews were given regarding the comparison of the IOR formula with the residual approach, although the latter cannot deal with the dualistic assessment. This section is designed to fill that gap by analyzing productivity growth with residual measurement for the three major sectors A, I, and S. Measurements of sectoral GR are not completely reliable due to data limitations. Nevertheless, broad patterns can be distinguished by careful use of the results relevant to this assessment. An overview is given by Table 5.4.

Industry versus Agriculture
What is most amazing is the unexpected phenomenon that the residual growth rate of industry is lower than that of agriculture (GRi < GRa) for the major range of developing economies. Apart

Table 5.4
Sector Components of Residual Growth by Group, 1960–1980

(%)

(A)	Agriculture		Industry		Services		Aggregate	
	Gya	GRa	Gyi	GRi	Gys	GRs	Gy	GR
I	0.4	0.08	0.5	–0.20	–0.5	–1.01	1.1	0.23
II	1.4	1.01	3.4	1.16	1.6	–0.22	2.5	1.03
III	3.4	2.90	3.2	1.42	1.7	0.81	3.8	1.89
IV	3.5	2.48	3.6	1.17	2.4	0.75	3.1	1.36
V	4.1	1.44	3.7	1.72	1.6	0.74	3.1	1.57

(B) Weighted

	GRa/Gya	waGRa	GRi/Gyi	wiGRi	GRs/Gys	wsGRs	Sectoral Sum Residual	Reallocation Effects
I	17.5	0.04	–4.0	–0.03	?	–0.41	–0.40	0.63
II	62.9	0.33	40.0	0.28	–0.6	–0.10	0.51	0.52
III	73.7	0.82	44.4	0.37	22.4	0.38	1.57	0.32
IV	70.6	0.37	32.5	0.27	15.4	0.37	1.01	0.35
V	34.1	0.07	46.5	0.67	26.3	0.42	1.16	0.41

Source: DE, op. cit., Tables 4.1 and A2.1.
Remarks: i) wa, wi, and ws are sectoral shares of output.
ii) The residual terms are not rounded, for the sake of later discussion.

from group II, the generally expected pattern GRi > GRa can only be seen in group V, representing developed economies. The performance of weighted magnitude is even more impressive: waGRa continues to be distinctly greater than wiGRi throughout all groups of developing countries. Reallocation effects are discussed below. Excluding this term, the relation of productivity growth and residual growth is presented for the three sectors. The following points are notable. The magnitude of productivity growth and residual growth in agriculture (GRa) appears much greater than usually expected. By sector of industry, the level of residual growth appears lower than usually expected in relation to its high level of productivity growth for the groups of developing countries. Finally, in the service sector, as expected, both productivity and residual tend to increase at a slower pace. However, as shown in Table 5.4, panel B, the contribution of residual growth to the aggregate is unexpectedly sizable in the latter segment in group average. These are the major issues, among others, of particular concern in the examination and interpretation that follow.

The same phenomena cannot be found in the historical path of presently developed economies. Table 5.5 briefly reviews Japan's case. GRi is distinctly higher than GRa through all periods. In addition, GRi is also larger than the aggregate residual growth GR through all periods without exception. It can be contended that this is atypical and due to Japan's exceptionally fast pace of industrialization. The present authors, however, do not necessarily think so. For example, the historical records of the UK show that the ratio GRm/GR (manufacturing in this case) is sustained over unity

Table 5.5
Residual Growth, Aggregate, Industry and Agriculture, 1887–1976 on Phase Average, Japan

	GR	GRi	GRi/GR	GRa
1887–1904	0.8	1.1	1.36	0.95
1904–1917*	1.8	2.1	1.16	1.36
1917*–1938	1.6	2.9	1.79	0.67
1954–1965	5.0	6.7	1.34	2.97
1965–1976	4.9	5.5	1.17	1.80

Source: From *DE*, *op. cit.*, Table A2.3, except GRa, which is from Kazushi Ohkawa and Hirohisa Kohama, *Lectures on Developing Economies: Japan's Experience and Its Relevance* (Tokyo: University of Tokyo Press, 1989), Table 1.7.
Remark: *is 1919 for agriculture.

since 1856 in five-period averages except for 1937–1951, the abnormal period.[2] The ratio GRi/GR derived from cross-sectional data by group is −0.87 (I), 1.17 (II), 0.75 (III), 0.86 (IV), and 1.10 (V).

For most developing economies the ratio is under unity on group average. The ratio can be over unity for individual countries with faster industrialization, however. The Republic of Korea is one such example,[3] although data for other similar cases are limited. At any rate, a ratio under unity generally characterizes the pattern of postwar developing economies from the industrialization standpoint.

Thus it is important to confirm such characteristics of developing economies. Is it possible to explain substantively the above-mentioned pattern of residual growth in agriculture derived from the estimates here? Or is it due to overestimates of GRa? The answer is of course negative, but requires detailed explanation. Two points made in *DE*, chapter 4, are relevant. First, the rate of productivity growth tends to be almost equal between agriculture and industry so far as most developing economies are concerned. Second, it is important to recognize that this near equality is achieved despite the basic difference in technology type between the two sectors. The implication of these two points is clarified below. When measuring residual growth using the output approach, it may be convenient to use the following conventional formulae for simplified treatment.

Industry: $GRi = \alpha i(GYi - GKi) + \beta i(GYi - GLi)$; and

Agriculture: $GRa = \alpha a(GYa - GKa) + \beta a(GYa - GLa)$
$$+ \gamma(GYa - GB)$$

(B and γ stand for land area and output elasticity of land, respectively).

The major purpose in using these formulae is to elucidate the compositional difference of residual growth between the two sectors. The performance of two groups, III and IV, is of special interest since their residual growth of agriculture is estimated to be higher than that of industry. In these two groups, the rate of productivity growth is nearly equal between the two sectors, that is, $GYi - GLi = GYa - GLa$. βa is somewhat greater than βi (this issue is discussed later), so that GRa should be greater than GRi,

---

[2] For details, see *DE, op. cit.,* Table A2.3 and its explanation.
[3] For details, see *DE, op. cit.,* Table A3.5 with its explanation.

Table 5.6
Rates of Productivity Growth in Agriculture, 1960–1980

(%)

	GYa	GYa – GB	GLa – GB	GLa	GB	Gyi
I	0.4	1.5	1.1	1.3	0.2	0.5
II	1.5	1.8	0.3	1.7	1.4	2.9
III	3.4	4.0	0.6	1.1	0.5	3.2
IV	3.5	3.1	−0.4	−0.7	−0.3	3.6
V	4.1	1.6	−0.5	−3.0	−0.5	3.7

Source: Gyi (GYi – GLi) from *DE*, *op. cit.*, Table A2.4; Gya (GYa – GLa) and all other agricultural terms are from *DE*, Table A2.5.

even if the effects of other terms are entirely ignored. The land term is specific to agriculture and operates to augment GRa further, since under a limited expansion of land area, output growth is realized by increasing current inputs to augment the function of land. Table 5.6 summarizes the relevant cross-sectional data for all groups.

Particular attention is paid to the rate of land productivity growth GYa – GB. Its pattern is an inverse U-shape: in the former segment it increases but it decreases in the latter, with group III being the turning point. During the former segment it is greater than the rate of labor productivity growth Gya, but the inequality is reversed during the latter segment. (For comparison, the growth rate of labor productivity of industry Gyi is added in Table 5.6.) Since Ya/La = (Ya/B)·(B/La), the difference in growth rate between per land and per labor input in agriculture is given by GLa – GB. The labor engaged per unit area is very high for group I, and yet the growth rate tends to increase during the former segment while it decreases during the latter segment. These are all simple indicators but suggest important implications. The productivity growth changes from the former to the latter segment suggest that in the former segment scale-neutral, BC technology plays a dominant role, while in the latter segment the dominant role shifts to scale-positive M technology. These are responses to changes in GLa – GB, although the effects of factor price changes cannot be covered in this simple approach. This shift in type of farming technology coincides with changes in the relative inequality of productivity growth rates between per land and per labor input mentioned above. It also indicates the actual contribution made by progress in BC technology. Viewed historically, this phenomenon has not been

Table 5.7
Historical Pattern of Productivity Growth in Agriculture: Selected Cases of
Presently Developed Countries

(Annual rates, %)

(A) In Added Value: Japan			(B) In Wheat Units			
	Gya	GYa – GB			Gya	GYa – GB
1887–1904	1.31	0.93	Japan	1880–1945	1.55	0.72
				1945–1980	5.07	4.64
1904–1919	2.05	1.15	Denmark	1888–1945	1.24	1.26
				1945–1980	5.49	2.50
1919–1938	1.09	0.66	France	1880–1945	0.88	0.61
				1945–1980	6.61	3.25
1954–1965	5.17	2.36				

Sources: A is from Kazushi Ohkawa and Nobukiyo Takamatsu, "Capital Formation,
Productivity and Employment," *IDCJ Working Paper No. 26*, March 1983, Table
2; B from Yujiro Hayami and Vernon Ruttan, *Agricultural Development: An International Perspective* (Baltimore: Johns Hopkins University Press, 1971), Appendix
B (2, 3 and 4).

Remarks: B is per male worker. The average annual rate of growth is determined by
a simple bridge between two years, demarcating two periods.

observed in the long path of the agricultural development of presently developed nations. It is a newly emerging pattern in contemporary development. No further elaboration is needed, but some
selected examples are shown in Table 5.7.

Japanese agriculture is widely accepted as presenting a classic example of BC technology development in rapid leveling up of yield,
although the rate of land productivity growth was slower than that
of labor productivity growth (Table 5.7, panel A). For international
comparison, three other countries were selected (panel B). Except
for prewar Denmark and postwar Japan, the rate of land productivity growth is much slower than that of labor productivity growth.
These are "favorable" land productivity cases, and in most other developed nations the difference must be much greater.

Finally, differences in initial levels of productivity and technology
in agriculture between contemporary developing countries and presently developed countries should be addressed. The initial level of
the former cannot be estimated reliably and directly but it can be
assumed to be extremely low since, despite the near-equal rates of
productivity growth, agricultural productivity relative to that of in-

dustry is distinctly lower than in developed countries, even in recent years. This implies that modern BC technology can be diffused under traditional conditions.

The above give supporting evidence for and an acceptable explanation of the greater GRa in contemporary developing economies. Critical comments on possible overestimates of GRa are dealt with separately in the Technical Notes at the end of this subsection.

The next topic concerns the entire development path and compares agriculture and industry in depth. In the process, sectoral characteristics of technology diffusion and of the conditions under which it occurs are clarified in more detail. Industrialization has often been thought to be nearly equivalent to economic development. Recently, however, the significance of the important role played by agriculture has been recognized, although the authors contend that this is not sufficient to evaluate agriculture correctly. A balanced view of agriculture should begin with productivity performance figures, as given in Table 5.8.

The significance of the near-equality in the productivity growth

Table 5.8
Productivity Growth: Agriculture versus Industry

(%)

		GYa	GLa	Gya	GYi	GLi	Gyi
I		1.7	1.3	0.4	5.2	4.7	0.5
II	Average	3.2	1.8	1.4	6.7	3.8	2.9
	E	4.2	1.8	2.4	7.8	4.5	3.4
	F	2.4	1.9	0.5	5.7	3.2	2.5
III	Average	4.4	1.1	3.4	8.0	4.8	3.2
	E	4.5	0.5	4.0	9.5	5.1	4.4
	F	4.3	1.7	2.6	6.4	4.2	3.2
IV	Average	2.8	−0.7	3.5	6.6	3.0	3.6
	E	3.2	−1.4	4.6	8.3	3.5	4.8
	F	2.4	−0.1	2.5	4.8	2.5	2.3
V	Average	1.1	−3.0	4.1	4.4	0.7	3.7
	E	0.6	−3.8	4.4	5.2	1.0	4.2
	F	1.5	−2.1	3.6	3.7	0.3	3.4

Source: *DE, op. cit.*, Tables 4.1 and 4.3, in averages of values of the 1960s and 1970s.

Remarks: For subgrouping, see Remarks to Table 5.15 for details. The criterion is the rate of macro productivity growth (E greater, F smaller).

rate witnessed between agriculture, Gya, and industry, Gyi, has been emphasized.[4] This is a characteristic feature of the postwar pattern of development insofar as the average observations by group are concerned. The discussion is not repeated here, but the relevant terms GYa, GLa, GYi, and GLi are listed for reference in Table 5.8. Subgrouping in terms of macro productivity growth rate Gy is used here. (There are 58 countries as listed in the Remarks to Table 5.15.) Each group is divided into two subgroups, E (greater Gy) and F (smaller Gy), making an equal number in each group. For I, however, the data are not sufficiently reliable to do so. In both industry and agriculture, the level difference in rates of productivity growth is sizable and distinctly shows E > F without exception through all groups. The magnitude of productivity growth rate tends to be nearly equal between industry and agriculture in subgroups E and F. A noticeable exception to this regularity is group II, as explained in section III in terms of the preprimary phase. This near equality in subgroups is an important finding, and through the path of development the cross-sectional data indicate meaningful performance through subgroup comparisons. With respect to E, Gyi shows a tendency of acceleration from 3.4 in II toward 4.8 in IV, followed by a slight decline in group V. Analogous to Gyi in this subgroup, Gya presents a tendency of acceleration from 2.4 in II toward 4.6 in IV, also followed by a slight decline in group V. With regard to subgroup F, the pattern is different, in sharp contrast to that of E. Gyi shows no tendency to increase, remaining at a low level of 2.2–2.5, and followed by a distinct surge in group V. Gya in subgroup F also remains at a low level of 2.5–2.6 (except for being very low in II as mentioned previously), followed by a sharp increase in group V.

These imply a notable phenomenon characteristic of the postwar path of development. During most of the path the gap in productivity growth rates between subgroups widens rather than narrows. A tendency to narrow the gap can only be seen toward group V, representing developed economies. Therefore a simple average observation would be misleading due to the overwhelming effects of subgroup E. The subgrouping here is simple, and if data on the distribution of the magnitudes of Gyi and Gya were available for individual nations, the range of the gap would be greater.

These findings are a major challenge for the present analysis.

---

[4] For details, see *DE, op. cit.,* chapter 4, in the last subsection of section II: Productivity Growth in Two-sector Comparison.

How can they be interpreted consistently? Relying on the relevant findings in the preceding analysis, a semihypothetical assumption is made that the contribution of the conventional inputs results in no sizable difference between subgroups, whereas the contribution of nonconventional factors constitu es the major productivity difference between subgroups, and that this pattern is essentially the same for both industry and agriculture. The assumption is relevant to, if not dependent upon, the subgroup performance (A versus B) determined in chapter 1, section I. It generally stems from the basic notion that productivity growth can be analyzed in terms of the relation of PC, production capacity, representing conventional inputs, to SC, social capability, pertaining to nonconventional inputs. Therefore, the assumption proposed above implies that at almost equivalent PC, in subgroup E a higher level of SC operates, while in subgroup F a lower level of SC operates. Because this is assumed for both industry and agriculture, the SC-PC relation is not sector-specific but common for each nation's society.

An attempt is made below, not to provide exact measurements as proof of the assumption, but rather to quantify its implications in order to examine its plausibility in relation to the relevant terms. Relevant data for industry are listed in Table 5.9. In the aggregate approach at the outset of this chapter, the simple formula $Gy = GR + \alpha Gk$ was used. Here, the same formula $Gyi = GRi + \alpha iGki$ is applied to industry, but the relation of the terms differs substantially. In the aggregate case all three terms involved are estimated independently (although the last one is conditional) for subgroups. In the sectoral approach, GRi is not available as an independent estimate. Thus, the procedure is to derive GRi under an assumption about $\alpha iGki$. In Table 5.9 the results of applying the same $\alpha iGki$ value obtained for the average in each group are given. No data are available on the variation of αi between subgroups, so that this assumption implies that the rate of growth of capital intensity Gki is equal between subgroups as follows: I, 1.5; II, 3.4; III, 3.3; IV, 4.6; and V, 5.2.

The tendency to increase through all groups, in particular between III and IV, is distinct. This appears to be consistent with the proposed notion that the international element in technology diffusion operates noticeably in the sector of industry presented in the present model. However, can it be said that its level and tendency make essentially no difference between the two subgroups? The authors are inclined to give an affirmative answer due to the overview from aggregate analysis and reasons specific to this sector. In chap-

Table 5.9
Semihypothetical Estimates of Residual Growth by Subgroup: Industry

	Gyi	αGki (Gyi − GRi)	GRi	GRi/Gyi	GLi	GKi	GYi
I		0.5	0.75	−2.0	−4.0	4.7	6.2	5.2
II	Average	2.9	1.74	1.16	40.0	3.8	7.3	6.7
	E	3.4	1.74	1.66	48.8	4.5	8.0	7.8
	F	2.5	1.74	0.76	30.4	3.2	6.7	5.7
III	Average	3.2	1.78	1.42	44.4	4.8	8.1	8.0
	E	4.4	1.78	2.62	59.5	5.1	8.4	7.5
	F	2.2	1.78	0.42	19.1	4.2	7.5	6.4
IV	Average	3.0	2.43	1.17	32.5	3.0	7.9	6.6
	E	4.8	2.43	2.37	49.4	3.5	8.1	8.3
	F	2.3	2.43	−0.13	−5.6	2.5	7.1	4.8
V	Average	3.7	1.98	1.72	46.5	0.7	5.9	4.4
	E	4.2	1.98	2.22	52.9	1.0	6.2	5.2
	F	3.4	1.98	1.42	41.8	0.3	5.5	3.1

Source: GYi, GLi, Gyi are reproduced from Table 3.12 for the sake of convenience. Capital's income share αi from *DE, op. cit.*, Table 1.7. GKi is from *DE, op. cit.*, Table A2.4.
Remarks: Gki = GKi − GLi. αGRi is derived by Gyi − αiGki.

ter 1, section I, the impression was given that the behavior of K/Lw pertaining to the aggregate economy showed little difference between subgroups A and B. Comparisons of GKi and GYi listed in Table 5.9 make it clear that the magnitude of inequality (GKi − GYi) tends to be greater in F and smaller in E for all groups without exception. The capital-output ratio generally tends to increase in all subgroups with the slight exception of E, Group IV. In this general tendency, the behavior of the capital-output ratio appears to be more favorable in E and less favorable in F. This is an acceptable pattern because the rate of productivity growth is greater in E and smaller in F, and it is probable that the above-mentioned pattern of the capital-output ratio takes place in association.[5]

Considering that the assumption of equal GKi is thus mainly acceptable, the magnitude of GRi, the rate of residual growth in the sector of industry, listed in Table 5.9 can be illuminating. Its magnitude is far greater in E than in F through the major portion of de-

[5] In *DE, op. cit.*, chapter 1, ΔK/ΔY, the incremental value of the capital-output ratio was found to be smaller in subgroup A and higher in subgroup B.

veloping economies. In this respect it is particularly notable that the gap narrows sharply in V, the developed economies. From group II to III and III to IV, GRi of subgroup F tends to decline, with its value in IV becoming negative. This tendency is due to the operation of decelerating factors, and its decline is indispensable in making the shift to the developed state. The rate of technology diffusion may roughly and conditionally be approximated by the ratio GRi/Gyi. With respect to E, the rate accelerates, but decelerates in F, making a sharp contrast. In this respect special attention is drawn to the latter segment. Its group average has a dip in IV and after that again tends to increase in V. The ratio regarding subgroup E also presents the same pattern. With regard to the reasons for such patterns, views differ among economists. It is the view of the present authors that the shift to higher levels of PC due to technological requirement by capital intensification makes it more difficult to raise the ratio GRi/Gyi. This difficulty is largely solved in V but not in IV.

For agriculture, one would like to apply the same assumption, that there is no difference between subgroups with regard to the contribution of conventional inputs. However, in doing so, a difficulty specific to agriculture is met in the form of the production activity of land (B). Corresponding to the case of industry, the rate of productivity growth Gya is decomposed as follows (where γ is elasticity of output with respect to land):

$$Gya = GRa + \alpha a(GKa - GLa) + \gamma(GB - GLa).$$

Therefore, if the magnitude of $\alpha a(GKa - GLa)$ can be assumed approximately equal between subgroups, the effects of the term $\gamma(GB - GLa)$ can differ considerably. At this stage, available data by subgroup are limited not only for GKa but also for GB. But data for GLa are available and its subgroup difference often appears significant. Therefore it is assumed that GB is nearly equal among subgroups; that is, the magnitude of $\gamma(GB - GLa)$ may differ due to GLa difference on the one hand, while on the other, with regard to $\alpha a Gka$, the same level (group average) can be applied for both E and F, implying that Gka tends to be greater in E than in F due to the difference in GLa between subgroups. These results are summarized in Table 5.10. The residual growth in agriculture GRa shows an inverse U-shape in group average: increasing in the former segment and decreasing in the latter. Analysis by subgroup reveals that this pattern is created by GRa of subgroup E, with the turning point being at group III. Although data are limited, GRa of subgroup F

Table 5.10
Semihypothetical Estimates of Residual Growth by Subgroup: Agriculture

		Gya	αaGka	γ(GB − GLa)	GRa	GRa/Gya	GLa
I		0.4	0.65	−0.32	0.07	17.5	1.3
II	Average	1.4	0.62	−0.09	0.88	62.9	1.8
	E	2.4	0.62	−0.01	1.79	75.0	1.8
	F	0.3	0.62	−0.02	−0.30	(−)	1.9
III	Average	3.4	0.52	−0.21	2.47	73.7	1.1
	E	4.1	0.52	0.00	3.58	87.3	0.5
	F	2.6	0.52	−0.41	1.50	57.7	1.7
IV	Average	3.5	0.90	0.13	2.47	70.6	−0.7
	E	4.6	0.90	0.34	3.36	73.0	−1.4
	F	2.4	0.90	−0.06	1.56	65.0	−0.1
V	Average	4.1	1.95	0.75	1.40	34.1	−3.0
	E	4.3	1.95	0.99	1.46	34.0	−3.8
	F	3.6	1.95	0.48	1.13	31.4	−2.1

Sources: GYa, GLa are reproduced from Table 5.6 for the sake of convenience. GKa, GB, αa, βa, and γ for group average are from *DE, op. cit.*, Table A2.5.

Remarks: i) αa(GKa − GLa) is calculated for each group average using GKa and GLa. GRa is calculated as Gya−(αaGka)−γ(GB − GLA). Due to the relatively small capital income share (12–21%) its effects are moderate, whereas γ(GB − GLa) is of considerable value for higher groups, although it is negligible for the former segment.

ii) GRa in group average deviates somewhat from its subgroup averages. Such inconsistency may not distort the broad interpretation made here.

appears very low in the former segment, but during the latter segment it becomes relatively high, making the subgroup gap narrower, particularly in group V. These tendencies are distinctly shown by the performance of the ratio GRa/Gya in subgroup comparison.

In dealing with productivity growth earlier, it was noted that the difference between subgroup Gyi and Gya behavior was nearly parallel. In general terms the results of decomposition reveal a parallel subgroup gap between GRi and GRa (compare Tables 5.9 and 5.10). To that extent different levels of national SC can be recognized between the two goods-producing sectors. However, a closer look at the figures reveals certain deviations from this tendency through groups of developing economies. Focusing on subgroup F, with respect to group II GRi > GRa but for groups III and IV GRi is extremely small, while GRa remains at normal levels. In V GRi > GRa. In this major segment of the development path the levels of SC in subgroup F appear to be especially inferior in industry relative to agriculture. This raises the problem of interpreting sectoral components of SC in relation to PC.

The absolute levels of GRi and GRa are not directly comparable in reference to the SC concept. GRa is often greater than GRi in the present measurements, because of the different properties of technology and organization. The larger GRa essentially stems from the diffusion of high-yielding varieties (HYV) of rice, wheat, corn, etc., which is made possible by fulfilling the required institutional-organizational conditions as well as by providing facilities such as irrigation and drainage. From the viewpoint of international technology diffusion, the importance of local R&D efforts cannot be denied due to the location-specific nature of farming technology, unlike the case of industry. The decline of prices of current inputs, such as fertilizers and insecticides, is a crucial condition for the domestic diffusion of technology of this type. This rough outline of an actual complex situation shows that the relation between SC and PC in agriculture appears to be specific because the required conditions differ from those for the case of manufacturing. In short, fulfillment of the required conditions may make it possible to diffuse improved BC technology without remarkable upgrading of the PC level. This basically results from the contribution of land, a natural resource, although it actually operates with the accumulated effects of investment in land, the major portion of PC in agriculture. The subgroup differential is essentially based on the balance (E) versus imbalance (F) between SC and PC, respectively. The latter is mainly caused by the insufficient level of SC as compared to PC. This is the application of the authors' original proposition derived from macro observation. Here, with regard to agriculture, what is important is not to reject this basic proposition but to give an adequate interpretation to it by taking into account the conditions specific to agriculture. Thus the current inputs play a significant role, as discussed in chapter 2, section III.

The HYVs can be called carriers of new technology of the BC type, analogous to the case of manufacturing, for which PDE is the carrier of new technology in international technology diffusion of the M type. This was not sufficiently recognized by the classical doctrine on technological progress in agriculture. In understanding the human and organizational capability elements in SC, special significance is given to progress in organizations and institutions. Small farmers cannot achieve more efficient farming without the support of local public activities in extending R&D achievements. The GRa gap between subgroups has been noted, but practical knowledge for comparing each subgroup case is limited. However, with regard to the scope and speed of HYV promulgation, empirical research results are available.[6] According to these, HYV promulgation from larger- to smaller-scale farmers occurred smoothly. As was once asserted during the initial diffusion process, differentiating factors operated among larger- versus smaller-scale farmers. The largest gap noted in group II may perhaps be aggravated by initial differentials in the subgroup F nations. Due to a smoother promulgation process in groups III and IV, however, the subgroup gap becomes much narrower in conditional estimates for these two groups: the GRi gap between E and F is far wider in industry than in agriculture, except for group II.[7]

Technical Notes

The purpose of this section is to reexamine the procedure for estimating GRa in response to critical comments. What is characteristic of agriculture is directly represented by the land term $\gamma(GYa - GB)$, but the relative magnitudes of αa, βa, and γ are also have significant effects in comparison with αi and βi in industry from the present point of view. Any overestimates of GRa would stem from these effects. In *DE*, Tables A2.4 and A2.5, the components of the measured GRi and GRa are presented but are not reproduced here to save space. Focusing on the effects of estimates using "imputation," possible distortions may result from this procedure. In estimating the proxies of output elasticities of factor inputs, the mixed incomes of farm households are evaluated by prevailing wages in deriving the conceptual βa. Nonwage income is thus partially treated as if it were wage income. Suppose βa^* is the result of applying the assumption of near equality between labor's marginal product and prevailing wages, $\beta a > \beta a^*$ to the extent of imputation. To the extent of the difference $d = \beta a - \beta a^*$, αa and/or γ must be greater. βa is adopted here instead of βa^*. This imputation proce-

---

[6] Yujiro Hayami and Vernon Ruttan, *Agricultural Development* (Baltimore: Johns Hopkins University Press, 1971), V, II, "Growth and Equity in Agricultural Development."

[7] The subgroup difference $(E - F)$ in its ratio (%) to the group average is calculated as follows (from Tables 5.9 and 5.10):

	II	III	IV	V
GRi	77.6	154.9	213.6	46.5
GRa	237.5	84.2	42.9	22.1

Table 5.11
Effects of Imputation on Agricultural Residual Growth, 1960–1980

(%)

	αa* (1)	GYa – GKa (2)	(1) × (2)	βa* (3)	Gya (4)	(3) × (4)	GRa*	GRa
I	21.8	−5.1	−1.11	48.4	0.4	0.19	−0.47	0.08
II	22.1	−3.6	−0.80	49.7	1.5	0.72	0.48	1.01
III	22.4	−0.8	−0.18	43.2	3.4	1.47	2.49	2.99
IV	23.9	−3.0	−0.72	43.6	3.5	1.53	1.82	2.48
V	31.0	−5.2	−1.61	39.9	4.3	1.72	0.59	1.44

Source: *DE*, Table A2.5.
Remarks: $αa^* = αa + 10.0$, $βa^* = βa − 10.0$.
  For V, this assumption cannot flatly be applied. The figures for this group are only for reference.

dure appears to fit the reality when examining income equilibrium between peasant households and workers in rural districts. Nevertheless, it may be worthwhile to examine the statistical effects of this procedure.

The effects may better be checked using the case of capital rather than land, because $GYa − GB$ is positive and the negative effects of d would be cancelled out considerably, while $GYa − GKa$ is negative and αa is relatively small and would reveal the effects distinctly. This may approach reality since a number of capital components, such as farm buildings, livestock, and perennial plants may be at issue. The magnitude of d cannot be specifically estimated and it is flatly assumed to be 10%. The results are shown in Table 5.11.

In conclusion, the test shows a decline in GRa and it is recognized that imputation makes GRa greater than would otherwise be the case. However, its effects as seen in the difference $GRa − GRa^*$ are not sufficiently large to alter the argument that GRa is distinctly higher than GRi, particularly for the two groups III and IV which constitute the major portion of developing economies under consideration.

Services and Reallocation Effects

In evaluating the service sector and reallocation effects, first the significant role played by the service sector in postwar developing economies in terms of output-income and labor employment should be emphasized. In this regard, the historical experience of presently developed nations cannot necessarily be used as the standard of analytical judgment. Due to the limited possibility of making technological progress in this sector, its role in forming residual growth is usually expected to be small and insignificant. However, as shown in Table 5.4, panel A, the estimated GRs for the latter segment is of considerable magnitude. This does not necessarily mean that this sector is less important in clarifying the character of structural changes relevant to technological progress in developing economies. This is particularly true if its effects are considered along with the reallocation effects of labor, because the two are closely related. GRs, the growth rate of residual in the service sector, is a residue measurement (aggregate minus goods-producing sector), so that it may contain more estimate distortions, especially with respect to lower groups. With some reservations, it can be stated that for lower groups it appears insignificant. However, attention is drawn to the considerable magnitude sustained in groups III, IV, and V. Due to the increase in the output weight of services, the weighted value wsGRs shown in Table 5.4, panel B becomes even greater than wiGRi, the corresponding value of the industrial sector in groups III and IV. The reallocation effect stems from shifts to labor from a sector of lower productivity to a sector of higher productivity. This is treated as a component of aggregate residual growth; because it stems from the operation of nonconventional factors, although this is not a direct result of technological progress. The estimated magnitude of reallocation effects shown in Table 5.4, panel B is sizable. In lower groups I and II, this is the greatest component of the aggregate residual growth, although it tends to decrease toward higher groups.

Following the above overview, a specific conceptual framework is needed to proceed with analysis because the nature of the problems differs from the case of goods-producing sectors. Since there has been no previous attempt to analyze the service sector comprehensively by subsector, the following two concepts are introduced here: facilitating activities and differential structure. Both pertain to the formation of the domestic market structure.

According to the present analysis, the function of the service sector is "facilitating" the activities of goods-producing sectors in the market, and it thus can be called a facilitating sector. Without specifying the different functions of service subsectors such as transportation, communications, finance, trade, and services in the narrow sense, the activities of this sector are generally defined in this overview for the sake of elucidating the common characteristics of services found in developing economies. The facilitating function is most relevant to advancing the domestic market mechanism of the economy, which contributes to promoting the domestic process of technology diffusion in industry and agriculture. The possibility of making progress in technology and organization in various subsectors, particularly transportation and communications, is recognized, but in this sector as a whole the significance of such indirect contribution must be emphasized. The residual emanating from this activity is a phenomenon relevant to allowing enhanced operation of the market mechanism. Thus the residual stems from a situation where no direct technological progress is expected. Views may differ among economists regarding how to interpret the operation of nonconventional factors. It is the view of the authors that they operate organizationally in a broad sense. It is beyond the present scope to discuss the details of the process of improving market mechanism operation, but the tendency to weaken the differential structure is relevant to organizational activities, as described below.

The second concept concerns labor reallocation. Clarification of sectoral differences in labor's marginal productivity would contribute to explanations of this phenomenon. Labor reallocation pertains to the differential structure in terms of labor's marginal productivity (MP), since the MP difference is sustained as a structure. The path of economic development in general tends to reflect the differential structure, as MP cannot be equalized between sectors. This is conventionally treated as a distortion from equilibrium from the viewpoint of the competitive operation of the market mechanism. This is not rejected, but the conceptual framework used here to treat the development process is toward equilibrium, while disequilibrium tends to be a sustained state of development. The reallocation effects resulting from labor shifts pertain to this differential structure. As the service sector plays the greatest role in this process, reallocation effects are treated together with services.

MP cannot be measured accurately without systematized data. It can be assumed that wages = MP by sector average, but systematic wage data are also lacking. To solve this problem, ratios, wa/w, wi/w, and ws/w (where w stands for aggregate average of wages) can be estimated using estimated labor income shares by sector and aggregates. These are shown in Table 5.12, panel A[8] together with related terms in panel B.

---

[8] The formula is $\Theta a \cdot \beta a / \beta = wa/w$ for agriculture, where Θa stands for the ratio of per worker product of agriculture to that of aggregate. wi/w and ws/w can be calculated similarly.

Table 5.12
Sectoral Differentials of Wages and Distribution of Wage Earnings

(%)

	(A) Wage Ratios		(B) Wage Income Distribution				
	A/I	A/S	S/I	A	I	S	Aggregate
I	0.15	0.20	0.75	52.8	15.1	32.1	100.0
II	0.19	0.19	1.02	35.3	21.6	43.1	100.0
III	0.40	0.32	1.28	30.6	28.6	40.8	100.0
IV	0.36	0.35	1.02	16.7	33.3	50.0	100.0
V	0.48	0.37	1.29	4.3	34.8	60.9	100.0

Source: A from *DE*, *op. cit.*, Table 2.7 and B calculated by weighted βa, βi, and βs from *DE*, Table 1.7.
Remark: For the estimation procedure, see main text.

The level of marginal product of labor MP in agriculture, approximated by average wages, is generally low in developing economies and extremely low in the former segment, groups I and II, as observed in its ratio to that of industry and/or services. The differential structure and its changes are thus quantified. The differential does not disappear when and where the ratio becomes unity, however. Due to differences in labor quality, composition of labor, regional prices, etc., at a certain inequality, wa < wi or wa < ws, substantive equality would be achieved in nominal terms, as indicated by the ratio of group V. Even in this group, however, countries with structural differentials are involved. At some point the inequality in the MP ratio may virtually disappear. This does not imply that all successful development paths have a trend for the differential to narrow, as illustrated by Japan's case.[9] A tendency for ratios A/I and A/S to increase through groups, as shown in Table 5.12, does not necessarily indicate the pattern over time of developing nations. Nevertheless, particular attention is drawn to the extremely low

[9] Japan is a country in group V in which the differential structure is sustained. The ratio A/I is estimated as follows:

1897–1903	39.5	1931–1938	26.4
1904–1918	33.9	1953–1969	25.2
1919–1930	30.9		

(These figures are based on βa from Kazushi Ohkawa and Nobukiyo Takamatsu, *IDCJ Working Paper No. 26, op. cit.*, Appendix Table 1; and *LTES*, Vol. 1, *National Income*, Table 3.5, p. 56).
The ratio shows a long-term trend of decline, indicating no turn toward higher levels.

level of groups I and II because this is characteristic of the preprimary phase structure (to be explained in section III), and this structure was not present in the historical path of presently developed nations.

Apart from in group I, the ratio S/I is greater than unity. This may cast doubt on whether labor MP is actually higher in services than in industry. In view of the aggravated underemployment in the so-called informal service sector, this doubt is legitimate, as the MP of workers is below the normal level by definition. On the other hand, however, in the formal sector MP levels are very high in services, reflecting the competitiveness of the service sector. Thus on average the ratio can be somewhat greater than unity.

The sectoral distribution of aggregate wage income is given in Table 5.12, panel B. This term is derived from the conventional concept of share distribution of income. Its aggregate is equal to labor's income share β and its sectoral value is expressed as its component. For example, regarding agriculture it is $\beta a \cdot Ya/Y$. As expected, two tendencies are seen: a sharp decrease for agriculture versus a considerable increase for industry. In services the distribution percentage of wage income is the largest through all groups except group I and shows an increasing trend, finally reaching a level over 60% in group V. The highest level of relative income of S in V is often pointed out as characterizing postindustrial economies, but the figures in panel B indicate that its highest level is sustained throughout the path of developing economies.

Under the sustained differential structure, the reallocation effects are estimated by use of the wage income distribution obtained above as the aggregate MP increase and taking the effects of sectoral shifts of labor into account.[10] The rate of increase in GLs is greater than that in GLi even in the former segment, and the difference becomes distinct in the latter segment. Thus, the "contribution" of sector S to reallocation effects continues to be overwhelmingly greater than that of sector I, except for III, as shown in Table 5.13. Furthermore, an interesting sectoral pattern is witnessed. The negative values of agriculture tend to increase during the former segment, but begin to decrease during the latter segment. With the pattern of this inverse U-shape, the positive values of industry change correspondingly, apart from the negative value in V. Unlike this pattern for goods-producing sectors, the higher positive values of the sector of services sustain an increasing trend throughout all

---

[10] The simple formula $\beta s \cdot (Ys/Y) \cdot (GLs - GL)$, etc., is used.

Table 5.13
Sectoral Relevance in Forming Reallocation Effects

(%)

	I	S	A	Sum
I	34.9	77.8	−12.7	100.0
II	32.7	88.5	−21.2	100.0
III	84.4	100.0	−84.4	100.0
IV	45.7	117.1	−62.8	100.0
V	−29.3	161.0	−31.7	100.0

Source: *DE*, Table A2.6.

Table 5.14
Reallocation Effects of Labor and Sectoral Relevance, Japan, 1908–1964

(%)

Period	Re	Re/GR	Sectoral relevance			
			I	S	A	Sum
(1) 1908–1917	0.51	27.7	41.2	76.5	−17.7	100.0
(2) 1918–1931	0.50	74.6	36.0	76.0	−12.0	100.0
(3) 1932–1938	0.60	17.6	81.8	26.8	−8.0	100.0
(4) 1955–1964	1.47	20.8	63.4	57.3	−20.7	100.0

Source: Kazushi Ohkawa, "Industrial Structural Change and Macro-Productivity Growth," Chapter 4, Tables 4-3 and 4-4, in *Nihon Keizai no Kozo* (Structure of the Japanese economy) (Tokyo: Keiso Shobo, 1974).
Remarks: i) The two postwar periods, 1955–1961 and 1962–1964 were treated separately in the original measurements. The weighted averages are listed for 1955–1964 in the table.
ii) Public utilities are included in S, not in I.

groups. In group IV the contribution of I has already been replaced by S to a certain extent, and this is strengthened toward group V.

Evaluation of the reallocation effects thus measured should be in terms of comparison with the effects determined from the historical records of presently developed countries. This is beyond the present scope, although an attempt is made here for the case of Japan. Table 5.14 presents a summary of the measured results of Japan's historical experience, arranged to be comparable to the figures for contemporary developing economies. The magnitude of reallocation effects Re during the prewar period is stable at 0.50–0.60 and appears larger than those of groups III and IV in the latter segment. However, its ratio to residual growth Re/GR is close to those of the latter segment, apart from period (2), which is atypically high due to a serious downswing of the economy. No comparable figures can be derived for the segment of groups I and II. As Japan had no experience of the preprimary phase, records during the primary phase may be a useful reference. Regrettably, no reliable data are available for periods earlier than (1). The authors speculate, however, that Re might be very small, perhaps in the range of 0.2–0.3, for the primary phase.

The pattern of Re determined based on cross-sectional data may thus be interpreted as follows. The dominant role played by Re in forming the residual is characteristic of contemporary developing economies, in the preprimary phase in particular, and furthermore this role is sustained to a certain extent in the primary phase. In the secondary phase, no noticeable pattern can be seen for developing economies, so far as the aggregate ratio Re/GR is concerned.

With regard to sectoral relevance, in Japan's case for periods (1) and (2), the service sector's contribution is distinctly greater than that of industry. Period (3) is atypical due to artificial industrialization resulting from military mobilization. The figures in Table 5.13, as compared to figures for Japan, largely indicate that a greater role was played by the service sector, particularly during the latter segment. This appears to endorse the contention that the service sector plays a major role in postwar developing economies.

III. Demarcating Phases in Developing Economies

In section I, demarcation of two major phases, primary and secondary, was suggested conditionally at the end of the discussion on the model of the dualistic traditional versus modern sector. Methodologically, the demarcation is based on the comparative application of two approaches: the IOR formula and residual measurements. In section II, in terms of the three conventional major sectors, the relation between productivity growth and residual growth was observed. This was carried out under the assumption that agriculture represents the traditional and industry the modern sector, treating the function of services as facilitating the activities of these goods-producing sectors. In this section we attempt to integrate these into a meaningful framework so as to elucidate the characteristics of development phases of contemporary developing economies. Why is the residual approach not used primarily for phasing? The answer is that recognition of the fundamental forces operating to cause a shift in phases is one thing and statistical demarcation is another. The upgrading of the SC level pertains to the former and the problem of determining the turning point pertains to the latter. Since no turning point can be expected in the SC level due to its basic property, this section is concerned with the latter.

Development phases can be demarcated by various criteria depending upon the purpose of analysis. The criterion here is Gy − Gw, the growth term of Y/Lw, and the representative term in the present approach. Section I gave detailed description of its pattern together with the patterns of its compositional terms Gk − Gw and GY − GK. For consistency, Gy − Gw should be used for clarifying the path of changes in the development pattern and mechanisms under dualistic structure. Due to data restraints, however, this is not possible. The rate of sectoral productivity growth Gy is used as the major term, leaving Gw as a term to be assessed separately. For Gw, the well-known approach for identifying the turning point is based on real wage performance of unskilled workers, or changes in the labor market mechanism. In the present case, the change in the mechanism of development with a dualistic structure is the focus, and the wage approach should be incorporated into it.

No attempt to do this is made here, however, since the major purpose is to ascertain the performance of productivity growth, elucidating the process of technology diffusion in the dualistic structure. Wage performance is taken up in relation to it, as attempted in the model in chapter 1. As discussed in terms of the differential structure, sectoral wage differentials and their changes are notable. Changes in the wage ratios agriculture/industry and agriculture/services broadly correspond to structural changes in the present sense (Table 5.12).[11] Thus, it is necessary to clarify in depth the mechanism of dualistic development, because the preceding discussion was limited to group averages. Below, pattern variance by subgroup is described in comparison with sectoral differences in productivity growth using the sectoral pattern of "difference indicators" for sectoral disaggregation of macro rates of productivity growth.

---

[11] The turning point in wage performance may come in the former interval of the secondary phase, but cannot systematically be identified as at present no data are available for estimating wages in real terms for contemporary developing economies except the Asian NIEs.

Sectoral Differences in Productivity Growth

It is presumed that the changing pattern of the role played by the traditional versus the modern sector is a major factor in changes in the growth mechanism. Changes in the sectoral contribution must be clarified in the framework of productivity growth. The difference indicators for the three major sectors, Da, Di, and Ds, are used for this purpose. These are calculated as the difference between the weighted rate of output growth and weighted rate of employment change. Let w and v stand, respectively, for the weight (ratio of sector to aggregate in output) in the former and for the weight (ratio of sector to aggregate in employment) in the latter, and we have

$$Da = waGYa - vaGLa;$$

$$Di = wiGYi - viGLi;$$

$$Ds = wsGYs - vsGLs,$$

presuming the sum Da + Di + Ds is the aggregate rate of productivity growth. Table 5.15 summarizes these results. Panel A identifies the regular pattern of industrialization by changes in Di throughout the entire rising levels of Y/L in group averages. Starting with an extremely low value of less than 0.5 in group 1, it shows a trend of acceleration toward group V, where it reaches the high of more than 1.5 with no deviation for any group. As industry represents the modern sector, the approach by Y/L level is acceptable for present purposes as the central pattern of sectoral contribution to macro productivity growth. In comparison, Da tends to increase up to group III along with Di, but then declines toward group V. In the service sector it is difficult to single out any regular pattern.

In terms of the figures by subgroup, the magnitude of each sectoral indicator is greater for E and smaller for F without exception throughout the entire range. This is expected from the previous examination of simple sectoral Gy by subgroup, but amplification is needed here, since the difference in sectoral Gy between E and F represents a difference not only in the modern sector but also in the traditional sector. The nonassociated factors operate in common for both, and are not merely results of differences in degree of industrialization.

Table 5.15, panel B illustrates the magnitude of difference in each sectoral indicator within each group. First Di and Da are compared, followed by Di and Ds comparison, respectively. The difference in Da is greater than the difference in Di in groups II and III, while the

Table 5.15
Sectoral Difference Indicators, 1960–1980

	(A) Sectoral Indicators			(B) Difference between Subgroups (E − F)		
	Da	Di	Ds	Da	Di	Ds
I Group average	−0.30	0.48	0.20			
II Average	−0.29	1.09	2.05			
E	0.03	1.35	2.18	0.64	0.52	0.33
F	−0.61	0.83	1.85			
III Average	0.68	1.16	1.43			
E	1.06	1.28	1.69	0.76	0.23	0.53
F	0.30	1.05	1.16			
IV Average	0.70	1.44	1.58			
E	1.02	1.88	1.67	0.63	0.88	0.19
F	0.39	1.00	1.48			
V Average	0.57	1.51	0.98			
E	0.71	2.04	1.30	0.28	1.09	0.63
F	0.43	0.98	0.67			

Source: *DE*, *op. cit.*, Table 4.10.
Remarks: i) Originally the difference indicators were calculated for two periods: 1960–1970 and 1970–1980. Simple averages of these two are listed in the table.

ii) Subgroups E and F are clarified in terms of macro productivity growth Gy in order to reveal variations due to the operation of nonassociated factors within each group (Gy is higher for subgroup E and lower for subgroup F). Nations actually classified are as follows (number of countries in parentheses). Data for group I are not sufficiently reliable to apply this procedure.

Group I (10)		Malawi, Burma, Tanzania, Benin, India, Nepal, Ethiopia, Somalia, Madagascar, and Niger
Group II (12)	E (6):	Pakistan, Bolivia, Philippines, Thailand, Kenya, and Ivory Coast
	F (6):	Sierra Leone, Senegal, Sudan, Sri Lanka, People's Republic of the Congo, and Mozambique
Group III (12)	E (6):	Republic of Korea, Turkey, Egypt, Syrian Arab Republic, Tunisia, and Malaysia
	F (6):	Nicaragua, Morocco, Paraguay, El Salvador, Honduras, and Colombia
Group IV (12)	E (6):	Brazil, Portugal, Yugoslavia, Dominica, Greece, and Singapore
	F (6):	Peru, Jamaica, Mexico, Costa Rica, Uruguay, and Argentina
Group V (12)	E (6):	Japan, France, Belgium, Germany, Denmark, and Finland
	F (6):	Netherlands, UK, Canada, Norway, Sweden, and USA

reverse is true for groups IV and V. No data are available for group I, but the inequality of the former type may prevail. This is relevant to the demarcation of the primary and the secondary phase proposed earlier. In the primary phase the difference in Gy between E and F stems from agriculture dominating over industry, whereas in the secondary phase the reverse holds. Straightforward comparison between Di and Ds appears difficult. With respect to the latter segment the difference is greater for Di and smaller for Ds. However, for the former segment the inequality appears mixed: in group III the difference is greater for Ds than for Di, but in group II the reverse is witnessed. Examination of the periods (1) and (2) mentioned in the Remarks to the table reveals that the former pattern is found for both groups II and III in period (1), and the latter pattern is seen in period (2). The latter may be a distortion, and the regular pattern may be similar to that found in comparison of Da and Di. If this is accurate, it can be argued that the rationale for comparing industry and agriculture can be applied to phase demarcation in the entire economy.

It was found previously that the percentage contribution of residual growth to productivity growth in agriculture is distinctly higher than that in industry. Therefore, the above argument should be tested in terms of the difference in residual growth between subgroups. As described above, however, residual measurements are possible only by semihypothetical procedures. Table 5.16 shows such approximations.

To be comparable to the difference indicators for productivity growth, the residuals are weighted in the same way in order to determine the magnitude and differences by subgroup in terms of contribution to the aggregate. Tables 5.9 and 5.10 illustrated sectoral performance of the residual and its relevant terms, and the figures in Table 5.16 can be understood in relation to those. The crucial pattern identified here is that the difference between subgroups (E − F) is greater in agriculture than in industry during the former segment (groups II and III), while it is reversed in the latter segment (groups IV and V), where it is distinctly greater in industry than in agriculture. The pattern change between the two intervals is definite in this case, whereas in the former case of productivity growth it was somewhat conditional. The nonassociated factors seem to operate differently in contributing to sizable variations in the activity of nonconventional factors among nations, while showing a regular shift from the traditional to the modern sector. The demarcation of the two major phases appears to be confirmed as correct.

Table 5.16
Weighted Residual Growth and Its Difference Between Subgroups:
Agriculture versus Industry

		Agriculture		Industry	
		waGRa	Difference (E − F)	wiGRi	Difference (E − F)
II	E	0.58	0.67	0.41	0.25
	F	−0.09		0.16	
II	E	1.02	0.64	0.62	0.52
	F	0.38		0.10	
II	E	0.54	0.10	0.79	0.83
	F	0.44		−0.04	
II	E	0.06	0.00	1.05	0.63
	F	0.06		0.42	

Source: For GRa and GRi, Table 5.10 and Table 5.9, respectively. The output
weights wa and wi are from the original data in *DE, op. cit.*, Table 4.10.
Remark: Averages of figures for interval (1), 1960–1970, and (2), 1970–1980.

The phases demarcated by changes in Y/L levels based on cross-
sectional data are acceptable insofar as nonassociated factors operate
to a limited extent. In such a case, the trend of increasing Y/L levels
shown by cross-sectional data is a roughly acceptable substitute representing the historical performance of the development path illustrated by the data series over time. However, the findings above do
not show such a case. The effects of nonassociated factors appear to
be sizable and necessitate additional examination. Phase demarcation essentially pertains to individual countries, and subgroup procedures cannot substitute, although they can yield useful information.
Below, further examination is attempted based on the performance
of each sector through groups. This is a "vertical" approach, while
the approach pursued above is a "horizontal" one, since subgroup
differences within the same group are the focus.

Crucial Turning Points in Sectoral Growth
The preceding discussions clarified the performance of sectoral productivity growth. Viewed from the same aggregate standpoint, the
difference indicators Da, Di, and Ds are used to identify the turning
points in sectoral performance. Table 5.15 gives numerical figures
for these three indicators with variations between subgroups. In this
vertical approach, the pattern of changes in each indicator while
Y/L is leveled up can be determined. The first issue is to search for

regularity in turning point formation, and the second is to interpret its relevance to phase demarcation. Two turning points are identified which are crucial in understanding the entire development path. The first point is identified for agriculture, and pertains to demarcating the preprimary phase specifically for the possibility of lower groups initiating modern economic development. The criterion is technically defined by the negative value of Da, the difference between the weighted rate of output growth and that of labor in agriculture. The first turning point can be reached by achieving Da = 0.

The second depends on the relation between industry and services and is identified by Di = Ds. This concerns the possibility of clearing the last hurdle before becoming a developed economy. These two are crucial points due to the particular difficulty in achieving the required rate of technological progress. The importance of technological progress during development in the interval between cannot be ignored, but once the growth mechanism fulfills the necessary conditions, the required rate of technological progress is generally achieved. This assertion is based on the performance of growth in terms of output, productivity, and the residual, which present an inverse U-shaped pattern through groups in terms of Y/L level (chapter 1). Once an economy initiates progress along the development path, it can accelerate its rate of growth by realizing trend acceleration. However, this path cannot necessarily be sustained as an economy comes closer to being developed, since a dip is usually identified toward the final phase.

The problem of agriculture in the preprimary phase can be summarized as how the economy proceeds from the initial situation of waGYa < vaGLa to waGYa = vaGLa, the first turning point, where the pattern of the initial interval is represented by a converted form

$$wa(GYa - GLa) < (va - wa)GLa.$$

The required pattern of agricultural growth to arrive at the first turning point is for a greater rate of productivity growth to be sustained over the rate of labor employment increase, subject to the placement of this sector in the macro economy (represented by the weights wa and va). This formula is useful to examine productivity performance in relation to employment in the path leading up to the first turning point. Numerical illustration is given in Table 5.17.

Table 5.17, panel A shows that Da is negative not only in group I but also in group II. A positive value is found for the first time in

Table 5.17
Agriculture in the Primary Phase Leading Up to the First Turning Point

(%)

	GYa	GLa	Gya	waGYa	vaGLa	Da	waGya	(va − wa)GLa
(A) By group								
I	1.7	1.3	0.4	0.84	1.08	−0.24	19.9	43.7
II	3.2	1.8	1.4	1.01	1.31	−0.30	44.2	72.4
III	4.5	1.1	3.4	1.23	0.57	0.66	92.8	26.6
(B) By subgroup								
II E	4.2	1.8	2.4	1.36	1.31	0.05	78.0	60.5
F	2.1	1.8	0.3	0.63	1.31	−0.68	9.0	77.2
III E	4.5	0.5	4.0	1.28	0.27	1.01	1.14	13.1
F	4.3	1.7	2.6	1.09	0.32	0.27	0.65	58.7

Source: Background data from *DE*, *op. cit.*, Table 4.10, panel A and panel B, averages of period 1), 1960–1970 and period 2), 1970–1980.
Remarks: i) For group I data for subgroup formation are not available.
 ii) For E and F, see main text.

group III. This indicates that the first turning point is found somewhere between II and III. In group I the inequality shown by the formula above exists and is sustained to group II because waGya increases but (va − wa)GLa increases more. From group II to group III, the pattern changes, and the magnitude on the left-hand side becomes distinctly greater than the magnitude on the right-hand side of the formula. This appears consistent with the above supposition that the first turning point occurs between groups II and III.

It should be noted that the turning point emerges in the performance of GLa, the rate of increase in the labor force engaged in agriculture. It increases from 1.3 in group I to 1.8 in group II but begins to decrease to 1.1 in group III. In the above formula this contributes substantially both to increasing the left-hand magnitude and to decreasing the right-hand magnitude. The increase in GYa, the growth rate of agricultural products, is recognized, but this is a sustained pattern from I to II by 1.5 percentage points and from II to III by 1.3. So far as this change is concerned, the performance of GLa appears more influential. Since the rate of increase in the aggregate supply of the labor force is estimated to increase from group I to group III (2.0 in I, 2.4 in II, and 2.9 in III), the possibility of sectoral reallocation effects discussed in section II is at issue here because the changing GLa pattern is undoubtedly due to the greater rate of labor shift from agriculture to the nonagricultural sector.

In Table 5.17, panel B, the difference in the magnitude of Gya is decisive between E and F, and is positively associated with that of Gy. The factor responsible for this difference appears to vary from group II to III: in the former it is GYa, the rate of output growth, while in the latter it is GLa, the rate of increase in labor engaged in agriculture. Although no data are presented for group I, it is supposed that a pattern similar to that for group II would be witnessed. The striking evidence is that Da is slightly positive in E but distinctively negative in F. Negative Da is witnessed for the group II average, and it is clear that this results from the effects of subgroup F. Toward group III the positive Da in E increases sharply, and in subgroup F its negative value becomes positive although only marginally. The different performance of these terms in the above formula provides additional evidence, as shown in the right-hand column of Table 5.17. In E and F, a negative value of Da occurs in group I.[12]

These findings are relevant to phase demarcation. Based on previous growth observations, the first turning point was assumed to fall between groups II and III. But now it should be located as follows. With respect to subgroup E, the first turning point is identified toward the end of the path leading to group II, whereas for subgroup F that point emerges between groups II and III, perhaps near the midpoint leading to group III. Phase demarcation is essentially concerned with the historical development path of individual nations, and generalizations are only possible when the patterns of individual nations can be assumed to be similar. Subgrouping such as is done here may help to determine degrees of similarity. All developing economies must reach the point Da = 0, but the time dimension appears to vary considerably; this variation in time is the core issue in development phasing. The example of subgroups E and F illustrates that the time difference is almost 1.5 times the length of the average group path.

In summary, in the case illustrated by subgroup F, the shift from the preprimary to the primary phase is prolonged compared to the case illustrated by subgroup E. Achieving more rapid phase shift is the objective of initiating development, so that such prolongation must be avoided in the process of moving from the primary to the secondary phase.

In reaching the second turning point, the technological progress

---

[12] It becomes clear that in the preceding macro approach (Table 5.14) the extremely small magnitude of Gyt, productivity growth of the traditional sector, and the negative value of Gyt − Gwt are mainly caused by the effect of negative Da.

Table 5.18
Industry versus Services at the Second Turning Point

(A) By group   (%)

	GYi	GLi	Gyi	wiGYi	viGLi	Di
Industry						
III	8.0	4.8	3.2	1.89	0.73	1.16
IV	6.6	3.0	3.6	2.20	0.76	1.44
V	4.4	0.7	3.7	1.77	0.26	1.51
	GYs	GLs	Gys	wsGYs	vsGLs	Ds
Services						
III	6.4	4.7	1.7	2.69	1.26	1.43
IV	6.1	3.7	2.4	3.11	1.53	1.58
V	4.4	2.8	1.6	2.39	1.41	0.98

(B) By subgroup

		GYi	GLi	Gyi	wiGYi	viGLi	Di
Industry							
III	E	9.5	5.1	4.4	2.25	0.97	1.28
	F	6.4	4.2	2.2	1.54	0.49	1.05
IV	E	8.3	3.5	4.8	2.78	0.90	1.88
	F	4.8	2.5	2.3	1.61	0.61	1.00
V	E	5.2	1.0	4.2	2.45	0.41	2.04
	F	3.7	0.3	3.4	1.09	0.11	0.98
		GYs	GLs	Gys	wsGYs	vsGLs	Ds
Services							
III	E	6.6	5.1	1.6	3.07	1.38	1.69
	F	6.1	4.0	2.1	2.30	1.14	1.16
IV	E	6.7	4.0	2.7	3.25	1.58	1.67
	F	5.5	3.4	2.1	2.95	1.47	1.48
V	E	4.7	2.5	2.2	2.43	1.13	1.30
	F	4.1	3.1	1.0	2.36	1.69	0.67

Source: For GY, GL, and Gy, *DE, op cit.*, Tables 4.1, 4.6, and 4.7; and original data
    for computing from *DE*, Table 4.10, panel C.
Remark: The slight difference between this table and *DE*, Table 4.10, is due to
    revision of the original data.

required for a more rapid phase shift must be achieved in industry in relation with services. This is defined as $Di = Ds$ or $wiGYi - viGLi = wsGYs - vsGLs$; see relevant data in Table 5.18. During the secondary phase, Di shows a sustained increase toward full industrialization (0.48 in I and 1.09 in II), as generally expected. Thus phase demarcation is usually based on a shift from light to heavy industry or the like, without considering its relation to other sectoral performance. However, the authors do not follow this convention and thus additionally examine services in relation to industry. The characteristics of the service sector in postwar developing economies have been pointed out; at this juncture the significance of two aspects should be mentioned: its sustained greater contribution to aggregate productivity increase and its competitiveness vis-à-vis industry.[13]

Analogous to the previous case of agriculture, Table 5.18, panel A shows the pattern of services by group. Surprisingly, Ds is greater than Di through groups III and IV, the main interval of industrialization. As expected, vsGLs, the weighted rate of employment increase in services, is far greater than wiGLi, the weighted rate of increase in industry. Along with this, wsGYs, the weighted growth rate of output in services, remains greater than wiGYi, the weighted growth rate of output in industry. The latter overwhelms the former, resulting in $Ds > Di$. In group V the sustained inequality is eventually reversed, that is, $Di > Ds$. This reversal is not due to the change in the relation of the weighted growth rate of output but to the change in the relation of the weighted rate of employment between the two sectors. Simply put, viGLi in V becomes extremely small. It is assumed that the second turning point occurs between groups IV and V.

As in the case of agriculture, observations based on group averages are useful but decisive in terms of phasing. Panel B of Table 5.18 shows observations by subgroup. Attention is drawn to the relationship between the growth rate of productivity and that of labor employed in sectoral comparison (Gyi, GLi versus Gys, GLs). The variation in GLi positively associates with that of Gyi (concurrent pattern), while between Gys and GLs no regularity can be found,

---

[13] In the macro performance of $Gy - Gw$ (Table 5.1), the modern sector plays the dominant role. The sectoral approach helps to clarify certain aspects of the mechanism of changing productivity-employment relationships during the secondary phase, when the performance of Gym is explained by competitive development of industry and services, rather than simply by industrialization.

either positive or negative (mixed pattern). This view is valid for the subgroups under consideration. For Gyi, E is nearly twice as great as F, yet for GLi the same inequality E > F is also sustained through the three groups. However, for Gys, E > F for IV and V, but in a positive relation with GLs in IV and in a negative relation with GLs in V. Furthermore, F > E for Gys in III, in a negative relation with GLs. The reason for this cannot be specified, but in general the main factor responsible in services is demand for output and labor rather than technological change. With regard to industry, technology change is the major factor responsible for the concurrent pattern. However, for the purpose of the present discussion, another pattern is considered, that is, the tendency of sharp decrease in GLi in both subgroups. In the introductory part of this section, groups IV and V were described as having greater GK – GL compared to the preceding segment. The effects of capital intensification must therefore be taken into account.

In subgroup E the point Ds = Di is assumed to occur between group III and group IV, because Ds > Di in the former changes to Di > Ds in the latter and this reversed inequality is stronger in group V. In subgroup F the inequality Ds > Di remains in group IV. The point Ds = Di should occur if possible toward the end of the path leading to V, and the reversed inequality Di > Ds should also be achieved along that path.

Analogous to the first turning point, such measures as the inequality Ds > Di illustrate a problem but do not provide a solution from the standpoint of development phasing. The significance, however, is that the time required to change from Ds > Di to Di > Ds must vary between individual nations. Since a rapid shift is the objective of development, this is crucial for nations lagging behind. As suggested previously, the problem stems essentially from the difficulty in achieving technological progress in industry in order to fulfill the prerequisites. The figures in Table 5.18, panel B, show that in E the magnitude of Di increase accelerates toward group V, whereas in F it tends to be sustained at a lower level. In essence, this indicates the capability difference in capital intensification on the final path toward becoming a developed economy.

Although integration of turning points by sector forms a generalized phasing framework, as detailed in chapter 7, the characteristics of the contemporary path of development are described here and suggestions made for futher studies. First, the primary phase is characterized by heavy pressure to remain in the preprimary subphase. The secondary phase is characterized by pressure to sustain the pattern Ds > Di over the long term. The former implies that upon arriving in group III, an economy can virtually eliminate the pressure of negative Da. The latter implies that in the interval between groups IV and V, an economy can eventually achieve the pattern Di > Ds by overcoming the pressure of Ds > Di.

These characteristics of contemporary developing economies can be elucidated clearly in comparison with the historical patterns of presently developed nations. The phenomenon of preprimary pressure cannot be identified for these nations, except for Italy around the turn of the century. The pattern Di > Ds was achieved much earlier in their history. For example, in Japan's case the second turning point, Di = Ds, is seen at the initial interval of the secondary phase, even based on the most conservative view.[14] Such comparisons, however, require careful qualification. The group average pattern of developing nations cannot legitimately be compared with one country's historical path of development. As suggested by subgroup observations, wide differentials characterize the multiple patterns of contemporary developing nations. On the one hand, one country in subgroup E may have no preprimary subphase and may arrive at the second turning point much earlier than others, similar to Japan's case.[15] On the other hand, one country in subgroup F may have a prolonged preprimary subphase and no likelihood of arriving at the second turning point. Therefore, in addition to comparative interpretation of the standardized pattern with the historical records of presently developed nations, the widely differentiated paths of contemporary developing economies should be examined based on the patterns of individual countries.

Two elements are at work: the initial interval and telescoping effects. The preprimary subphase characterizes late-latecomers. The initial situation features abrupt industrialization in which the time dimension is crucial: the later its start the stronger its effect. A number of African countries and some Asian countries classified as belonging to groups I and II are typical cases. The response to the pressure of this initial interval varies among nations. A favorable response is made by some nations and an unfavorable response by

---

[14] For more detailed treatment, see *DE*, chapter 4, in particular Tables 4.11 and 4.12.

[15] For example, according to *DE*, Appendix III, the Republic of Korea seems to have arrived at the second turning point in the beginning of the 1970s. This is much earlier than the dates assumed from the average of subgroup III, E, to which Korea belongs.

others. In subgroup observations with respect to group II, E represents the former and F represents the latter. The positive effects of the telescoping process can accelerate the pace of phase shift, but cannot be generalized uniformly over the entire path of development. Instead, its effects contribute to the creation of wider differentials among developing nations. By subgroup, telescoping effects operate strongly in E and weakly in F for both agriculture and industry. In broad terms, in the primary phase telescoping is dominant in agriculture, while in the secondary phase it is dominant in industry.

6

Productivity Growth and Labor: Employment and Product-Income

The relationship between technological progress and conditions of labor, i.e., employment and income, has only partially been explored in the preceding chapters. This relationship represents an analytical challenge since no *a priori* hypothesis can usefully be made based on either theories or historical knowledge of presently developed nations. In light of preceding clarifications of initial conditions and the sustained differential structure of employment on the one hand, and the multirange structure of technology diffusion in the disequilibrium process composed of international and national elements on the other, the relationship in contemporary economies differs significantly from that determined historically. Empirical study can yield some information, although the unemployment problem cannot be dealt with due to lack of data.

The conventional framework includes "growth and equity," including income distribution, size and share, and the issue of poverty in its coverage of the conditions of labor. The problem is dealt with here using the framework for production activities used in chapter 4, observing the patterns of productivity growth, both macro and sectoral, on the one hand, and the changes in the conditions of labor on the other in order to determine the relationship between the two. This is based on the recognition that empirical observation is most important in this study area, in particular due to the crucial role played by residual growth in determining productivity growth. No *a priori* relationship has been established between employment change and the effects of nonconventional factors. The pace of technological progress is assumed to be roughly indicated by the rate of productivity increase supplemented by residual growth, although such estimates are too general. The size distribution of income is beyond the scope of the present study because it is not directly related to productivity. The specific issue of the lowest income groups

213

(poverty) will briefly be mentioned so far as it pertains to production activity in agriculture.

Thus three aspects of the conditions of employment are selected for study: first, employment itself (section I); second, sectoral inequality of product per worker (section II); and third, share distribution in industry and farmer's income in agriculture (the Annex). For the first, the Y/Lw formula in the productivity approach is used.

The cause and effect identification between productivity and employment is a controversial issue; the significance of sectoral performance in this regard is emphasized. The pattern of changes in sectoral product per worker is a classic problem, clarified by Kuznets in terms of convergence versus divergence. The differential structure approach is an especially important theme in the framework of this chapter. In the present assessments, the subgroup approach is relied upon since the operation of nonassociated factors other than the Y/L level is significant.

I. Productivity and Employment: Relation to Rates of Change

Debates on "trade-off" have often focused on the relation of labor employment to productivity in relation to the option of technology type (capital-intensive versus labor-intensive) in manufacturing development. This notion is important but is controversial due to conceptual vagueness. The present authors think that the problem requires cautious treatment in analysis: the nature and scope of the two objectives and the terms of comparison should be precisely specified. Here the issue is presented in the terms of rates of change in both productivity and employment. Furthermore, the relationship between the two should be determined by comparing the three major sectors. This approach is not always adequate, but adopted here due to the linkage of productivity growth with the major theme of technology diffusion.

Concluding propositions were made in *DE*, chapter 4,[1] with respect to the characteristics of respective sectors (industry, "concurrent"; agriculture, "reversal"; and services, "mixed") in the relation between productivity growth and employment change. "Concur-

[1] Kazushi Ohkawa, in collaboration with Katsuo Otsuka and Bernard Key, *Growth Mechanism of Developing Economies: Investment, Productivity and Employment* (Tokyo: International Development Center of Japan/International Center for Economic Growth, 1993).

rent" means a positive and "reversal" means a negative association between the two, and "mixed" implies no regular association either positive or negative. These are deduced from empirical observations using the approach in comparisons of the rate of productivity growth Gy and employment increase GL in 1960s and 1970s averages. This simple procedure is adopted because the speed, rather than the type, of technological progress is the major issue. The conventional method of approaching this issue is using crude elasticity, $\eta =$ GL/GY, but the authors do not think that this is adequate.[2]

The findings from the simple procedure are essentially valid. Below they are amplified by dealing with the data more systematically. The two variables GL and Gy should be treated independently rather than assuming *a priori* any cause-and-effect relationship, because the situation may differ among sectors. On the one hand, for example, in the sector of industry, employment change grasped in terms of GLi can be assumed to be determined by the tempo of capital formation and type of technology adopted by individual enterprises, and in the sectoral aggregate it is determined by the speed of widening and diffusing of such enterprises. On the other hand, the rate of productivity change viewed in terms of Gyi can be assumed to be determined by two components: the output effects of the rate of capital intensity growth GKi $-$ GLi, and the rate of residual growth GRi. At this simplified dimension the measure is composed of two elements: performance of individual enterprises and the pattern of sectoral aggregate formation. The role of conventional inputs is relevant to what is described above with regard to GLi, but more important is the recognition that the effect of nonconventional inputs is not related to GLi in any sense, but is measured as the residual GRi. Therefore, no direct measures can be conceptually conceivable for the relationship between GLi and Gyi as long as GRi cannot be treated separately from Gyi. If reliable measurement

---

[2] This originally stems from the formula Gy = a + bGY *à la* N. Kaldor along the lines of the Verdoorn Law that aims at clarifying a different aspect of the problem. GY is the independent variable, representing the market demand side as shown by its converted version GL = a' + b'GY. Furthermore, $\eta =$ GL/GY is a crude elasticity pertaining to this formula, ignoring the magnitude of interception a'. Judging from the results of its application to Japan's historical series of manufacturing and other sectors, this formula is useful from this point of view but the effects of interception are significant (Kazushi Ohkawa and Henry Rosovsky, *Japanese Economic Growth: Trend Acceleration in the Twentieth Century* [Stanford, CA: Stanford University Press, 1973], chapter 4). An analogous approach using $\eta' =$ GL/Gy is not acceptable either in concept or as a computational procedure.

of GRi can be made, the relation between Gyi and conventional inputs can be discussed in various ways. This issue is serious, because in developing economies the magnitude of GRi relative to that of Gyi is significant, and observation by subgroup is indispensable for analysis. Nevertheless, fully reliable measurement by subgroup is difficult.

Given these circumstances, a compromise is required. The device used here is to observe the difference (δ) in GLi and Gyi, respectively, between subgroups E and F, used in the preceding analysis, and to compare these two in order to clarify the relationship between productivity and employment. The residual approach is supplementary. All the measured results for the industrial sector are listed in Table 6.1. Panel A lists the original terms, and panel B δi, the difference between subgroups.

In observing the average of two periods in panel A the relation between the two appears to change regularly. For example, the ratio Gyi/GLi tends to increase across all groups on average. Furthermore, Gyi shows a straight line of increase across all groups from 0.5 in I to 3.8 in V. However, GLi appears to present an inverse U-shape: increasing in the former segment (I is statistically questionable) while decreasing in the latter segment. Thus the relationship between Gyi and GLi differs between the former and the latter segment, although this should be confirmed by time series. Attention is drawn to the performance of δi, which essentially makes no such changes between the two segments.

What is noticeable is that the rate of employment increase is greater in E and smaller in F through all groups without exception. With this preliminary information, the performance of δi, the indicator in the column of averages in panel B, including group V, should be examined. The rate of employment increase GLi is definitely greater in E than F for all groups without exception. However, the rate of productivity growth Gyi also tends to be greater in general (in particular in groups III and IV) as compared to F. This is exactly what was previously called a "concurrent pattern" in industry, pointing out the parallel difference in Gyi and GLi between subgroups. An important finding thus derived is that a greater rate of productivity increase can be realized by leveling up the rate of employment increase, instead of leveling it down (trade-off).

To what extent does this proposition represent regular, steady performance? The available data cover only two decades, which is not long enough to answer the question. For the time being, the performance of periods (1) and (2) can be examined carefully.

Table 6.1
Employment Increase and Its Relation to Productivity Growth: Industry
(Annual rate of growth, %)

Group	(1) 1960–1970 GLi	Gyi	(2) 1970–1980 GLi	Gyi	Average GLi	Gyi
(A)						
I	4.4	1.9	5.0	−0.9	4.7	0.5
II Average	4.5	3.8	3.1	1.9	3.8	2.9
E	5.2	3.9	3.7	2.8	4.5	3.4
F	3.9	3.7	2.5	1.0	3.2	2.4
III Average	4.3	3.8	5.1	2.8	4.7	3.3
E	4.8	5.4	5.3	3.4	5.1	4.4
F	3.7	2.2	4.6	2.2	4.2	2.2
IV Average	2.6	5.1	3.4	2.0	3.0	3.5
E	3.3	6.2	3.6	3.4	3.5	4.8
F	1.9	4.0	3.1	0.6	2.5	2.3
V Average	0.7	5.3	0.6	2.3	0.7	3.8
E	1.2	5.6	0.8	2.6	1.0	4.1
F	0.1	4.9	0.4	2.0	0.3	3.5
(B)						
II	1.3	0.2	1.2	1.8	1.3	1.0
III	1.1	3.2	0.7	1.2	0.9	2.2
IV	1.4	2.2	0.5	2.8	1.0	2.5
V	1.1	0.7	0.4	0.6	0.7	0.6

Source: *DE*, *op. cit.*, Table 4.6.
Remark: δi stands for the difference E − F, as for GLi and Gyi, respectively.

Table 6.1, panel A, shows that the average concurrent pattern is reflected in the performance during the 1970s, but not necessarily during the 1960s.

The difference in Gyi between subgroups is influential in creating the variance between periods 1 and 2; The Gyi difference tends to be relatively narrower in 1 but becomes much greater in 2. This is conceivably because the pace of technological innovation varied between E and F in the 1970s, when a less favorable environment for developing economies prevailed, than in the 1960s.

Panel B shows that the pattern presented by δi in periods 1 and 2 is exactly the same as identified above for the average. In comparing the two periods, the difference in GLi becomes smaller from 1 to 2, that in Gyi appears to become larger. Knowledge is too limited to discuss the reasons for such changes over time, but for the present analytical purposes attention should be drawn to the fact that the causes of the changing magnitude of difference between subgroups appear to differ between employment and productivity and tend to operate independently to a considerable extent.

The present procedure is an unavoidable compromise in methodology, since reliable decomposition of the effects of conventional inputs and residual growth are not available for the sector under consideration. Nevertheless, it is strongly suggested that the role played by residual growth GRi is significant, as suggested by δi variance between subgroups. Table 5.9 illustrated this point by making semi-hypothetical estimates. Two cases are examined here: case 1 assuming the same rate of capital intensity increase GKi − GLi for E and F (as above but with data adjustments); and case 2 approximating its possible variances between subgroups by use of the macro data on GK used conditionally in chapter 1. These are estimated for the average of the two periods as summarized in Table 6.2.

This exercise is useful in determining the order of magnitude and hence the significance of residual growth. Case 1 is hypothetical in a technical sense and may be an extreme case, while case 2 is closer to the reality. However, based on the technical procedure briefly explained in the Remarks, case 2 may not necessarily reflect actual conditions. Preceding analysis showed that the rate of capital formation and related terms do not appear to cause much variance between subgroups. Actually case 2 shows a not necessarily regular relation of capital intensity growth between subgroups. In groups II and IV, E > F, but in groups III and V, F > E. Apart from the slightly different group V which represent developed economies, why is a reverse pattern seen for group III? The answer is not clear, but the rate of residual growth GRi is clearly greater in E than in F without exception through all groups in both case 1 and case 2. In the industrial sector the magnitude of Gyi is thus considerably influenced by GRi. Therefore the notion of a direct option for technology type, i.e., greater or smaller Gki, may not be realistic due to the influence of GRi. Taking this a step further, it could be argued that the greater GLi is the result of greater GRi. The authors do not share this view, however. It is true that in the cross-sectional context of subgroup comparisons an association is recognized between the two, and this may be found in changes over time as well. There is no theoretical basis for asserting any cause-and-effect relationship between the two, however.

The service sector is dealt with using the same concept and proce-

Table 6.2
Relation between Employment Increase and Residual Growth and Related
Terms: Semihypothetical Estimates, Industry

Group		GLi	GRi		GKi − GLi	
			Case (1)	Case (2)	Case (1)	Case (2)
II	E	4.5	1.9	1.7	2.9	3.3
	F	3.2	1.0	1.3	2.9	2.4
	Difference	1.3	0.9	0.4	0.0	0.9
III	E	5.1	2.9	3.0	2.8	2.6
	F	4.2	0.7	0.4	2.8	3.4
	Difference	0.9	2.2	2.6	0.0	0.8
IV	E	3.5	2.8	2.1	3.9	5.2
	F	2.5	0.3	0.7	3.9	3.0
	Difference	1.0	2.5	1.4	0.0	2.2
V	E	1.0	2.6	2.6	4.2	4.1
	F	0.3	1.8	1.7	4.2	4.3
	Difference	0.7	0.8	0.9	0.0	−0.2

Source: i) GKi from the data for *DE, op. cit.*, Table A2.4, with adjustments.
ii) GLi and Gyi are from *DE*, Table 3; αi is from *DE*, Table 1.7. (Originally βm: labor's income share in manufacturing. This is used by assuming that $\alpha i = 1 - \beta i$.)
iii) Macro GK − GL is from Table 1.1, panel A.
Remarks: i) The conventional simple formula $Gyi = GRi + \alpha i(GKi - GLi)$ is used with the same value of αi for E and F.
ii) In case 1, GKi − GLi is assumed to be the same. In case 2, the macro data of GK − GL for subgroups A and B are used to approximate roughly the subgroup differences between E and F by applying the ratios to the group average. The varied subgrouping criteria may not matter much.

dure as for industry, and the results are presented in Table 6.3. Panel A gives averages of the two periods. The performance of GLs and Gys was discussed previously in detail, but here attention is focused on the relation of the two terms. The ratio Gys/GLs tends to be much smaller for services than for industry, with relatively stable trends though groups, including V. This is the combined outcome of GLs > GLi and Gys < Gyi through groups. Although it can be said that this is characteristic of postwar developing economies, the authors do not necessarily agree because GLs > GLi is observed also in the historical path of presently developed nations except Japan (*DE, op. cit.* Tables 4.11 and 4.12). Furthermore, why does employment in services tend to increase faster than in industry despite its much slower productivity growth rate? The facilitating activity of the service sector is largely carried out labor-intensively except for

Table 6.3
Employment Increase and Its Relation to Productivity Growth: Services
(Annual rate of growth, %)

	(1) 1960–1970		(2) 1970–1980		Average	
Group	GLs	Gys	GLs	Gys	GLs	Gys
(A)						
I	4.5	−0.9	5.3	−0.1	4.9	−0.5
II Average	4.1	2.5	4.7	1.2	4.4	1.9
E	4.6	2.7	5.2	1.2	4.9	2.0
F	3.6	2.2	4.1	1.2	3.9	1.7
III Average	4.8	1.0	4.6	2.4	4.7	1.7
E	4.2	1.9	4.3	2.8	4.3	2.4
F	5.3	0.1	4.9	1.9	5.1	1.0
IV Average	3.2	2.8	4.2	2.0	3.7	2.4
E	3.3	3.2	4.6	2.3	4.0	2.8
F	3.0	2.5	3.7	1.6	3.4	2.1
V Average	2.8	2.5	2.8	0.7	2.8	1.6
E	2.6	3.4	2.4	1.0	2.5	2.2
F	3.1	1.5	3.1	0.4	3.1	1.0
(B)						
II	1.0	0.5	1.1	0.0	1.0	0.3
III	−1.1	1.8	−0.6	0.9	−0.8	1.4
IV	0.3	0.7	0.9	0.7	0.6	0.7
V	−0.5	1.9	−0.7	0.6	−0.6	1.2

Source: *DE*, *op. cit.*, Table 4.7.
Remark: δs is the subgroup difference (E–F).

modern transportation and communications. At the same time, the contribution of residual growth via technological progress in enhancing productivity growth in services is much more limited. In addition to this basic property, it must be noted that in postwar developing economies higher level of per worker product has been sustained by this sector.[3]

In performance by subgroup, the ratio Gys/GLs has a greater value in E than in F for all groups with a slight exception in group II, which is essentially the same pattern as in industry. In this

[3] No sectoral wage data are systematically available for comparison between sectors S and I, but ws > wi may be sustained on average except in the case of underemployment. A comparison of $\theta s \cdot \beta s/\beta$ with $\theta i \cdot \beta i/\beta$ (θs and θi are sectoral levels of Y/L relative to the aggregate) shows ws > wi (see chapter 4, section II).

case also it could be expected that this must be the general result of a combined greater GLs and greater Gys in E than in F, but the expectation is not met. As clearly shown in panel B by δs, in the "average" column for groups III and V, GLs, the difference, is instead greater in F than in E. This is a notable difference as compared with industry. Is it possible to give a consistent interpretation?

The service sector is multicompositional, and it is difficult to treat it using simplified methods. However, the relationship between employment and productivity growth differs from the case of industry and this difference must generate the pattern. In period performance, for δs two different cases in GLs are recognized: greater in E than in F for groups II·and IV and the reverse for groups III and V. This must be regular performance characteristic of this sector. The former case is concurrent, analogous to industry, and the latter case is reversal, unlike industry, indicating a trade-off relation between employment increase and productivity growth. This is relevant to the reason why this sector was characterized earlier by a "mixed" pattern.

It can be interpreted simply that the effects of underemployment tend to be stronger in the service sector in addition to the operation of the same forces as in industry. By subgroup comparison, when and where the underemployment factor works more strongly the reversal pattern emerges, whereas when the latter factors operate more effectively the concurrent pattern is seen. The magnitude difference of Gys between subgroups tends to be remarkably greater in the former case, while it is smaller in the latter case. This suggests, although indirectly, that the degree of underemployment is greater in the reversal pattern by subgroup comparison. This interpretation pertains to the major segment of developing economies. In group III in particular the negative value of δs reaches 0.8 for GLs on average of the two periods and this is combined with 1.4, the greatest value of Gys difference. However, the effects of technological progress and the output demand change in the goods-producing sector appear to be much more influential in E (treated by GYg in *DE*, Table 4.7) in such cases. Thus greater employment increase GLs in F reduces Gys there. The group V pattern is similar to that of group III, but the meaning differs. In developed economies, the demand for labor undergoes a structural shift from industry to services, and a negative value of δs does not necessarily indicate underemployment.

In the case of agriculture, the pattern is different due to technological character. The relation between labor employment change and productivity growth is that of reversal. In this respect it resembles to a certain extent the case of the reversal pattern in services, due to the similar reason that agriculture is a reservoir of underemployment. However, viewed from the long-term observation of labor employment, what is peculiar to this sector is a trend of decrease in GLa toward negative magnitude in groups IV and V. In making comparisons by subgroup, δa, the difference between Gya and GLa, is applied, respectively, between E and F. The measured figures are listed in Table 6.4 and evidently endorse the present view of the reversal relation as shown by the average performance through the two decades of periods 1 and 2. Through all the groups the value of δa is negative for GLa with the minor exception of II, while showing a distinctly greater positive value with respect to Gya without exception. It should be noted that this relation is identified irrespective of

Table 6.4
Employment Changes and Their Relation to Productivity Growth: Agriculture

(Annual rate of growth, %)

		(1) 1960–1970		(2) 1970–1980		Average	
Group		GLa	Gya	GLa	Gya	GLa	Gya
(A)							
I		1.4	0.6	1.3	0.1	1.4	0.4
II	Average	1.6	1.7	2.0	1.0	1.8	1.4
	E	1.8	2.6	1.8	2.2	1.8	2.3
	F	1.4	0.8	2.2	−0.2	1.8	0.3
	a	0.4	1.8	−0.4	2.4	0.0	2.1
III	Average	1.1	3.5	1.1	3.2	1.1	3.4
	E	0.6	4.0	0.3	4.1	0.5	4.1
	F	1.5	3.0	1.9	2.2	1.7	2.6
	a	−0.9	1.0	−0.6	1.9	−1.2	1.5
IV	Average	−1.0	4.2	−0.4	2.7	−0.7	3.5
	E	−1.5	5.2	−1.2	3.8	1.4	4.5
	F	−0.5	3.2	0.4	1.6	−0.1	2.4
	a	−1.0	2.0	−1.6	2.2	−1.3	2.1
V	Average	4.0	5.3	−1.9	2.7	−3.0	4.0
	E	−4.7	5.7	−2.9	3.0	−3.8	4.4
	F	−3.3	4.8	−0.9	2.4	−2.1	3.6
	a	−1.4	0.9	−2.0	0.6	−1.7	0.8

Source: *DE*, Table 4.5.

possible differences in technology type: scale-neutral BC type in the former segment and increasing weight of the scale-effective type toward the latter segment. By period observation no major distortion of this pattern is found except in group II in the 1960s, when GLa is greater in E than in F, which results in $\delta a = 0$ on average of the two periods. The specific reason for this is not clear, although underemployment due to the overabundance of labor may be relevant. Generally, however, the pattern identified is essentially regular.

In trying to interpret δa performance, it is necessary to discuss the general characteristics of agriculture in postwar developing economies. It is characterized by two seemingly contradictory phenomena: an unprecedentedly high rate of residual growth GRa, and aggravated underemployment. The former pertains to Gya and the latter to GLa. The effects of the well-known Green Revolution can be comprehended quantitatively by the residual growth GRa, which is estimated to be greater than usually expected. The ratio GRa/Gya ranges from 70% to 80% for developing economies, a much higher percentage in comparison with industry, GRi/Gyi (chapter 5). Subgroup estimates are not sufficiently reliable, but judging from the figures derived by semihypothetical estimates (Table 5.10) the authors are convinced that the difference in GRa is dominant in determining the positive magnitude of δa for Gya shown in Table 6.4.

The underemployment situation can be approximated by measuring marginal productivity of labor MP, assuming that it is nearly equal to the prevailing wage rate—in the case of agriculture, the prevailing wages in rural districts, wa. This is underemployment in the conventional sense of MPa < wa, the first category in the present analysis. Developing economies are characterized by differentials of MP between the modern and traditional sectors, forming a disequilibrium state of the aggregate economy. Sectoral reallocation is thus an important phenomenon. Although not strictly conventional, the notion of underemployment can also be applied in this intersectoral sense. Due to the use of estimates by imputation, the first category of underemployment defined in intrasectoral terms cannot be discussed here, but for the second category defined in intersectoral terms rough approximation is possible. The ratio (%) of wages in agriculture to the average wage level in the nonagricultural sector is estimated as follows:

I	II	III	IV	V
17	19	36	36	43

Considering the differences in labor quality, regional prices, etc. the MP differential should be adequately discounted, as pointed out in chapter 4. The Mp gap remains sizable, in particular for groups with lower Y/L levels. As discussed in chapter 5, population pressure is sustained with limited land and this is the basic cause of underemployment. Estimates of GLa − GB (where B stands for land used for farming) are as follows in terms of average annual rate of change:

I	II	III	IV	V
1.1	0.3	0.6	−0.4	−3.5

Until group III, land for agriculture expands to some extent, but the number of workers engaged in agriculture increases even more. The initially unfavorable man-land ratio thus operates as a more aggravating pressure. Together with technological progress, decreasing MPa of labor input continues to operate.

In interpreting the relationship between GLa and Gya via δa, the authors argue that the reversal pattern should not be viewed as a dependent relationship. For example, one may assert that on the one hand, a smaller (greater) rate of GLa contributes to a higher (lower) rate of productivity growth Gya, because the pressure of underemployment is weaker in E (stronger in F). This assertion cannot be completely rejected, but Gya and GLa are determined almost independently of each other. As approximated in Table 5.10, the subgroup difference of Gya is mainly determined by the residual growth. As an additional illustration, if the ratio GRa/Gya of group average is simply applied to subgroups, GRa would be as follows:

	II	III	IV	V
E	1.7	3.4	3.4	1.5
F	0.2	2.2	1.8	1.3
Difference	1.5	1.2	1.6	0.2

With respect to technological advance of the BC type there is almost no evidence that GRa tends to be greater (smaller) in association with smaller (greater) GLa, although this may be the case when scale-effective technological advance of the M type becomes more dominant toward group V. For the major segment of developing economies, therefore, in terms of the magnitude of δa, GLa is essentially determined by factors other than Gya. Since the difference in the aggregate rate of labor force increase between subgroups is minor, the rate of sectoral reallocation of labor must be the most significant of factors. The effects of reallocation of labor are treated as forming residual growth in the present framework, and it is measured on the basis of the lower level of MPa in agriculture as compared with marginal productivity of the other two sectors I and S. Here the magnitude of GLa relative GLi and GLs represents the labor-absorption power of the nonagricultural sector.

Table 6.5 lists relevant terms in average estimates for 1960–1980. The effects of reallocation are greater in E than in F with the minor exception of group IV. Particularly noteworthy is that the weighted magnitude of employment increases in the nonagricultural sector (sum of columns 2 and 3) and is distinctly greater in E than in F through all groups without exception, which exactly corresponds to the difference in vaGLa between subgroups, as expected. With respect to the changing position of labor absorption power between sectors I and S by subgroup, the stronger position of S in group II

Table 6.5
Sectoral Labor Allocation and Reallocation Effects by Subgroup, 1960–1980

(%)

Group		vaGLa (1)	viGLi (2)	vsGLs (3)	Sum of (2) and (3)	Reallocation Effects
II	E	1.22	0.55	0.98	1.53	0.71
	F	1.40	0.33	0.65	0.98	0.35
	Difference	−0.18	0.22	0.33	0.55	0.36
III	E	0.29	0.97	1.38	2.36	0.32
	F	0.91	0.49	1.14	1.63	0.28
	Difference	−0.62	0.48	0.21	0.69	0.04
IV	E	−0.49	0.90	1.58	2.48	0.13
	F	−0.04	0.61	1.47	2.08	0.16
	Difference	−0.45	0.29	0.11	0.40	−0.03
V	E	−0.51	0.41	1.13	1.54	0.62
	F	−0.22	0.11	1.69	1.80	0.13
	Difference	−0.29	0.30	−0.56	−0.26	0.49

Source: Weighted rates of labor changes are from *DE*, *op. cit.*, Table 4.4, and reallocation effects are from *DE*, Table A2.8.

Remark: Weights va, vi, and vs are the percentage shares of employment to the total estimated average employment in 1960, 1970, and 1980, respectively.

results in a shift to the dominant role played by sector I in the major segment of developing economies, III and IV; in group V a major shift occurs to the service sector.

In concluding this subsection, the following remarks are warranted. First, the conventional notion of a trade-off in the growth relationship between productivity and employment is misleading mainly because it ignores the effects of residual growth due to non-conventional factors. The role played by residual growth in determining variance in productivity increase is significant in goods-producing sectors by subgroup comparison. Based on this, it is assumed that the different performance observed between subgroups can be a rough proxy to substitute for scheduled observation of variant relationships between productivity growth and employment changes in a given economy. This argument is perhaps debatable, but it is the view of the authors that attempts to link changes in employment directly with the pattern of production factor inputs are not valid.

Second, on the employment side, due to the sustained differential structure, special consideration must be given to underemployment of the second category for agriculture and services. It is contended that a smaller rate of macro productivity increase tends to accompany greater pressure aggravating the problem of underemployment, assuming the same conditional interpretation of schedule variance as above is acceptable. Although there is difficulty in estimating directly the degree of underemployment of the first category, we suggest that reallocation effects deserve attention in this regard. Its greater (smaller) magnitude indicates a greater (smaller) degree of improvement in the differential structure. For example, in group II it is 0.71 for E versus 0.35 for F (Table 6.5). To that extent the sectoral difference in marginal productivity tends to narrow, with the effect of reducing underemployment. Conceptually, this is treated as another type of residual growth in aggregate measures, since the effect is the result of nonconventional factors. Therefore the combined effects of the two kinds of residual growth should be considered in this problem area characterizing contemporary developing economies.

Third, it may appear that the macro approach is meaningless in this study area due to the essentially different growth relationships between productivity and employment in the three major sectors. In reality, a global viewpoint is required, as illustrated by the discussion on reallocation effects, i.e., the relationship between productivity growth and employment change in each sector should be aggregated to provide a global picture. Statistically this can be achieved by weighting the magnitude of sectoral productivity growth and that of sectoral employment change to determine the sectoral contribution of each to macro performance. This is discussed in detail in the subsequent section. The significance of the role played by the service sector from this point of view in terms of employment and productivity is illustrated below in numerical values (%) by group average:

	I	II	III	IV	V
Employment (vsGLs)	26.3	30.6	50.0	73.7	88.2
Productivity (Ds)	52.6	71.9	43.7	42.5	32.0

(Ds is the difference indicator used in chapter 5.)

The weighted rate of employment increase (vsGLs) shows a trend of acceleration toward groups with higher Y/L level, and the pattern of the weighted rate of productivity increase (Ds) deserves particular attention. Except for group V, it sustains fairly high levels, despite its limited rate of technological progress. Except for group I it is greater than Di, the corresponding value of industry (II 53.1, III 35.4, and IV 38.7). This eloquently illustrates the necessity of the aggregate viewpoint.

II. Productivity Growth and the Sectoral Inequality of Product Per Worker

The relationship between productivity growth and sectoral inequality of product per worker is controversial. One view holds that technological progress in the modern sector leads to rapid productivity growth there, but is accompanied by a greater inequality in the level of per worker product in the traditional sector. This trend is called "divergence." Another view, however, argues that such unfavorable effects on the traditional sector do not always occur and that the rate of per worker product increase in the traditional sector becomes greater than that in the modern sector, depending upon the pace of technological progress and changes in the conditions of employment. This is the trend called "convergence." The factors actually responsible for determining divergence or convergence in the development path are complex, and no theoretical hypothesis can be made *a priori*. Empirical research has been done in this study area, following Kuznets's pioneering work, but certain points remain to be clarified. This is particularly so with respect to contemporary developing economies. The results of the authors' recent studies were described in *DE*, chapter 3, in which the significance of the difference recognized between the historical records of presently developed nations and contemporary developing nations is emphasized with special regard to initial conditions that influence divergence or convergence. Amplification of this is attempted in this section conceptually and empirically. As a preliminary, a simple coefficient of inequality of the level of per worker product itself is derived (static) and then it is treated in terms of its rate of growth (dynamic). Its relationship with productivity growth is investigated by subgrouping, first by the degree of industrialization and second by productivity growth, analogous to the procedure in section I.

In the previous analysis the major procedure was in terms of sectoral ratio, first agriculture versus nonagriculture, and second industry versus services. As a whole a trend of convergence is seen for contemporary developing economies as the level of Y/L increases by group in cross-sectional data, despite the maintenance of the differential structure. How is this possible? This question is answered by clarifying the significance of the given initial conditions using integrating indices, instead of sector ratios. In order to do so, a simple formula is used for the three major sectors A, I, and S:

$$3\varepsilon = \mid \frac{wa}{va} - 1 \mid + \mid \frac{wi}{vi} - 1 \mid + \mid \frac{ws}{vs} - 1 \mid, \qquad (1)$$

where w and v stand for the share of product and that of labor, respectively. This is derived from

$$(wa - va)/va + (wi - vi)/vi + (ws - vs)/vs, \qquad (1')$$

which explicitly treats the difference of output share and labor share (relative productivity) of each sector corresponding to the labor employment size of each sector as indicated by its share. The coefficient ε, indicating the performance of divergence versus convergence, thus essentially sums up these sectoral values by measuring the changes in employment distribution among sectors. Table 6.6 summarizes the results for the group average.

The pattern of change in coefficient ε across groups shows a sharp trend of convergence through the 1960s and 1970s. Although the cross-sectional data cannot be interpreted to indicate directly the pattern over time, such a distinct trend of convergence is characteristic of contemporary developing economies. The initial conditions bequeathed by colonialism and the abrupt start of modern develop-

Table 6.6
Sectoral Inequality of Per Worker Product by Group, 1960–1980

Group		(1) 1960–1970	(2) 1970–1980	Average
I	wa/va − 1	−0.80	−0.40	−0.39
	wi/vi − 1	2.95	4.04	3.50
	ws/vs − 1	3.08	2.36	2.72
		2.14	2.27	2.20
II	wa/va − 1	−0.56	−0.57	−0.57
	wi/vi − 1	0.99	1.00	1.00
	ws/vs − 1	1.84	1.38	1.61
		1.13	0.98	1.06
III	wa/va − 1	−0.44	−0.46	−0.45
	wi/vi − 1	0.38	0.32	0.35
	ws/vs − 1	0.64	0.45	0.55
		0.49	0.41	0.45
IV	wa/va − 1	−0.59	−0.50	−0.55
	wi/vi − 1	0.38	0.40	0.39
	ws/vs − 1	0.40	0.22	0.31
		0.46	0.37	0.42
V	wa/va − 1	−0.44	−0.45	−0.45
	wi/vi − 1	0.01	0.03	0.02
	ws/vs − 1	0.12	0.06	0.09
		0.19	0.18	0.19

Source: *DE, op. cit.*, Table 3.2, where the data are given as $\theta a = wa/va$, etc., for three years, 1960, 1970, and 1980.
Remark: ε is one-third of the absolute values by sector.

ment are major causes. Comparisons with the historical pattern of presently developed nations cannot be made systematically, but, for example, the same coefficient of inequality measured for Japan shows a much slower trend of convergence: The magnitude of inequality of product per worker may be affected positively by the degree of industrialization because the level of productivity in industry must be much higher than that in agriculture. If were actually the case, the coefficient of sectoral inequality of product per worker would be greater in C and smaller in D. The results of this investigation are summarized in Table 6.7.

A closer look at the trend demarcates two ranges in terms of the magnitude of ε: I, II, and III, IV. On average in periods 1 and 2, the first range, 2.20–1.06, the magnitude is large with a distinct decline; the second range, 0.45–0.42, is smaller with a slow change to-

Table 6.7
Sectoral Inequality of Per Worker Product by Subgroup: Share of Industrial
Output, 1960–1980 Averages

Group	Subgroup	wa/va − 1	wi/vi − 1	ws/vs − 1	
I	C	−0.40	1.67	2.76	1.61
	D	−0.38	5.95	3.30	3.21
II	C	−0.57	1.07	1.38	1.01
	D	−0.54	1.62	2.19	1.45
III	C	−0.54	0.51	0.67	0.57
	D	−0.42	0.73	0.71	0.62
IV	C	−0.61	0.72	0.38	0.57
	D	−0.53	0.17	0.33	0.34
V	C	−0.31	0.05	0.04	0.13
	D	−0.38	0.06	0.15	0.20

Source: DE, op. cit., Table 3.10.
Remark: Averages of C and D do not necessarily coincide with the corresponding
figures in Table 5.6 due to differences in data and procedure.

ward V (0.19, or close to zero). These two ranges of developing
economies are relevant to phase demarcation as discussed below. By
sector the major part of the coefficient changes stems from industry
and services, while the negative magnitude of the agricultural component changes little across the entire group. This indicates that the
low level of product per worker engaged in agriculture tends to be
generally sustained despite the trend of convergence in developing
economies.

As suggested by the procedure used in section I, analysis is concerned with the difference in inequality patterns between subgroups,
since the authors believed that the inequality of per worker product
cannot be assumed to be associated solely with differences in Y/L
level. Thus nonassociated factors are at issue, and various subgroup-
ings should be tested. The degree of industrialization (indicated by
output share of industry) is first taken up using subgroups C and D,
with greater and smaller share, respectively, in selected countries.[4]

[4] Selected countries (the total number of countries is shown in parentheses).

Group I	C:	(5)	Malawi, Madagascar, India, Somalia, and Tanzania
(10)	D:	(5)	Ethiopia, Nepal, Niger, Benin, and Burma
Group II	C:	(6)	Pakistan, Bolivia, the Philippines, Thailand, Kenya, and
(12)			Ivory Coast
	D:	(6)	Sierra Leone, Senegal, Sudan, Sri Lanka, People's
			Republic of the Congo, and Mozambique

Contrary to expectations, the value of ε is greater for D than for C through all the groups except group IV. How should these patterns be interpreted for developing economies? By sector component, as expected, the difference in agriculture contributes least to forming such patterns, whereas the components pertaining to industry and services are influential; the difference between C and D is large in particular for lower groups I and II. This suggests the effect of abrupt, often heavy, industrialization including mining: despite smaller output share a distortion toward higher-productivity firms might emerge in subgroup D as compared to C. The initial inequality is greater in services for D due to its more influential position. This initial situation tends to be overcome by the normal, more competitive pattern of industrialization toward the latter segment. This is speculative and further examination is needed, including the reason for the exception of IV. But at least the trend of convergence can broadly be applied between sectoral inequality and the degree of industrialization.[5]

In the preceding discussion, the approach using formula (1) was "static" in the sense that sectoral inequality is measured at the given

Group III (12)	C:	(6)	Korea, Turkey, Nicaragua, Egypt, Morocco, and Syrian Arab Republic
	D:	(6)	Paraguay, Tunisia, El Salvador, Honduras, Colombia, and Malaysia
Group IV (12)	C:	(6)	Brazil, Peru, Yugoslavia, Jamaica, Portugal, and Argentina
	D:	(6)	Dominican Republic, Mexico, Greece, Costa Rica, Uruguay, and Singapore
Group V (12)	C:	(6)	Japan, France, Netherlands, Belgium, UK, and Germany
	D:	(6)	Denmark, Canada, Finland, Norway, Sweden, and USA.

[5] In *DE, op. cit.*, chapter 3, the same procedure using formula (1) was applied also to the case of subgrouping in terms of aggregate productivity growth rates: E (higher) versus F (lower), the subgrouping to be adopted in the approach that follows. The results, taken together with the present results of the preliminary approach by subgrouping in terms of C versus D, are interpreted as broadly consistent in showing a trend of covergence.

The numerical values of ε are as follows (from *DE*, Table 3.10):

	II	III	IV	V
E	0.99	0.50	0.34	0.26
F	1.24	0.77	0.54	0.18

In this case IV shows a regular pattern, but V appears somewhat exceptional.

state of the relationship between product share and labor share observed on average for the period under consideration. Actually, however, the sectoral levels of per worker product are changing. Therefore it is desirable to search for an alternative formula that can measure the changing state. This requires "dynamic" approaches, among which the simplest and most operational is a formula in growth terms. Sectoral comparisons of per worker product are made in terms of growth rates, meaning that the inequality is not in levels but in the rate of growth of per worker product. This approach takes the same standpoint in that sectoral inequalities are aggregated with the weights of labor employment shares. This is done to provide the inequality coefficient in a sense analogous to the previous case, and the comparison of its sectoral values are also significant. The difference indicators Da, Di, and Ds were used for the purpose of demarcating the points of sectoral turn in chapter 5 (waGYa − vaGLa, etc.). Their distribution is simply obtained by the percentage to their sums, or macro productivity growth. This can be used effectively for the present purpose, together with the distributive shares of labor employment va, vi, and vs. The formula is thus proposed as follows:

$$\left|\frac{Da}{D} - va\right| + \left|\frac{Di}{D} - vi\right| + \left|\frac{Ds}{D} - vs\right| = 3\rho \qquad (2)$$

$$(D = Da + Di + Ds).$$

The main implication of this formula is simple, but a technical explanation is required. The purpose here is to determine 1) sectoral differences in growth rates of productivity (product per worker), and 2) sectoral distribution of labor employed, in order to derive the coefficient of inequality ρ. The development path encompasses changes in 1) and 2) not in parallel, but in varied combinations, and we attempted to clarify the pattern of such variations. An overview can be obtained from Table 6.8, which summarizes the averaged results for two periods, the 1960s and 1970s, with respect to group by Y/L level.

The magnitude of the inequality coefficient ρ presents a trend of sharp decrease through the former segment of developing economies, I–III, whereas in the latter segment the tempo of decline becomes moderate, even showing a slight increase from group IV to group V. This is broadly similar to the two-range pattern pointed out earlier for productivity growth and employment change. In the

Table 6.8
Productivity Growth and Sectoral Inequality of Per Worker Product by Group in 1960–1980 Averages

i) Difference Indicator

(percentage distribution, %)

Group	Da	Di	Ds	D (Sum)	Da	Di	Ds	D
I	−0.30	0.48	0.20	0.38	−79.0	126.3	52.6	100.0
II	−0.29	1.09	2.05	2.85	−12.9	39.4	73.5	100.0
III	0.68	1.16	1.43	3.27	20.8	35.5	43.7	100.0
IV	0.70	1.44	1.58	3.72	18.8	38.7	42.5	100.0
V	0.57	1.51	0.98	3.06	18.6	49.4	32.0	100.0

ii) Labor Share and Inequality Coefficient

Group	va	vi	vs	Sum	a	i	s	D
I	83.3	6.0	10.7	100.0	−162.3	120.3	41.9	114.8
II	72.8	10.5	16.7	100.0	−85.7	28.9	56.8	57.2
III	51.5	18.9	29.6	100.0	−30.7	16.6	14.1	20.5
IV	37.2	25.1	37.7	100.0	−18.4	13.6	4.8	12.3
V	6.4	40.3	53.3	100.0	12.2	9.1	−21.3	14.2

Source: *DE, op. cit.*, Table 4.10. Da, etc. are from panel C, and va, etc. from panels B and C.
Remark: ρ is ⅓ of the sum of absolute values of ρa, ρi, and ρs.

present case, a sectorwise comparison points out the following features for developing economies. In forming such a pattern of ρ magnitude change, the contribution of services ρs tends to be rather small while the contribution of the goods-producing sector ρi and ρa appears greater: ρi shows a completely straight trend of decline in positive magnitude, while ρa shows an almost corresponding movement in negative magnitude. However, a shift from IV to V accompanies noticeable changes in two points: in agriculture the value of ρa becomes positive, while in services the value of ρs becomes negative. This suggests structural differences in the sectoral inequality between developing and developed economies.

Thus as an overview the inequality in sectoral growth rates of per worker product definitely tends to narrow as Y/L level increases (convergence), so far as cross-sectional observation is concerned.

Next, the effects of nonassociated factors are examined by subgroup. Subgrouping in terms of productivity growth rate used in the preceding section also fits this purpose. By definition, macro productivity growth is greater (smaller) in E (F), so that if the sectoral differential is greater (smaller) in E, the inequality performance is unfavorable (favorable). To clarify these possibilities, the same procedure can be applied as for estimating the figures in Table 6.8, essentially following formula (2). Table 6.9 summarizes the measured results. Because of the importance of time series, detailed data including changes over time are listed. Looking at panels B and C in the table for the average performance in the 1960s and 1970s, coefficient ρ (sum of the absolute values of sectoral ρ) presents a perfectly regular pattern of inequality (smaller in E, greater in F) through all groups. In other words, nations with greater (smaller) rates of macro productivity growth also have smaller (greater) magnitudes of sectoral inequality in growth rates of product per worker. This is an important finding, since it may be contrary to expectations.

The pattern determined is the result of the relation between the productivity growth pattern and the labor employment distribution (average va, etc., are shown in panel B of Table 6.9 for convenience of comparison). What is impressive is that all the sectoral productivity indicators, Da, Di, and Ds, are greater in E than in F throughout all groups. (There is a slight exception in group II for Ds.) This phenomenon is notable, but interpreting it is not easy and detailed investigation is beyond the present scope of analysis. However, it is recognized that two factors operate in forming sectoral productivity

Table 6.9
Sectoral Inequality in Growth Rates of Per Worker Product by Subgroup: 1960–1980

(A) Two periods   (%)

Group	Subgroup	(1) 1960–1970				(2) 1970–1980			
		Da	Di	Ds	Sum	Da	Di	Ds	Sum
II	E	(4.2)	(34.8)	(61.0)	(100.0)	(−0.7)	(41.4)	(69.3)	(100.0)
	F	(−12.6)	(33.4)	(79.1)	(100.0)	(−70.6)	(29.4)	(141.2)	(100.0)
		a	i	s		a	i	s	
	E	−65.9	23.2	42.7	43.9	−70.8	28.9	36.4	45.3
	F	−88.0	24.8	63.1	38.6	−142.6	19.6	123.0	95.1
		Da	Di	Ds	Sum	Da	Di	Ds	Sum
III	E	(27.3)	(36.5)	(36.0)	(100.0)	(21.7)	(34.9)	(43.4)	(100.0)
	F	(18.3)	(27.9)	(53.8)	(100.0)	(5.9)	(29.3)	(64.8)	(100.0)
		a	i	s		a	i	s	
	E	−26.1	20.6	5.5	17.4	−21.5	13.2	8.3	14.3
	F	−37.9	10.9	27.0	25.3	−14.8	9.1	34.7	29.0
		Da	Di	Ds	Sum	Da	Di	Ds	Sum
IV	E	(22.3)	(40.5)	(37.2)	(100.0)	(18.7)	(38.0)	(43.3)	(100.0)
	F	(16.2)	(39.0)	(44.8)	(100.0)	(6.8)	(29.3)	(63.9)	(100.0)

Table 6.9 (continued)

(A) Two periods

(%)

Group	Subgroup	(1) 1960–1970				(2) 1970–1980			
		Da	Di	Ds	Sum	Da	Di	Ds	Sum
		a	i	s		a	i	s	
	E	−20.2	17.3	2.9	13.5	−14.2	10.3	3.9	9.5
	F	−21.3	15.1	6.2	14.2	−24.0	6.4	17.6	16.0
		Da	Di	Ds	Sum	Da	Di	Ds	Sum
		a	i	s		a	i	s	
V	E	(17.4)	(45.2)	(37.4)	(100.0)	(15.8)	(51.7)	(32.5)	(100.0)
	F	(12.1)	(58.2)	(29.7)	(100.0)	(9.1)	(65.5)	(24.6)	(100.0)
		a	i	s		a	i	s	
	E	0.1	5.9	−6.0	4.0	6.8	11.4	−18.2	11.0
	F	2.9	19.4	−22.3	14.9	3.9	30.7	−34.6	23.1

(B) Summation on average of periods (1) and (2)

a) Difference indicator

		Da	Di	Ds	Sum
II	E	0.08	1.32	2.12	3.52
	F	-0.67	0.71	2.16	2.20
III	E	1.02	1.49	1.66	4.17
	F	0.32	0.77	1.59	2.68
IV	E	1.01	1.91	1.92	4.84
	F	0.37	1.01	1.46	2.84
V	E	0.64	1.67	1.30	3.61
	F	0.25	1.30	0.60	2.15

b) Percentage contribution (sum = 100)

		Difference Indicator			Labor Share		
		Da	Di	Ds	va	vi	vs
II	E	2.3	37.5	60.2	67.5	12.1	20.5
	F	-30.5	32.3	98.2	73.7	9.2	17.1
III	E	24.5	35.7	39.8	48.3	18.8	32.9
	F	11.9	28.8	59.3	53.0	18.6	28.5
IV	E	20.8	39.5	39.7	37.7	25.5	36.9
	F	13.0	35.6	51.4	34.2	23.4	42.5
V	E	17.7	46.3	36.0	14.4	38.6	47.1
	F	11.6	60.5	27.9	7.7	36.9	55.5

Table 6.9 (continued)

(C) Inequality coefficient

Component		A	I	S	(average)	(1)	(2)
II	E	−68.3	26.1	39.6	44.7	43.9	45.4
	F	−115.3	22.2	81.1	76.9	58.6	95.1
III	E	−23.8	16.9	6.9	15.9	17.4	14.3
	F	−41.0	10.0	31.0	27.3	25.3	29.3
IV	E	−17.2	13.8	3.4	11.5	13.5	9.5
	F	−20.8	10.8	11.9	15.1	14.2	16.0
V	E	3.5	8.7	−12.1	8.1	4.0	12.1
	F	3.4	25.1	−28.5	19.0	14.9	23.1

Source: GYa, GLa, etc. and wa, va, etc., share of output, and share of labor are from *DE, op. cit.*, Table 4.3.

Remarks: Da, etc. = (waGYa − viGLa), etc., are listed only in percentage distribution. The magnitudes slightly differ from those in *DE*, Table 4.10, due to a slightly different treatment of the original data.

ii) The averages of E and F do not necessarily coincide with the corresponding figures in Table 6.8 due to unavoidable differences in data coverage and procedure.

growth: one is the sector proper and the other the aggregate common to all sectors. In the present subgroup treatment, the latter operates more distinctly.[6]

The component behavior by sector in panel C with respect to services shows distinctly greater values in F than in E for the entire range of developing economies, whereas it is negative for group V. With respect to agriculture, distinct variance is noted. During the former range its negative value is greater in F than in E, but in V there is almost no difference between E and F. Its positive value in group V is particularly noted as the final shift in its sustained negative values through all groups of developing economies. This presents a sharp contrast to the service sector. Finally, for industry, it shows a regular, sustained reverse inequality greater in E than in F throughout all groups of developing economies and becomes the opposite in group V. Thus, in aggregate, coefficient ρ tends to narrow the difference between subgroups from lower to higher groups of Y/L level, sustaining the same pattern of inequality for the entire range of developing economies. However, it should be noted that in group V the range of subgroup difference appears to become somewhat wider. This is a combined effect of two factors: a wider range of difference in S and a reversed inequality in I (greater in F than in E).

With regard to the sectoral allocation of labor employment v, detailed observation is made in relation to productivity growth terms. For the sake of simplicity, data by subgroup are not listed in Table 6.9, panel A, but are given in the Annex. One aspect is noted here, however. Industry plays an influential role in increasing vi through groups by Y/L level, but has only minor effects in forming subgroup differences in vi. Regarding subgroup differences in labor allocation, services and agriculture play influential roles in forming countereffects. This is a regular pattern for all groups without exception, and is consistent with the results of measuring reallocation effects in chapter 5, section II. This contributes to forming larger ρ of F combined with similar tendencies of D performance except in group V.

All these findings provide useful knowledge but are not sufficient for the present purpose of inequality analysis. The point is not only

---

[6] Nonassociated factors appear to operate commonly to the three major sectors. The balance or imbalance between social capability SC and production capacity PC is the point at issue in this regard (cf. the relevant discussion in chapter 5).

the absolute level of the difference indicators but its relative aggregate in terms of labor employment distribution. The difference in the sectoral component of ρ between subgroups E and F must therefore be examined. Table 6.9, panel C, illustrates such differences as expressed by F–E:

	A	I	S
II	−47.0	−3.9	41.5
III	−17.5	−6.9	24.1
IV	−3.6	−3.0	8.5
V	−0.1	16.4	−16.4

In forming the sum ρ, sectoral regularity can be clearly witnessed with respect to subgroup pattern: agriculture and services are dominant and industry is minor for developing economies. This runs counter to the usual expectations, but is not uniform. It is strongly evident in group II but toward group IV it becomes distinctly weaker. In the developed nations composing group V, the pattern is reversed. Thus for developing economies the inequality difference mainly pertains to agriculture versus services, not industry. This appears different from the results based on the static approach. The authors believe what is derived from this growth approach is more significant in light of the reality of the development path, and that this is an important finding. Further analysis is needed, but viewed from the proposed conceptual framework the following statements can be made.

The two elements of technology diffusion are relevant to contemporary developing economies. In subgroup F development of the traditional element continues behind subgroup E, as distinctly shown by agriculture, and the traditional activities facilitating function of the service sector are assumed to correspond to that development. The difference tends to narrow as the Y/L level increases. The modern element, broadly represented by industry, results in a much narrower inequality between the two subgroups, against expectations. In addition, the difference in inequality in industry does not necessarily show a noticeable trend of increase or decrease from lower to higher groups.

Data on changes from the 1960s to the 1970s are listed in Table 6.9, panel A, and attention is drawn to ρ(1) and ρ(2) in panel C. Exactly the same pattern is seen for both $\rho(1)$ and $\rho(2)$ as was identified earlier in averages of the two periods. This means that the pattern indicated by the coefficient is basically sustained over time through the two decades and is a lasting characteristic of postwar developing economies. The figures for (1) and (2) in comparison appear self-evident, and no further explanation is required if cautious observation is made. What is described below is intended to aid such observation.

First, since the rate of aggregate productivity growth slowed down from period (1) to (2), is there any noticeable tendency of ρ to increase or decrease over time? Some economists may assert that the slowdown of productivity growth tends to create a greater magnitude of the inequality coefficient in an economy. This assertion is worth investigating because it must be known whether subgroup differences by the cross-sectional average observation are consistent with changes over time. The magnitude of ρ by group average is as follows:

Period	II	III	IV	V
(1)	51.3	21.3	17.0	9.4
(2)	70.2	21.8	13.8	17.6

Although the data for group I cannot be used for reliable estimates, the pattern appears generally consistent with that identified cross-sectionally apart from group IV. However, a closer look at the magnitude difference of ρ by subgroup, presented in Table 6.9, panel C, reveals that the greater magnitude of inequality coefficient in (2) than in (1) is clear for both E and F with regard to groups II and V, whereas for III and IV it is greater for F in (2) than in (1) but for E it is reversed. This mixed pattern is not inconsistent with the group average figures mentioned above. Subgroup E in groups III and IV retains relatively higher rates of productivity growth in period (2), which results in the reversed pattern. In the case of group III, it contributes to making only a slight difference in group averages of ρ, and in the case of IV it overwhelms the pattern of F in group averages. Thus the consistency appears conceivable, and the authors believe this is an important finding in that a slower rate of productivity growth (instead of a higher rate) tends to accompany a greater sectoral inequality in leveling up product per worker. This will be further dealt with below.[7]

The varied patterns of changes over time with regard to the sectoral components of ρ in subgroup comparison are noteworthy. The most conspicuous finding is a close positive association of changes between component A and aggregate ρ. As noted in comparison of panel A with panel B, for group II in both E and F components A and ρ increase from 1) to 2); for group III, in E both decrease but in F both increase; for group IV exactly the same pattern is discernible. In light of the statistical property of the coefficient, the other side of the coin is found for the nonagricultural sector. In view of the earlier findings on the performance difference between sectors I

---

[7]To save space in Table 6.9, detailed data on labor's sectoral allocation are not included. What follows is a supplement (sum = 100):

Annex to Table 6.9   Labor's Sectoral Allocation

Group		(1) 1960–1970			(2) 1970–1980		
		va	vi	vs	va	vi	vs
II	E	70.1	11.6	18.3	64.9	12.5	22.6
	F	75.4	8.6	16.0	72.0	9.5	18.2
	Difference	−5.3	3.0	2.3	−7.1	3.0	4.4
III	E	53.4	15.9	30.7	43.2	21.7	35.1
	F	56.2	17.0	26.8	49.7	20.2	30.1
	Difference	−2.8	−1.1	3.9	−6.5	1.5	5.0
IV	E	42.5	23.2	34.3	32.9	27.7	39.4
	F	37.5	23.9	38.6	30.8	22.9	46.3
	Difference	5.0	−0.7	−4.3	2.1	4.8	−6.9
V	E	17.3	39.3	43.4	11.4	37.9	50.7
	F	9.2	38.9	51.9	6.1	34.8	59.1
	Difference	8.1	0.4	−8.5	5.3	3.1	−8.4

Source: ILO, *Economically Active Population*, 1950–2025, 5 volumes.

The sectoral performance of labor's allocation appears to support the argument stated in the main text. First, with regard to the difference between subgroups, correspondence between agriculture va and services vs is witnessed, respectively, for the former segment (II and III) and for the latter segment (IV and V). In the lower groups, greater va corresponds to smaller vs in F than in E, and in the higher groups smaller va corresponds to greater vs in F as compared to E. From the former to the latter, the share of industry vi increases to a considerable extent, but its effect on forming the difference between subgroups appears rather minor. Second, with regard to the changes over time from period (1) to period (2), the normal effect of increasing vi is seen for all developing economies (a slight exception is F, IV) despite slowing down of productivity growth in the 1970s. However, here again a distinct correspondence between agriculture and services is seen: a decrease in va versus an increase in vs. With respect to group V, a new phenomenon of a decline in vi from (1) to (2) takes place and to that extent the influence of vs becomes much greater.

and S, the concern here is component I, for which the magnitude tends to decrease in general for both E and F in the three groups of developing economies. The magnitude of component S tends to increase for both E and F. The sole exception to these countering changes is seen in E in group II. The slowdown of productivity growth in the 1970s was essentially due to that of industrialization, making the performance of I understandable. What is characteristic of developing economies is the counterfunction of S. With respect to group V, as expected from previous observations, the sectoral pattern differs. In developed economies, A becomes positive and the negative magnitude is replaced by S. Associated direction of changes over time in this case is recognized between component S and aggregate ρ.

So far this explanation has been based on the empirical facts directly deduced from Table 6.9, panel A. The following is a further interpretation of the relevant phenomena thought important in view of the conceptual framework, in particular development phasing. The initial path characterized by the inequality waGya < vaGLa is called the preprimary subphase, specifically distinguished from the ordinary primary phase (chapter 5). Until the economy reaches the point of equality waGya = vaGLa, that is, Da = 0, agriculture operates negatively in forming aggregate productivity growth. During this preprimary subphase, the share of labor employed in agriculture is very great, so that the magnitude of the inequality coefficient must be extremely large. Due to data limitations, subgrouping is not possible for group I, but average group values for periods (1) and (2) can be calculated as follows, based on *DE, op. cit.*, Table 4.10:

	Da	Di	Ds	Sum
	−0.30	−0.48	0.20	0.38
Percentage distribution	−78.9	126.3	52.6	100.0
	va	vi	vs	
Percentage distribution	83.3	6.0	10.7	100.0
	A	I	S	ρ
	−162.3	120.3	41.9	100.0

Reservations must be made in terms of reliability, but the extremely large magnitude of ρ generally illustrates the actual initial situation in comparison with that in subsequent phases. In Table 6.9, panel A, a negative value of Da for II, E, was seen in the 1970s and for F in both the 1960s and 1970s. In other words, nations belonging to group II are at the preprimary subphase, except for E in the 1960s which passes the point Da = 0. The preprimary subphase is thus characterized by an extremely large magnitude of inequality coefficient. This stems mainly from the abrupt industrialization of economies traditionally structured by agriculture and services during the colonial period.

The second turning point is defined by the equality Di = Ds, as discussed in chapter 5. When an economy can reverse the path of Ds > Di to Di > Ds, it is moving toward the final, developed phase from the secondary phase. In Table 6.9, panel A, such moves are seen first in III, E, and second in IV, E, in period (1), although these change again to Ds > Di in period (2).[8] For group V, the pattern Di > Ds is established, which is characteristic of developed economies. Of particular concern here is the peculiar pattern of ρ changes: in both III, E, and IV, E, the aggregate value of ρ decreases from period (1) to period (2). This is peculiar because in all other cases the magnitude of ρ tends to increase, endorsing the view that a slower rate of productivity growth accompanies a greater sectoral inequality. Therefore, it is necessary to clarify the reason for the emergence of such a peculiar pattern. This pattern is the combined result of the maintenance of a regular pattern of changing labor employment allocation between sectors through periods (1) and (2) in developing economies, as is shown in the Annex to Table 6.9: va tends to decrease, while vi and vs tend to increase. Despite the slowdown of productivity growth, this normal pattern occurs, but as pointed out above the difference between E and F cannot be ignored. The peculiar pattern of these cases stems from the performance of D combined with the pattern of changes in v. Changes in the sectoral component of ρ between the two periods are as follows for these cases:

III, E:	A	I	S	IV, E:	A	I	S
(1)	−26.1	20.6	5.5	(1)	−20.2	17.3	2.9
(2)	−21.5	13.2	8.3	(2)	−14.2	10.3	3.9
Changes	−4.6	7.8	−2.8	Changes	−6.0	7.0	−1.0

[8] These are percentages of the sum. The original values are as follows:

		Di	Ds		Di	Ds
E, III	(1)	1.52	1.51	(2)	1.45	1.80
E, IV	(1)	2.32	2.13	(2)	1.50	1.71

The effects of the faster process of industrialization are clear. Changes in I are dominant, while changes in S are minor. In addition, A decreases corresponding to increases in I, in contrast to all other cases of developing economies. These illustrate the pattern of sectoral inequality, which is characteristic of the development path in the secondary phase defined in chapter 5. It is now clarified that the pattern we described previously with regard to the performance of group average is caused by a mixed treatment of different patterns by development phases. In light of this proposition, it is confirmed that the minor role in forming ρ played by the industrial sector is essentially a feature of the primary phase, which is characterized by Ds > Di.

The results of observations over time are generally consistent with those based on cross-sectional analysis by subgroup: slower (faster) rates of productivity growth result in greater (smaller) magnitudes of sectoral inequality of per worker product, not the reverse as often asserted.[9] Methodologically, observations by phase only partially prove the consistency, because data cover only two decades.

In conclusion, the following points in contemporary developing countries are noteworthy. First, a trend of convergence, rather than divergence, is the result of measurements using conventional formulae. However, this cannot be mechanically compared to the historical paths of presently developed countries. The effects of the different initial conditions are enormous. A distinct trend of convergence emerges mainly due to the enormously divergent initial situations.

Second, from the primary to the secondary phase a trend of convergence continues as Y/L is leveled up. However, more attention should be drawn to the range of divergence caused by nonassociated

[9] This suggests that the inequality is greater in downswing intervals and small in upswing intervals of the growth of the economy in general. Japan's historical records illustrate the plausibility of this proposition. Its coefficient of sectoral inequality of product per worker is estimated as follows:

Downswing	Coefficient	Upswing	Coefficient
1990–1914	0.63	1915–1922	0.49
1927–1933	0.71	1936–1940	0.55
		1955–1965	0.53

Source: *DE, op. cit.*, Table 3.12.

The procedure for measuring the coefficient is simply based on formula (1) but may broadly be comparable to those for developing economies, as this roughly corresponds to subgrouping. It is contended that in the possible intervals of downswing —for example, in the 1980s—the inequality would become greater in developing economies.

factors within the same Y/L level (subgroup observation in the present treatment). 1) Sectoral inequality of product per worker tends to be smaller for cases of faster productivity growth, while it is larger for cases of slower productivity growth. 2) Agriculture, together with services, plays a dominant role in creating such divergence, while the difference in industrial growth appears less significant than usually expected. In view of the argument stated in the concluding remarks to section I, this finding is particularly important in revealing the significance of the development of the traditional sector in the primary phase. 3) In shifting to the secondary phase, the effects of industrialization become more influential.

Third, viewed from the dimension of changes over time, greater inequality in sectoral product per worker is likely to occur at smaller rates of economic growth rather than greater rates.

Fourth, combining the results of observations in sections I and II, the authors argue that the role played by more rapid technology diffusion in determining the rate of productivity growth accompanies positive effects on improvement of the employment situation.

Annex: Labor Income Share and the Farmers' Lowest Income Level
Although no systematic attempt is made to deal with income distribution, two selected related topics are discussed here: changes in the share distribution for workers in industry in relation to technological progress and productivity growth; and farmers' income level in relation to changes in the sectoral inequality of product per worker.

The representative term Y/L_w in the simplified formula implies that L_w/Y has labor income share (β) as its reciprocal in a broad sense. More precisely, Y pertains to GDP at market prices so that any β value derived from it deviates from the true labor income share measured in terms of distributed income at factor cost. In dealing with long-term changes, however, it can be assumed that resultant deviations do not pose serious problems. Methodologically, the present formula β is not assumed to be a given variable in entrepreneurial production decision making, although Y/L_w is dealt with in the framework of the formula. The numerical values of labor income share in the industrial sector (β_i) along with those for Y_i/L_{wi} are estimated as follows by Y/L level by group:

	I	II	III	IV	V
β_i	50.6	49.9	45.6	47.5	61.6
Y_i/L_{wi}	197.6	200.4	219.3	210.5	162.3

In the dualistic structure model, the figures above represent the performance of the modern sector. It is reconfirmed that βi tends to decrease during the former segment (from I to III), and increase during the latter segment (from III to V and particularly from IV to V). These notable changes in βi trends conditionally characterize the general performance of worker income share in the primary and secondary phase.

The figures above are estimated averages for 1960–1985. No data are available on changes during that interval, but semihypothetical estimates of wage changes are made in terms of growth rates in deriving Gy – Gw (Technical Notes, chapter 1) for the macro economy. The rate of wage increases in the modern sector Gwm contained in those estimates is as follows in comparison with the rate of productivity growth in the relevant sectors (Gyi for industry and Gys for services):

	I	II	III	IV	V
Gwi	0.8	2.2	2.4	3.0	3.1
Gyi	0.5	2.9	3.2	3.6	3.7
Gys	1.1	1.6	1.7	2.4	2.5

It is presumed that in the industrial sector the relation of wages and productivity is given by Gwm and Gyi. The inequality Gyi > Gwm prevails throughout all groups except for group I, for which the data are less reliable. Technically, this inequality is the outcome of two assumptions: first that sectoral β is unchanged for the interval under review; and second that Gwm is determined as the combined effects of sectors I and S, excluding the part assumed to belong to the traditional sector. These are arbitrary assumptions, but the authors believe that inequality of growth rates is an essential phenomenon of the industrialization process. The effect of changes in sectoral structure are more clearly revealed by decomposing aggregate performance Gy – Gw (Table 1.1) but examination of the modern sector shows the following. In comparison between groups II and III and groups IV and V, roughly corresponding to the primary and the secondary phase, respectively, the degree of inequality measured by the ratio (%) (Gwm – Gyi)/Gyi is 24.1–18.8 in the former versus 16.7–16.2 in the latter. Although these estimates are approximate, they show that the inequality becomes narrower toward the secondary phase.

Gyi – Gwi performance was discussed in detail in chapter 2 in terms of Japan's historical experience. The tendency to increase along the innovative path or in the leading sector, and to decrease along the noninnovative path or in more traditional sectors, results in the relative stability of Gyi – Gwi over the long term. The reciprocal can be assumed here to be Gwi – Gyi. In contemporary developing economies, cross-sectional data suggest that the innovative process mainly occurs in the industrial sector during the preprimary phase. Labor wage income is thus generally determined in this context by phase demarcation. This provides a useful framework for dealing with the second topic, which essentially pertains to the traditional sector.

The objective of examining the level of farmers' income is to clarify the pattern of change in the so-called lowest wage income, which is an indispensable element in interpreting the results of measuring sectoral inequality coefficients of product per worker. The trend of convergence is characterized by an initial situation in which the product per worker in agriculture starts at an extremely low level, but how does it perform through the path of convergence? The answer to this legitimate question is combined with the performance of wage income of farmers, and is given by $\beta a \cdot \theta a$, where βa and θa stand, respectively, for the labor income share in agriculture and the ratio of per worker product in agriculture to that in the total economy. Since $\beta a = Lawa/Ya$ and $\theta a = (Ya/La)/(Y/L)$, we have

$$\beta a \theta a = wa/(Y/L). \tag{3}$$

Formula 3 is a crucial term that measures the level of farmers' wage income relative to the aggregate level of product per worker in the economy. The average numerical values (%) of these terms for the interval 1960–1985 are as follows:[10]

	I	II	III	IV	V
βa	58.4	57.7	53.2	53.6	49.9
θa	61.0	48.7	50.7	45.0	61.3
wa/(Y/L)	35.6	28.1	27.0	24.1	30.5

Surprisingly, the crucial ratio tends to decrease from group I to group IV, except from IV to V, despite the pattern of convergence. In developing economies, the wage income of farmers tends to de-

---

[10] βa from *DE, op. cit.*, Table 1.7; θa from Table 3.2.

cline relative to the aggregate level of per worker product, which shows a distinct increase through groups.

Although this is an extremely important finding, why is the ratio smaller in group IV than in group III? This is a legitimate question because the preceding discussion suggested that a shift from the primary to the secondary phase takes place from III to IV. The answer is that such a phenomenon occurs mainly due to the smaller weight of agriculture in aggregate data, and no contradiction arises in phase demarcation. The magnitude of labor income share β in the aggregate economy is approximated as follows (from *DE*, Table 1.7):

I	II	III	IV	V
53.0	51.4	48.9	51.2	69.0

The figures above include β_i, β_a, and β_s. The pattern of β is generally consistent with the phase demarcation; during the former segment it tends to decrease, while it tends to increase in the latter segment with no dip in group IV (cf. the previous discussion of $w_a/(Y/L)$). Specifically, from group III to group IV, despite a tendency for β_n to increase in the nonagricultural sector, β_a tends to decline. This explanation is acceptable as long as the estimated pattern of aggregate β is meaningful despite the dualistic structure of the economy.

The main problem is how to interpret the pattern of $w_a/(Y/L)$ thus estimated from the standpoint of assessing it as the "lower income." The prevailing view is that the problem of poverty stems mainly from the rural portion of the economy and basically pertains to the situation of those engaged in agricultural production. In the classical analytical framework the concept of subsistence level is basic. In the present framework, the imputation procedure uses w_a to estimate the level of mixed income of farmers, which is assumed to be equivalent to the wage earnings of workers employed in agriculture. It is further assumed that this imputed income can be treated as the lowest income in the rural as well as in the aggregate economy; this corresponds to the subsistence level in classical approaches in the analysis of contemporary developing economies, but differs in that it is not presumed constant *a priori* but is treated as a variable in the operation of the labor market mechanism.

Therefore with respect to the primary phase the pattern of decline in the labor income share in the modern sector occurs in association with the trend of decrease in the relative position of the lowest income in the traditional sector. The conventional theory of surplus labor explains the former phenomenon by assuming, for example, an unchanged subsistence level for the latter. Its significance as an initial condition is recognized, but it is suggested that the definition of surplus labor can be provided by the notion of lowest income as observed empirically in the market mechanism in the subsequent development path. In the secondary phase leading toward the developed stage, correspondence between alternate increases in aggregate β and the lowest income is seen, although it is not necessarily smooth, as illustrated by group IV. Further detailed investigation of income distribution variation is warranted.[11]

---

[11] An analogous approach is in the study area of size income distribution. The concept of lowest income is applied in relation to the total average level of family income in order to measure the coefficient of size distribution of income *à la* Parato. This attractive device also uses the wage earnings of workers employed in agriculture as an appropriate indicator of the lowest level of family income. This is relevant to the present approach. Toshiyuki Otsuki and Nobukiyo Takamatsu, "An Aspect of the Size Distribution of Income in Prewar Japan," *IDCJ Working Paper Series No. 09*, 1978.

7

Generalized Framework of Development Phases

I. Conceptual Framework

Developing countries are usually ranked by per capita income in efforts to evaluate the results of development efforts. Since the objective of development is to upgrade the welfare level of the people, such ranking is valid. However, from the analytical viewpoint use of this indicator has limitations, particularly because of its static nature. The preceding analysis presented an alternative in terms of changes in the pattern and mechanism of growth, that is, phasing. If factors associated with changes in the Y/L level operated dominantly, it would not be difficult to link production analysis with the income level approach through changes in the level of per capita income increase. As revealed by subgroup observation, however, factors not associated with the Y/L level are also influential throughout the development path. This suggests the necessity of an alternative approach, that is, phasing in terms of the changes in the operation of these factors as well.

Phasing in this dynamic sense should include changes in sectoral structure in relation to the macro performance of the economy. Methods of sectoral treatment, however, are not fixed, but vary depending upon the purpose of phasing. A simple example is the share of industrial (or manufacturing) output relative to GDP, which has been widely used to indicate the degree of industrialization. However, the output share alone does not show changes in the pattern and mechanism of growth and neglects changes in the employment structure. Focusing on changes in the sectoral structure, it is easy to see that changes in the share of industrial output (Yi/Y) also indicate changes in nonindustrial output (Yn/Y) decomposed to the output of agriculture (Ya/Y) and of services (Ys/Y). This common approach based on three major sectors can be extended to the subsectors of each. Since industrialization is not equivalent to economic development, the output shares of the three major sectors have been relied upon in analysis. In addition to output share, however, the corresponding labor employment shares must be determined. The authors thus specifically propose clarifying the changes in the relationship between output and employment in growth terms, combined with share changes, in relation to the macro growth of the economy. This was done in chapter 5 by adopting the "difference indicator (D formula);" here it is generalized in the phasing approach.

For simplicity, assume a two-sector economy composed of industry (i) and nonindustry (n). Macro productivity growth (Gy) is usually decomposed as follows:

$$Gy = (wiGyi + wnGyn) + \{(wi - vi)GLi + (wn - vn)GLn\}, \quad (1)$$

where w and v stand for output share and labor share, respectively. The term in brackets { } is called a "structural term." The D formula avoids the structural term and takes the output term (wiGYi + wnGYn) and labor term (viGLi + vnGLn) directly. Gy is thus shown as the difference between the two sectoral components (wiGYi − viGLi) and (wnGYn − VnGLn).

The authors contend that this formula, although simple, is appropriate to clarify changes in the pattern and mechanism of growth, that is, phase demarcation. Macro productivity as measured by Y/L is in a sense an abstract term. It can be thought of as aggregated sectoral productivity, but the legitimate weighting terms are unavailable. Use of output shares neglects the effects of structural changes as shown by Equation (1). The D formula avoids this procedure by treating the aggregate of output and labor independently in a decomposition of the conventional macro measures of productivity growth. The use of the growth term is intended to illustrate the dynamic process of development. Of the two input factors of labor and capital, the D formula is applied to capital, although that is not done here since the stress is on the importance of employment in the present context. Available data are limited, but it would be desirable to extend the D formula to include capital in future studies.

So far productivity indicators have been used for demarcating phases. What would the results be if the effects of nonconventional factors, or residual growth, were used? Unlike conventional measures of TFP, the residual growth in the present case is originally measured in terms of capital formation ($\Delta R/I$ or $\Delta R/\Delta K$). As shown in Table 1.1, its magnitude tends to increase distinctly from I to III in group average; by subgroup it is greater in A than in B through all groups. To the extent that the increase in residual growth serves as a general indicator of upgrading in the level of social capability (SC) of each nation, a shift in development phase will result from upgrading the capability level.

In addition to what was stated in chapter 5, note that basic understanding of the mechanism of growth pertains to its relation to production capacity (PC). Using I/Y, $\Delta R/Y$ or GR and GY $=$ GR $+$ GC can be derived, where GC stands for the growth rate of the sum of conventional inputs. It is easy to see that Gy is composed of two factors: GR and GC $-$ GL. (In neoclassical formulae this is expressed as Gy $=$ GR $+$ α(GK $-$ GL), where α stands for the output elasticity of capital.) Conceptually the former pertains to SC and the latter to PC. Because productivity is an indicator of the combined results of SC and PC operation, the clarification of interrelations between the two is extremely important in development analysis. It is difficult, however, to arrive at quantitative conclusions, particularly in a sectoral approach. Thus the productivity indicators are used here. Phase demarcation depends on statistical testing, for which testable indicators are needed. The D formula can be used for this purpose since it focuses on labor and its average productivity and is useful if interpreted accurately.

The meaning of a "generalized" framework of phase demarcation can be explained as follows. The actual process of development differs rather widely from one country to another so that no common pattern can be found in all. The variance stems from complex elements, such as sociocultural characteristics and political systems, as well as features including country size and initial historical conditions of modern economic growth. Emphasis on this aspect leads to negative evaluation of development in any generalized framework. Nevertheless, certain common patterns between developing nations can be discerned if the conceptual framework is appropriately formulated and flexibly applied. The framework should be applied to analysis of the development paths based on the market mechanism of growth, except in centrally controlled economies. This is the first condition.

The second condition concerns the sector approach. Cross-sectional data provide useful information for a sectoral approach along the lines suggested above. The minimum essential requirement for generalization is formulation of a two-sector basic model, consisting of the goods-producing sector and the service sector. The former is actually an integration of agriculture and industry and the latter is equivalent to the so-called tertiary sector. This differs from the conventional two-sector model that only takes industry and agriculture into account. The present authors believe that the facilitating activities of the service sector are of crucial importance in the path of development and that the conventional bias toward the goods-producing sector does not give a full picture of the entire mechanism of growth. The importance of services has already been discussed, particularly in identifying the second turning point (Di versus Ds), but here it is generalized for the entire path of development. Treatment of the first turning point as it pertains to Da is integrated into the treatment of the goods-producing sector below. In applying the D formula Dg (for the goods-producing sector) and Ds are the main focus, with the important difference in performance between Da and Di treated as a secondary approach.

It is beyond the present scope to compare comprehensively the characteristics of the two major sectors. The following points, however, must be recognized. First, the facilitating activities of the tertiary sector are felt in multiple subsectors, including transportation, communications, trade and commerce, financing, various personal services, etc., and are directly and/or indirectly related to the operation of market mechanisms. The output of the goods-producing sector can only meet final and/or intermediate demand through the operation of these service sector activities. At given times in development, the market operates differently in size, scope, and intensity. As development proceeds, operation of market mechanisms achieve a higher level and/or wider extent, combined with output growth of the goods-producing sector. Development of the tertiary sector should be sustained to support market mechanisms. The "output" of this sector estimated by national income accounts essentially yields the quantitative indicator of the sum of these facilitating activities.

The market is composed of two dimensions: domestic and international. Through the path of development the composition and relation of the two tend to change. Initially, domestic elements operate dominantly but infusion of the international element becomes stronger and wider through development. At the same time, the domestic market continues to operate significantly as international contacts expand, as illustrated by price system variance in individual countries by group classified by Y/L (for example, ppp measures). Such price variations are the result of domestic elements operating through the broad trend of internationalization. The conventional dichotomy approach distinguishing tradables versus nontradables is relevant here. No attempt is made to be precise in applying this concept to the present framework. Generally, however, the two major sectors, goods-producing (G) versus services (S), correspond to this dichotomy. As is well known, the domestic elements stem from the preference scale indigenous to each developing nation, and to that extent some of the products of sector G may be nontradable, whereas some of the outputs of sector S may be tradable, as suggested by recent trends. Yet by and large the two major sectors can be distinguished from the trade possibility aspect, which is indispensable in phase demarcation in the long-term perspective of development.

The arguments stated above concerning market structure do not imply rejection of competitive resource allocation in the domestic market. Instead, it is the view of the authors that competitive operation works between industry and services in the framework. Certain empirical evidence is found for labor (Table 5.12) in terms of the ratio of wages. The ratio services/industry (S/I) is slightly over unity through groups of varying Y/L level. The most conservative view is that in terms of marginal productivity of labor, industry and services appear competitive. In terms of capital return a corresponding situation can be envisaged. These pertain to average observations of sectoral aggregates in the given interval 1960–1980, yet provide evidence for the present conceptual formulation.

While multiple approaches to phase demarcation are possible, the authors have proposed the productivity approach, without rejecting other possibilities. The criteria chosen for demarcation can and should be multiple due to the fundamental nature of economic development. Trade patterns, labor markets, and capital investment, among other criteria, are used in phase demarcation to clarify different aspects of the development path for different analytical purposes. These are not exclusive but rather complementary.

The reason for proposing the productivity approach is simply that analysis of this aspect has been somewhat neglected in previous research on phasing. Therefore, its complementary relations with other types of phasing require explanations. At the present stage of study, however, this cannot be done systematically; the discussion in preceding chapters represents a partial response. First, for the aspect of changes in the labor market based on the dualistic structure (chapter 1), the importance of the relation between Gw (rate of increase in wages) and Gk (rate of capital intensity increase) was stressed. The changes recognized between the former and the latter segment in cross-sectional group averages indicate changes in the labor market. If more data become available in the future, this approach can be linked with the productivity approach to discuss the complementary relationship of the two. For the time being, it can be stated that the model appears broadly consistent with the present demarcation of primary and secondary major phases.

Second, with regard to capital investment, the conventional indicator I/Y (investment proportion) was once widely accepted to be the crucial criterion for phasing, influenced by Rostow's thesis. As was clarified in the preceding discussion (mainly chapter 1), however, it was found that changes in I/Y are not crucial in shifting phases. The importance of the role played by domestic investment is not denied, however. The criterion proposed in chapter 4 is import dependency of investment (in particular PDE). Its relation with the productivity growth pattern and secondary import substitution pattern should be explained further, as will be touched upon briefly in discussing the import pattern below.

Third, the trade pattern approach is most widely known and represents the conventional phasing method. Ohkawa previously selected this approach in analyzing East Asian development[1] and for Japan used it as the global framework in *OK*.[2] Research along this line, however, has not yet developed systematically for contemporary developing countries. Its relation with the outcome of the productivity approach as applied to domestic economies is a major problem to be clarified in the future. In section III, using cross-sectional data we attempt to determine the relation as a preliminary approach. While it can be assumed that changes in trade pattern reflect changes in productivity in the domestic economy, the present view is more flexible in assuming mutual influence from both sides.

Finally, recognizing all the aspects mentioned above, the "generalized" setting of phasing in this volume can be characterized as follows. The minimum essentials for clarifying structural changes in the long-term development path of economies are treated by relying mainly upon the operation of market mechanisms, without specifying any aspect other than productivity growth, the fundamental requirement of economic development. This generalized, basic approach does not specify the actual structural changes in trade,

---

[1] John C.H. Fei, Kazushi Ohkawa, and Gustav Ranis, "Economic Development in Historical Perspective: Japan, Korea and Taiwan," in Kazushi Ohkawa and Gustav Ranis, with Larry Meissner, eds., *Japan and the Developing Countries* (Oxford, UK: Basil Blackwell, 1985).

[2] Kazushi Ohkawa and Hirohisa Kohama, *Lectures on Developing Economies: Japan's Experience and Its Relevance* (Tokyo: University of Tokyo Press, 1989).

labor, and capital investment. Analytical complementarity with other approaches should be evaluated in this context.

II. Production: Productivity Approach

Cross-sectional Overview

Table 7.1 lists cross-sectional empirical data in a simplified form by Y/L level group estimated in 1960–1980 averages. First, the D performance differs distinctly between the earlier interval I–II and the later interval III–V. As shown in panel B, Ds is much greater than Dg in the former, whereas during the latter the inequality is reversed, with the difference increasing from group III to IV but not sustained to group V. The changes in the relation between the two sectors thus appear to have a certain regularity. Second, the pattern is a combined result of movement of the two components, output and employment, as shown in panel A. In terms of the contribution to forming the aggregate pattern, during the former interval the goods-producing sector (G) employs the majority of labor, while services (S) contributes to a very limited extent in terms of rate of increases. Nevertheless, the output contribution of services tends to be greater than G; it is almost equal in group I but tends to be greater in group II. This occurs due to an almost equally minor share of employment increases (in panel B, negative 0.90–0.95). In interval III–V, the picture changes. In group III, the labor term becomes equal, and there is a greater contribution of sector G than S with regard to output. Toward group IV the output term again becomes greater for sector S with a distinctly greater employment term for this sector. This pattern appears to be sustained up to group V. However, as mentioned above, Dg ceases to increase in comparison with Ds in group V, where new activity of the service sector emerges.

The group average observations thus suggest three distinctly different segments. If the factors associated with increasing Y/L level could be assumed to operate dominantly, these segments could be demarcated as forming different phases of development. Actually, in the cross-sectional approach often adopted in development analysis, such an interpretation would be valid. In the present approach, however, these findings are preliminary, although they suggest that the turning point may occur between II and III. The importance of the operation of nonassociated factors should be emphasized. Subgroup observations in terms of macro productivity growth were

Table 7.1
Difference Indicators (D) of Two Major Sectors, Goods-producing (G) and Services (S), with Components

(A) Sector measures   (%)

Goods-producing sector	wg	wgGYg	vg	vgGLg	Dg
I	64.4	1.60	89.3	1.40	0.20
II	54.5	2.50	83.3	1.70	0.80
III	52.9	3.30	70.4	1.45	1.85
IV	50.4	2.65	62.4	0.50	2.15
V	43.5	1.77	46.6	0.20	1.57

Services	ws	wsGYs	vs	vsGLs	Ds
I	35.6	1.60	10.7	0.50	1.10
II	45.5	2.85	16.7	0.75	2.10
III	47.1	2.95	29.6	1.45	1.50
IV	49.6	2.95	37.6	1.40	1.55
V	54.5	2.50	53.4	1.50	1.00

(B) Differences between sectors (G − S)

	Output	Employment	(Dg − Ds)
I	0.00	−0.90	−0.90
II	−0.35	−0.95	−1.30
III	0.35	0.00	0.35
IV	−0.30	0.90	0.60
V	−0.73	1.30	0.57

Source: Kazushi Ohkawa, in collaboration with Katsuo Otsuka and Bernard Key, *Growth Mechanism of Developing Economies: Investment, Productivity and Employment* (Tokyo: International Development Center of Japan/International Center for Economic Growth, 1993), Table 4.10.

Remarks: i) Value of the goods-producing sector is estimated as the sum of agriculture and industry for output and employment, respectively. The component differences are expressed as (wgGYg − wsGYs) and (vsGLs − vgGLg), where w and v are shares of output and labor, respectively.

ii) The figures are slightly different from the original ones in *DE*, Table 4.10, due to rounding and to the procedure of making direct averages of the estimated figures for two periods, 1) 1960–1970 and 2) 1970–1980.

Table 7.2
Difference Indicators (D) of Two Major Sectors, G and S, with Components: Subgrouping

(%)

		wgGYg	vgGLg	Dg	wsGYs	vsGLs	Ds	Dg − Ds
II	E	3.15	1.77	1.38	3.16	0.98	2.18	−0.80
	F	1.95	1.73	0.22	2.62	0.65	1.97	−1.75
III	E	3.60	1.26	2.34	2.32	1.38	0.94	1.40
	F	2.75	1.40	1.35	2.92	1.14	1.78	−0.43
IV	E	3.29	0.41	2.88	3.39	1.58	1.81	1.07
	F	1.96	0.57	1.39	3.03	1.47	1.57	−0.18
V	E	2.65	0.46	2.19	2.33	1.13	1.29	0.99
	F	1.30	0.13	1.17	2.83	1.69	1.14	0.03

Source: Original data for *DE*, *op. cit.*, Table 4.10.
Remark: A slight inconsistency exists between the group average figures in this table and those in Table 7.1 due to differences in dealing with the original data.

attempted in the preceding discussion in identifying sectoral turning points (chapter 5). The same procedure is adopted below with efforts made to integrate the two sectoral turning points into the newly introduced generalized framework. Table 7.2 is an extended, combined version of Tables 5.17 and 5.18.

The difference in growth pattern between two subgroups is fairly, if not perfectly, regular. Dg is distinctly greater in E than in F, whereas Ds tends to show a similar but narrower inequality, with an exception at group III. These patterns stem dominantly from similar variances in the output component for both sectors G and S because, as for the labor component, the difference is much narrower between the two subgroups. In light of these general features, the performance for the respective intervals demarcated earlier is examined below.

Although data are not available for group I, the figures for group II suggest the features of the first interval. In forming the remarkable inequality of Ds>Dg, F contributes much more than E, mainly due to the difference in output components. The preceding analysis of the negative values of Da (Table 5.17) is clearly relevant here. Toward group III, a notable difference is seen between E and F: in the former Ds > Dg becomes a reversed inequality, Dg > Ds, while in the latter the initial inequality Ds > Dg is sustained. If the turning point is at Dg = Ds, the previous group average observations suggest that it must be placed between II and III. This expectation is valid for subgroup E but not for subgroup F in which nonassociated factors are more influential. Recognizing this fact and integrating the results of the preceding analysis of the Da pattern, the authors would like to propose that point $Dg = Ds$ can be used for demarcating the preprimary phase, or the first subphase (a generalized label for the preprimary phase) of the primary phase. Countries classified as belonging to E achieve this point between II and III, but countries belonging to F lag behind in the first subphase.

Surprisingly, the inequality $Ds > Dg$ in F is sustained even to group IV, whereas the reverse inequality $Dg > Ds$ is distinctly realized in E. The latter pattern of F is identified for the first time in group V. With regard to subgroup F, the first turning point either may be expected to be realized late in the path from group IV to V or may not be realized at all throughout the entire path of development. This cannot directly indicate a demarcation for actual phasing, since it is merely an outcome derived from cross-sectional treatment, although it does present an important implication analytically.

By group average, it is known that the second subphase of the primary phase is featured by the inequality $Dg > Ds$ and that the difference $Dg - Ds$ tends to widen from III to IV. However, this tendency changes toward V. This preliminary knowledge should be extended by focusing on subgroup E, which is relevant along the path moving toward group V. In other words, a specific procedure is used to demarcate the secondary phase, leaving out subgroup F due to the above. The sectoral difference indicators of subgroup E present a distinct variance regarding the components of Dg, that is, Di and Da. In groups III and IV, both show significant magnitude (Di 1.28 and 1.88 and Da 1.06 and 1.00, respectively) but in group V the magnitude of Da becomes extremely low (0.15) while Di continues to increase (2.04). Discussion of the possibility of shifting to V should be focused on comparison of Ds and Di rather than Dg in this case.

The actual magnitude of Da in certain nations may be much greater, as discussed below in illustrating individual cases, but the present procedure is an analytical device using cross-sectional data. The preceding discussion on identifying the second turning point $Ds = Di$ (referring to Table 5.18) is now given its true analytical meaning. The observation made there pertained to both E and F as it was intended to provide preliminary information. The conservative phrase regarding F should be remembered: "The point of $Ds = Di$ is assumed to occur, if possible, toward the end of the path to V. . . . " What is crucial here is to reconfirm through the performance of subgroup E that the second turning point is expected to occur between groups III and IV. From there onward an economy begins to show the inequality $Di > Ds$, which characterizes the secondary major phase.

Japan's Historical Series and Cross-sectional Data from Selected Developing Countries
Subgroup observations can serve as an analytical device in using cross-sectional data because the problem of demarcating phases originally pertains to the historical development of individual countries. Simple average observation conceals wide variance between nations, however. This can be compensated for by applying two procedures: historical observation of Japan's case and illustrative treatment of selected developing countries for which cross-sectional data are available.

The data in Table 7.3 are arranged to cover the entire historical path of development, 1887–1965, excluding the interval distorted by World War II. The primary and secondary phases are demarcated by the point $Ds = Di$, which is identified in period 3 and includes the World War I years (panel A). Di is actually slightly greater than Ds, but possible distortions contained in the original data must be allowed for. It might be more accurate to state that the turning point is identified near the border between periods 3 and 4. During periods 1 and 2 the inequality $Ds > Di$ definitely prevails, while in periods 4 and 5 it is sharply reversed to $Di > Ds$, although the figures in 4 are somewhat distorted by artificially accelerated industrialization due to military expansion.

This application of the $Di = Ds$ criterion to Japan stems from the concept that Japan is a type of extended case of subgroup E in which the features of E identified previously in subgroup averages are presented more intensively and strongly. To that extent, the turning point is reached earlier than otherwise. What is more important is the finding that the cross-sectional phase demarcation is essentially endorsed by Japan's historical series. It has often been asserted that Japan's case is atypical or unique, but this view is not supported by the present phasing approach. In this sense, Japan's case can be labeled E^*. The demarcation of the two major phases has often been set at around 1919 based on economic research in terms of changes in the mechanism of the labor market (the so-called turning point). A broad coincidence is recognized between the present demarcation and the labor market approach. As men-

Table 7.3
Difference Indicators with Components: Historical Japan

(%)

	1887–1897 (1)	1897–1904 (2)	1904–1919 (3)	1919–1938 (4)	1955–1965 (5)
(A) Indicator					
Ds	1.00	1.12	1.18	0.83	3.97
Dg	0.61	1.23	1.53	2.57	7.63
Da	0.43	0.67	0.32	0.07	1.32
Di	0.18	0.56	1.21	2.50	6.31
(B) Output term					
wsGYs	1.32	1.53	1.58	1.27	4.92
wgGYg	1.11	1.58	2.05	3.28	8.13
waGYa	0.60	0.64	0.27	0.18	0.38
wiGYi	0.51	0.94	1.78	3.10	7.75
(C) Empolyment term					
vsGLs	0.32	0.41	0.40	0.44	0.95
vgGLg	0.50	0.35	0.52	0.71	0.50
vaGLa	0.17	−0.03	−0.05	0.11	−0.94
viGLi	0.33	0.38	0.57	0.60	1.44

Source: *DE*, *op. cit.*, Table 4.12.
Remarks: Transportation and communications are included in the sector of industry, instead of services. To that extent, underestimates of Ds versus overestimates of Di occur. No adjustment is possible to be consistent with the cross-sectional data on developing nations.

tioned in the preceding section, the latter is not attempted systematically here, although it is worth noting. Thus Japan's historical records illustrate possible cases of E* in contemporary developing countries, for example, the Asian NIEs, and it is possible for E countries, even those classified as group III in cross-sectional observation, to enter the secondary phase.

With regard to the primary phase, the point of dividing it into the first and second subphases, that is, $Dg = Ds$, can be identified for Japan's case between periods 1 and 2, in the early years of this century. $Ds > Dg$ in period 1, and it is reversed to $Dg > Ds$ in 2, even allowing for the statistical adjustment effects mentioned above. The phenomenon of negative Da is not seen in Japan's case, as in most historical Western cases, and yet the pattern $Ds > Dg$ is clear in period 1 because the magnitude of Ds is very high at the time of inaugurating modern economic growth. This is the same pattern identified earlier for groups I and II of developing economies, although the tendency of Ds – Dg to increase from I to II is not explicitly found in Japan's case. This finding is important as well, because not only the major phase demarcation but also subphase demarcation in the primary phase coincides in the cross-sectional and historical series.

Further examination of the output and employment terms in Table 7.3, panels B and C, endorse the statement above despite their different magnitude in Japan's case as compared to those in developing economies. It is known that Japan's path differs because of the much smaller rate of increase in the labor force supply. This is shown in Table 7.3, panel C, which can easily be compared with the corresponding figures in Table 5.2. For example, vaGLa shows negative values from as early as period 2 (the ratios of these to output terms are discussed later). Despite such variances, the proposed phasing deduced earlier from cross-sectional analysis can consistently be applied to the long historical development path of Japan.

In discussing data from selected developing nations, the two turning points are focused on. To begin with the second turning point, the Republic of Korea is first taken as a representative case of Asian NIEs. Table 7–4 presents relevant data.

The pattern Ds > Di in period 1 is converted to Di > Ds in period 2. A shift from the primary to the secondary phase is identified from the 1960s to the 1970s. A pattern similar to that induced from Japan's case is observed for the case of Korea. Comparisons of sectoral components between Korea and Japan in corresponding periods yield further evidence of a common pattern. In cross-

Table 7.4
Difference Indicators and Components: Republic of Korea, 1960–1980

(%)

	Da	Di	Dg	Ds
Indicator:				
(1) 1960–1970	1.46	2.23	3.69	2.66
(2) 1970–1980	0.84	4.18	5.02	2.22
Component:				
(1) wGY	1.51	3.84	5.35	3.85
vGL	0.05	1.61	1.66	1.19
(2) wGY	0.69	5.57	6.26	3.68
vGL	−0.15	1.39	1.24	1.46

Source: Original data are the same as for *DE, op cit.*, Table 4.10.
Remark: The calculation procedure is the same as for Table 7.1.

sectional analysis, Korea is classified as belonging to E of III, and can represent the shift marked by E*. No other such cases can be observed, although it is expected that Taiwan would present a pattern similar to Korea.[3] Thus the present formula can essentially be applied to East Asia with the addition of the preprimary phase indicated by E*.

How should the other representative countries classified as sub-group E be treated? Unlike the case of East Asia, these countries exhibit a wide range of variance in regional location, the role played by agricultural productivity growth (Da), and the degree of difference between Ds and Di with their component variance, among others. The answer to the above question differs accordingly. The difference between Ds and Di is selected here because it is directly relevant to the present line of discussion. The analysis of this aspect regarding E countries also contributes to clarifying the characteristics of East Asia using the common yardstick of a link between E and E*. This is important because it has often been asserted that the growth pattern of East Asia is unique and does not show the path of development observed for other regions. This view is not acceptable.

A more realistic interpretation can be made by comparing the patterns of the components of D, which can be done in several ways. The ratio $R = vGL/wGY$ for the two major sectors is used for the present purpose of economic analysis. The industrialization process is indicated by the leveling up of Di, but the same magnitude of Di can be achieved by varied ratios of Ri, $viGLi/wiGYi$, as against that of Rs, $vsGLs/wsGYs$. As compared to the "difference indicators," these ratios indicate more directly the degree of contribution of output and labor, respectively, to forming the macro pattern. In a comparative sense a greater ratio can be called labor-intensive and a smaller ratio capital-intensive. These are relevant to the treatment of the technology type related to the discussion on export promotion versus import substitution of manufactured goods in the case of Ri. In providing additional useful information, the ratio Ri/Rs indicates the magnitude of Ri, taking the level of Rs as the standard in treating individual countries. As stated previously, the output of S is

---

[3] With regard to Taiwan no comparable data are available from *World Bank Reports*. Calculation using data compiled by the Taiwan government reveals that the point Ds = Di emerges around 1969–1973 in terms of annual estimates. This corresponds to the case of Korea. However, after that until 1988 the inequality Ds > Da again occurs, although the difference remains moderate. Whether this is due to the statistical data or to substantial causes needs further scrutiny.

Table 7.5
Ratios of Components of Difference Indicators: Industry and Services, 1960–1980

(%)

		viGLi	wiGYi	Ri	vsGLs	wsGYs	Rs	Ri/Rs
Group								
I		0.25	0.75	0.33	0.50	1.60	0.31	1.06
II		0.44	1.56	0.29	0.82	2.89	0.28	1.04
III		0.73	1.89	0.39	1.26	2.69	0.47	0.83
IV		0.76	2.20	0.35	1.53	3.11	0.49	0.71
V		0.26	1.77	0.15	1.41	2.39	0.59	0.25
Subgroup								
II	E	0.46	1.79	0.26	0.98	3.16	0.31	0.84
	F	0.42	1.32	0.32	0.65	2.62	0.25	1.28
III	E	0.97	2.25	0.43	1.38	3.07	0.45	0.96
	F	0.49	1.54	0.32	1.14	2.30	0.50	0.64
IV	E	0.90	2.78	0.32	1.58	3.25	0.49	0.65
	F	0.61	1.61	0.38	1.47	2.95	0.50	0.76
V	E	0.41	2.45	0.17	1.13	2.43	0.46	0.37
	F	0.11	1.09	0.10	1.69	2.36	0.72	0.14

Source: *DE, op cit.*, Table 4.10, and original data.
Remark: The data are averages for periods 1 (1960s) and 2 (1970s).

largely nontradable and the production structure is basically deter-mined domestically, whereas the output of the industrial sector is largely tradable and its production structure is determined subject to international competition. Before examining individual cases, the performance of these ratios in cross-sectional terms is summarized in Table 7.5.

By group a regularity is witnessed: Ri tends to decrease, while Rs tends to increase, although with distortions at II for which the reason is not clear. The former is an expected pattern but the latter draws attention. Regarding the interval relevant to the present discussion, that is, III–V, the change between III and IV is rather slight, but from IV to V the change is remarkable, with a sharp decrease in Ri versus a distinct increase in Rs. Thus the magnitude of the ratio Ri/Rs tends to decline, in particular from IV to V. By subgroup the pattern appears mixed in comparison of E with F.

Two points with respect to the performance of subgroup E in the interval III–V are relevant to the present discussion. First, Ri tends to decline from 0.43 to 0.17 rather distinctly, whereas Rs remains nearly unchanged with a greater magnitude than Ri. This suggests that Rs can be taken as the domestic standard as mentioned above. Second, the ratio Ri/Rs tends to show a sharp decline from 0.96 to 0.37. Note that even its larger magnitude at group III is somewhat less than unity. Toward IV and V, the ratio becomes increasingly smaller.

In light of these findings, how can the East Asian experience be interpreted? How can the pattern characterized by E* in the productivity approach using the D formula be understood by this ratio analysis? Table 7.6 shows corresponding numerical values.

Two points are particularly noticeable in Table 7.6: common patterns and differences. A tendency for Ri to decline and Rs to remain relatively stable is apparent in Japan's historical records. The former appears to be sharper, as expected, for E*, and the latter is generally apparent even for E*. Within these long-term trends, however, the magnitude of Rs is smaller for both Japan and Korea than in cross-sectional averages of E countries. Thus the value of ratio Ri/Rs is distinctly higher in Japan's case for periods 1–3 as compared to cross-sectional values, and this is also the case for period 1 of Korea. The atypically low value in period 4 of Japan and perhaps in period 2 of Korea may be affected by rapid industrialization. Its magnitude remains over unity in East Asia in the path of $Ds > Di$, while in other developing economies in subgroup E it remains under unity

Table 7.6
Ratios of Components, Industry and Services—Japan and the Republic of Korea

(%)

Japan:	Period	(1)	(2)	(3)	(4)	(5)
	Ri	0.65	0.40	0.32	0.19	0.19
	Rs	0.19	0.27	0.25	0.35	0.19
	Ri/Rs	3.42	1.56	1.28	0.54	1.00
Korea:	Period			(1)	(2)	
	Ri			0.42	0.25	
	Rs			0.31	0.40	
	Ri/Rs			1.35	0.63	

Source: Japanese data from Table 7.3 and Korean data from Table 7.4.
Remark: For Korea, period 1 is the 1960s and 2 the 1970s (figures for earlier periods are unavailable).

Table 7.7
Ratio Performance of Selected Developing Countries in Subphase II, 1970s

| | (A) Difference Indicators | | | | (B) Ratio Indicators (%) | | |
	Da	Di	Ds	Dg	Ri	Rs	Ri/Rs
Kenya	1.06	1.60	2.24	2.66	0.21	0.18	1.17
Brazil	0.61	2.21	2.80	2.82	0.35	0.44	0.80
Colombia	1.39	1.35	2.11	2.74	0.31	0.41	0.76
Malaysia	0.98	1.49	1.69	3.47	0.40	0.53	0.75
Turkey	0.90	1.12	1.86	2.02	0.43	0.58	0.74
Philippines	0.23	2.52	1.31	2.75	0.11	0.41	0.27
Yugoslavia	2.24	2.26	1.04	4.50	0.14	0.54	0.26
China	−0.50	3.48	0.50	2.98	0.14	0.38	0.37

Source: The same original data as for the preceding tables on cross-sectional analysis.
Remark: The computation procedure is the same as for Table 4A.5 and 4A.4, but due to insufficient data, other devices are applied for the Philippines and China.

for the intervals relevant to the present discussion. To that extent, the difference between E* and E is recognized, although this does not endorse the view that the East Asian pattern is atypical.

To support the discussion of other E countries, the data listed in Table 7.7, panel A, show difference indicators, and panel B shows ratio indicators to illustrate the patterns of other countries on the path toward the second turning point Di = Ds during the 1970s (period 2). Countries are selected for which indicators show the inequality Dg > Ds, possibly located in the second subphase of the primary phase and covering various regions. Da is added for reference, although it is not directly discussed here. Countries are listed in order of the magnitude of the ratio Ri/Rs. Yugoslavia and China are added for the sake of comparison.

In panel A, the pattern Ds > Di is not identified for the Philippines, Yugoslavia, and China. In the latter two countries distortions could be caused by nonmarket mechanisms, but this reasoning cannot be applied to the Philippines. Has that country arrived at the secondary phase, or does this mean that the proposed formula of phasing cannot be generally applied? The results of the ratio indicator approach shown in panel B help to answer this question.

In Table 7.7, panel B, which is relevant to the majority of selected countries, the pattern of ratio indicators tends to endorse earlier findings comparing cross-sectional data and those for East

Asia. Although component values are not listed in the table to save space, the Ri/Rs ratio is under unity for other E countries in comparison with the pattern of period 1 in Korea identified above. The level over unity for Kenya may not be an exception as this can be thought of in light of the pattern of group II (Table 7.5) and Japan's historical records for the primary phase. However, the case of the Philippines presents a notable exception. Why does it have an extremely low level, close to that of Yugoslavia? This illustrates an important issue in applying the present formula: the ratio approach is indispensable to test the general validity. It is not possible to place the Philippines in the secondary phase. This judgment is based on the view that there is a distortion at the primary phase from the commonly recognized "normal" path of development, essentially based on the operation of market mechanisms. The case of China presents a typical case of distinct distortion brought about by a centrally controlled economy. Yugoslavia is a mixed economy and cannot be judged simply. Yet a common feature occurs: small Ri and Ri/Rs for both China and Yugoslavia. The Philippines should not be seen as a socialist distortion; the distortion stems from the forces working against normal operation of market mechanisms. It is represented by its components. The magnitude of Ri is extremely low, implying a remarkably capital-intensive type, and the level of Rs is not atypical but similar to that of Brazil or Colombia.

The concept of the "normal" path of development is based on empirical facts systematically obtained in historical perspective. The present phasing approach aims to establish the normal path in light of cumulative forces that lead an economy toward subsequent phases. Too much industrialization creates distortions from this normal path. In this regard the smaller magnitude of the ratio Ri/Rs for the majority of selected E countries as compared to East Asia does not necessarily mean "too much" industrialization, but is rather interpreted as normal. Two elements contribute to forming such a pattern: on the one hand, the telescoping effects in the international technology diffusion process induce smaller Ri values; on the other, greater Rs values are due to the domestic situations of developing nations.

Subphase I of the Primary Phase

The relevance of the pattern of East Asia, as represented by Japan's historical records, to contemporary developing economies appears limited in determining the first turning point as compared to the second. Point $Dg = Ds$ is found between periods 1 and 2 in Japan, and during period 2 Ds remains greater than Di (Table 7.3). From information obtained from cross-sectional comparison, it can be expected that this pattern is common with respect to the first subphase of the primary phase of contemporary developing countries. However, the underlying conditions differ, as is specifically revealed by analysis of agriculture in the discussion on the "crucial turning points in sectoral growth" in chapter 5. The negative value of Da is a crucial issue. Here the inequality between Ds and Dg is dealt with in a generalized formula, but the negative value of Da is most influential in leading an economy to the inequality Ds > Dg (Da + Di).

Thus the problem at issue is whether it is possible to integrate these findings into the present phasing to determine the normal path of initial development. An illustration of individual cases is indispensable and provided in Table 7.8. For all selected countries, the value of Da is negative or near zero. This does not mean that all countries in subphase I are in such a situation. The inequality Da > Di, the pattern shown in 1 in Japan's case, also exists (for example, in Mali). However, the number of such cases is limited. Only two countries in Africa are listed, against expectations. A number of African nations show negative values of Da, but in most this occurs along with negative values of Di and/or no sign of positive economic growth. The data require no further analysis. The selec-

Table 7.8
Difference Indicators and Component Ratios: Countries in Subphase I, 1970–1980

	(A) Difference Indicator				(B) Ratio Indicator (%)		
	Da	Di	Ds	Dg	Ri	Rs	Ri/Rs
Pakistan	−0.23	0.97	1.67	0.74	0.16	0.43	0.37
Niger	−2.05	2.53	1.82	0.48	0.07	0.13	0.54
Bolivia	0.12	2.08	4.15	2.20	0.15	0.24	0.63
Lesotho	−0.32	1.00	4.47	0.68	0.47	0.57	0.82
Thailand	−0.14	2.03	2.57	1.89	0.20	0.24	0.83
Mexico	−0.73	0.83	1.36	0.10	0.64	0.55	1.16
India	−0.11	0.60	1.32	0.49	0.32	0.24	1.33

Source: The same original data as for the preceding tables on cross-sectional analysis.
Remark: The computation procedure is the same as for the preceding relevant tables, but weights used for deriving the ratio are proxies for some countries.

tion is thus made so as to judge the inequality $Dg < Ds$ in a meaningful manner. The selected countries are listed in order of the magnitude of the ratio Ri/Rs. They belong to groups I and II in cross-section except for Mexico which belongs to IV, F. Why is Mexico such an exception? In previous treatment of the criterion $Ds = Di$ all of subgroup F was excluded because $Ds > Di$ is sustained toward V. Mexico represents such a case.

In Table 7.8, panel A, the point is the composition of Dg, that is, Di and Da. In forming the smaller magnitude of Dg the contribution of Da plays a decisive role. Could this be a result of the specific selection of the representative countries? The answer is no, since previous cross-sectional analysis by group averages showed a negative value of Da not only for group I but also for group II (in II, $Ds = 2.05$ versus $Dg = 0.50(Di = 1.09,\ Da = -0.29))$. The figures in Table 7.8 represent this feature mainly from two aspects: the behavior of industrialization indicated by large Di (note that in 1 and 2 in Japan, Di was much smaller); and the backward situation of agricultural development. A simple indicator of the relation between the two sectors can be given by $Di - Da$. The absolute value of this difference is affected by the rate of macro productivity growth, so that the difference should be relative to the sum of all sectoral indicators. The calculated values of individual countries range broadly from 31 to 50% apart from the atypical highs of Mexico and Niger. The corresponding values calculated from Table 7.7 range from 0 to 11% except for the atypical highs of the Philippines and China. The significance of this is thus easily illustrated and should be clarified by the ratio approach.

To begin with the ratio indicators, Table 7.8, panel B shows that the magnitude of Ri is generally very small. A greater value would be expected for these countries as compared to countries in subphase II, because the historical records of Japan show greater figures for earlier than for later phases and the majority show a range of 0.21–0.43 for selected nations in subphase II (Table 7.7). The value of Ri listed in Table 7.8 ranges from 0.07 to 0.32 except for Lesotho and Mexico. The reason is that in cross-sectional data (Table 7.5) Ri is 0.29 for group II (E 0.26 and F 0.32). These values are smaller than those for group III (E 0.43 and F 0.32). Viewed from these average figures, Ri in the table is unexpectedly small. Second, cross-sectional ratio Ri/Rs (Table 7.5) is over unity for I and II in group averages, so that its level under unity means a bias toward industrialization. Substantively this means a relatively less labor-intensive or more capital-intensive pattern insofar as Rs in each country is assumed to be given by its domestic market mechanism. The argument is analogous to that in the previous case of distortions, illustrated by the Philippines and others. The very small value of Ri for China is associated with a negative value of Da (Table 7.7). This leads to the second point. It is tempting to conclude that a distortion toward industrialization of this type would contribute to a negative value of Da, worsening the situation of agriculture under the macro pattern of productivity growth. This conclusion appears accurate, although the actual mechanism responsible cannot be clarified by such an approach.

To examine the validity of the conclusion suggested above, the case of Pakistan is examined to illustrate the combined operations of factors. Table 7.9 lists numerical values in period 1, the 1960s, in comparison with those in period 2 which are reproduced from Table 7.8.

Pakistan is a typical case of shift from a normal pattern (positive value of Da close to that of Di) to a distorted pattern (negative value of Da). In period 1 Dg > Ds, although only slightly, and this is reversed drastically to Ds > Dg in period 2. The component ratio Ri/Rs is well over unity in the 1960s. A much smaller value occurs because of this drastic shift to period 2, the combined result of a drastic decline in Ri and an increase in Rs. The rate of annual increase (%) in the total labor force increased from 2.1 in period 1 to

Table 7.9
Pakistan: Indicators and Ratios Comparing Period (2) with Period (1)

(%)

	Da	Di	Ds	Dg	
Indicator					
Period 1, 1960–1970	1.13	1.15	2.19	2.28	
Period 2, 1970–1980	−0.23	0.97	1.67	0.74	
Component					
wGY (1)	2.16	1.80	2.66		
(2)	0.85	1.16	2.95		
vGL (1)	1.03	0.45	0.56		
(2)	1.18	0.19	1.28		
					Ri/Rs
Ratio R (1)		0.28	0.21		1.33
(2)		0.16	0.43		0.37

Source: Same as for Table 7.8
Remark: Data available for period 1 are limited for other countries.

2.8 in 2 and increased from 1.7 to 2.0 in agriculture and 2.6 to 5.7 in services. On the contrary it decreased from 2.5 to 1.0 in the industrial sector. Thus the changes in sectoral values of vGL listed in Table 7.9 occur corresponding to those in sectoral output components wGY. A drastic decline in waGYa is particularly noted. Further detailed examination is required, including the external negative pressure caused by the oil crises and other factors, but what is clear even through such simple treatment is that a "backward movement" associated with industrialization bias takes place in countries located around subphase I. The conclusion mentioned above thus appears to be endorsed.

However, it can be risky to make sweeping generalizations along this line. The level of ratio Ri/Rs is in fact over unity for Mexico and India in Table 7.8, panel B. It cannot necessarily be asserted for these cases that negative Da occurs in association with industrialization of a less labor-intensive type. While additional examination of the actual situation is needed, it can be stated that in making the value of Da negative, backwardness in agricultural development itself plays an important role as well. Generally, despite the Green Revolution, positive effects in agriculture occurred in a differentiated manner. In group averages the effects appear to be very limited in groups I and II and become noticeable from group III onward, but the difference between subgroups becomes sizable. This is due to the differentiated pace of technological progress, although the rate of increase in the labor force engaged in agriculture is important.

In summary, despite the differences identified as compared with the East Asian pattern, the present concept of a normal path of development can be applied in terms of subphase I, assuming that the notion of development phasing in a generalized framework is acceptable. The authors believe that the normal path around subphase I common to all relevant countries should at least achieve a positive value of Da. This is an indispensable requirement for arriving at the first turning point Dg = Ds. It is not necessary to achieve Da > Di, the pattern presented by Japan's historical records. It is difficult to ascertain the precise mechanism of achieving balance or imbalance between Da and Di, although the importance of the pattern of industrialization should be emphasized. Possible differences in initial conditions and topology, in particular natural resource endowment, between countries must also be considered. A negative value of Da, however, is most indicative of imbalance between the industrialization process and agricultural development in the earlier stage of the primary phase.

III. Phases by Trade Pattern

As stated in section I, the authors' research on phase demarcation started with East Asian trade patterns. As summarized in *OK*, lecture I, the series of shifts from phase 1 to 5[4] was empirically observed throughout the entire process of industrialization. The "affinity" of the East Asian region was the basis for identifying the common pattern of shifting phases, although some modifications in the sequence were made for individual countries. This phasing is useful for analysis of other developing countries in comparison with Japan's experience. Granted, additional modifications are sometimes needed in applying the pattern to other countries in different regions. For example, the primary export substitution phase is often omitted in countries with richer natural endowments for agriculture.[5] However, no systematic investigation of individual cases has yet been carried out on international phasing in terms of changes in trade patterns.

Cross-section data compiled for the productivity approach can be used for comparative observation of changes in trade patterns with those in productivity performance. The following three points must be noted, however. First, the trade pattern is observed in growth terms, instead of in terms of static comparative advantage. Second, observation of the sequential process of exports and imports is essential, although it is beyond the present scope to treat them separately. Third, as touched upon in section I, it cannot be assumed *a priori* that trade patterns are merely the reflection of the productivity pattern. This approach pertains to the supply side but

[4] Phase 1 is traditional export expansion; 2, primary import substitution; 3, primary export substitution; 4, secondary import substitution; and 5, secondary export substitution.

Actually, Japan's case is as follows. 1: 1870–1900, 2, 3: 1900–1919, 4: 1919–1960, and 5: 1960–1975. These can be compared with the phase demarcation based on productivity indicators shown in Table 7.3. The comparison cannot be made precisely, but the two generally appear to coincide: 1900 and 1919 appear to be the two demarcating years. This illustrates the problems to be clarified in this section for developing economies.

[5] Regarding the effects of topological differences, see *OK, op. cit.*, lecture I, section I, Comments.

Table 7.10
Exports and Domestic Productivity: Rate of Growth in the Goods-producing Sector, 1960–1980

(%)

Group	GX* (1)	Dg* (2)	Difference (1) – (2)	Dg – Ds
I Average	1.4	0.9	0.5	−0.7
II Average	2.3	2.6	−0.3	−1.3
E	3.4	3.4	0.0	−0.7
F	1.2	1.8	−0.6	−1.7
III Average	4.9	4.2	0.7	0.5
E	5.8	4.8	1.0	0.7
F	4.1	3.6	0.5	0.1
IV Average	5.0	4.3	0.7	0.6
E	7.6	5.9	1.7	0.2
F	2.4	2.8	−0.4	−0.1
V Average	6.9	4.5	2.4	0.8
E	7.6	4.8	2.8	0.9
F	6.3	4.2	2.1	0.7

Remarks: i) GX* is the weighted sum of GXm and GXa, from Table 7.11.
ii) Dg* is the weighted sum of Da and Di, from Table 7.11, excluding Ds.
iii) Dg − Ds, from *DE, op. cit.*, Table 4.10.

the demand side has international effects, as implicitly assumed in treating phase shifts.[6]

Exports
The basic concept of treating export expansion is that it is possible, by raising productivity in producing commodities, to meet demand. Merchandise exports growth GX must have a positive association with Dg, instead of aggregate D including Ds. Beyond that, due to what is called "specialization" of exports, the former tends to be higher than the latter. How are these phenomena dealt with in the present framework? Table 7.10, specifically designed for the goods-producing sector instead of the macro economy, presents the relevant data pertaining to the export of agricultural products GXa and that of manufactures GXm.

[6] This type of approach was previously developed in *DE, op. cit.*, "Incorporating Trade Patterns with Phasing in the Domestic Productivity Structure," section III, chapter 1. The idea is essentially the same, but the procedure of analysis and explanation is revised.

First, by group average, the rate of export growth GX* (weighted sum of sectoral exports GXa and GXm) tends to increase toward groups of higher Y/L level, although there is a slowdown at group IV. This corresponds exactly to the trend of increase in the productivity growth of the goods-producing sector, which is shown by Dg*, the weighted sum of Da and Di, in Table 7.10. The magnitude of GX* is mainly greater than that of Dg*, and the difference between the two tends to show a trend of increase toward groups of higher Y/L. The slowdown noted above at group IV also emerges in this case. The term Dg − Ds is listed in the table for the purpose of examining the possible relationship between exports and the productivity indicator pattern. By group averages it is only possible to say generally that in the former segment with the Ds > Dg pattern, I–II, GX* is smaller, whereas in the latter segment with the Dg > Ds pattern the difference is much greater, although in general these seem to suggest the existence of an interrelation between the export growth pattern and the productivity growth pattern.

By subgroup approach, it was previously clarified that E leads and F follows in shifting phases. This is simply indicated by the difference in the magnitude of Dg − Ds in Table 7.10, where it is distinctly greater in E than in F. The difference E − F is 1.0 (negative) in II, 0.6 in III, and 1.3 in IV, followed by a negligible value of −0.2 in V. The relation between this phenomenon and export behavior should be determined. As is shown in the table, GX* is greater in E than in F through all groups without exception. This exactly corresponds to the pattern of Dg − Ds. Furthermore, the difference shown in Table 7.10 between GX* and Dg* shows a notable regularity in subgroup comparison: it is greater in E than in F without exception. The higher rate of productivity growth suggested earlier for export specialization cannot be quantified, but the magnitude of this difference suggests its order. Specialization intensity is greater in E than in F through the entire interval except for I for which the data are less reliable. Finally, of particular concern is the relation to the activity of services in the domestic economy. Its competitive nature in relation to industry in the domestic economy was pointed out earlier, especially concerning the application of the Di − Ds criterion. The corresponding difference identified in subgroup comparisons between GX* − Dg* and Dg − Ds seems to endorse the present proposition. The stronger position of Ds is indicated by a distinctly smaller magnitude of Dg − Ds in subgroup F, exactly corresponding to the very poor behavior of export specialization (near zero) in this subgroup. A reverse correspondence is witnessed for subgroup E.

Thus it is suggested that a competitive relation operates between the domestic activity of services and export performance in the international market, although no direct evidence can be provided. To approximate the actuality, the goods-producing sector should be decomposed into industry and nonindustry, with agriculture representing the latter. For exports the corresponding decomposition is GXm and GXa. GXm pertains to exports of manufactures and GXa to exports of agricultural products excluding other nonmanufactures. These are for the sake of convenience but the authors believe such an approximation is permissible for present analytical purposes.[7] The conventional phasing in terms of export pattern can be grasped as representing the path of changes in the relation between GXa and GXm: the phase of initial export expansion of traditional goods pertains to GXa and the phases of primary and secondary export substitution pertain to GXm. Through the normal path, GXa will first increase and then decrease, whereas GXm will start at a slower pace than GXa but soon increase to a higher level, which accelerates toward later phases. This pattern is simply indicated by changes in the magnitude of GXm − GXa. The issue is to examine the relation between these and phasing in terms of productivity indicators. Two factors must be considered: share changes in GXm and GXa and export specialization, discussed above. Table 7.11 presents data compiled for this purpose, using weighted GXm and GXa versus weighted Di and Da.

In group averages, unweighted GXm tends to increase from I to III and to decrease toward V. However, weighted GXm* shows a trend of increase throughout all groups. Unweighted GXa shows a trend of increase with a distinct dip at IV, but its weighted magnitude GXa* tends to increase during the former segment, followed by a decrease in the latter segment. Thus the linear trend of increase in GXm* versus the inverse U-shape of GXa* present the real pattern of GXm − GXa. The weighted indicators of domestic productivity Di* and Da* show a corresponding pattern: a trend of increase in Di* versus an inverse U-shape of Da*.

The export specialization briefly discussed above implies complex contents including the effects of international demand, but it can be assumed simply that the rate of productivity growth of subsectors specializing in exports must be greater than that of the total sector concerned. The differences listed in Table 7.11 suggest specializa-

---

[7] Exclusion of minerals from nonmanufactures makes it difficult to discuss the effects of natural resource endowment in general.

Table 7.11
Exports and Domestic Productivity: Decomposed into Manufactures and Agricultural Products, 1960–1980

(%)

Group	GXm (Simple)	GXm* (Weighted) (1)	GXa (Simple)	GXa* (Weighted) (2)	Di* (Weighted Indicators) (3)	Da* (4)	Difference (1) – (3)	Difference (2) – (4)
I	5.0	0.3	1.3	1.1	0.8	0.1	−0.5	1.0
II Average	6.5	1.1	1.9	1.2	2.3	0.3	−1.2	0.9
E	7.7	1.4	3.4	2.0	2.4	1.0	−1.0	1.0
F	5.2	0.8	0.3	0.4	2.2	−0.4	−1.4	0.8
III Average	13.8	2.9	4.2	2.1	2.6	1.0	0.3	0.5
E	19.0	4.0	4.0	1.8	2.8	2.0	1.2	−0.2
F	8.6	1.8	4.3	2.3	2.4	1.2	−0.6	1.1
IV Average	10.8	3.5	2.8	1.5	3.0	1.4	0.5	0.1
E	13.1	5.4	3.3	2.1	4.0	1.9	1.4	0.2
F	8.5	1.6	1.0	0.8	2.0	0.8	−0.4	0.0
V Average	7.4	5.7	4.9	1.2	3.9	0.6	1.8	0.6
E	8.0	6.2	5.7	1.4	4.1	0.7	2.1	0.7
F	6.9	5.2	4.2	1.1	3.7	0.5	1.5	0.6

Source: GXm and GXa (simple) are from *DE, op. cit.*, Table 6.10 (original data from *World Development Report*). Di* and Da* are weighted Di and Da from *DE*, Table 4.10.

Remarks: i) "Other primary" in the *World Development Report* is assumed to be agricultural products. Dm cannot be estimated and Di is used as a proxy. The product of mining is included in Di, but note that the main oil producers are originally excluded in the cross-sectional approach.

ii) GXm* and GXa* are weighted by the share in the sum of Xm and Xa on average of 1960 and 1980. Di* and Da* (weighted productivity indicators) are calculated using the shares of output and labor, respectively, in the goods-producing sector excluding the service sector.

tion effects in this sense. The difference regarding manufactures, (1)–(3), tends to change from a negative value in the earlier segment to a positive value in the latter segment with an increasing trend. The difference regarding agricultural products, (2)–(4), shows a relatively greater positive value with a decreasing trend except for V. Taken together, changes in specialization activities appear to exhibit the expected pattern.

Among subgroups, the inequality of the terms under consideration is E > F with a minor exception for GXa at group III. The degree of differences, period 1–3 and 2–4, in manufactures shows no sizable inequality of negative values in II, but for the major interval of industrialization, a noticeable difference is seen between E and F. E has a distinctly greater positive value without exception, whereas negative values occur for F except in V. Specialization activity thus differs in intensity between subgroups, as expected.

Having thus clarified the relation between exports and domestic productivity, with regard to manufactures it becomes possible to treat the criterion $Di - Ds$ in phasing by integrating exports in subgroup observation. The previous discussion was centered on subgroup E, for which the variance of the magnitude of $Di - Ds$ is confirmed as follows:

	II	III	IV	V
E	−0.83	−0.59	0.11	0.74
F	−1.02	−0.11	−0.48	0.34

Subgroup E has a greater magnitude of $Di - Ds$ than F, with an exception at group III. This corresponds to the pattern identified above regarding exports. The shift from the primary to the secondary phase, from $Ds > Di$ to $Di > Ds$ (E earlier, F later), accompanies a corresponding pattern of export growth of specialized manufactures. The degree of specialization can vary widely even in the same subgroup, although export of "machinery and transportation equipment" (PDE) in its ratio (%) to total manufacturing exports can be a useful indicator. Its average by subgroup is as follows in 1980 (data from *World Development Report, op. cit.*):

	III	IV	V
E	22.2	27.3	43.3
F	1.6	17.4	43.0

The difference between subgroups is distinct, with a tendency to narrow toward group V. This corresponds to the shift of the economy to the secondary phase, suggesting the path toward secondary export substitution.

On export of agricultural products, the column of the difference period 2–4 in Table 7.11 provides useful information, in particular for the former segment in cross-sectional observation. Export specialization is very intensive. The widely known problem of agriculture emanates from the competitive relation between cash crop cultivation for export versus food production for domestic consumption. Specialization often means organizational differences, e.g., commercial-plantation versus peasant farms. The problem of negative Da identified earlier stems from this situation. Even the weighted indicator Da* shows a negative value for F, II. Although supporting data are not available, for F, I, its negative value must be greater. It is important to note that the relatively greater value of GXa* (Table 7.11, column 2) is achieved under peasant production.

Imports

In conventional phasing with regard to trade pattern there are two major phases: primary import substitution and secondary import substitution. Both pertain to manufactures. In the authors' view, "import expansion" should be added as the initial phase to approximate more closely the reality of contemporary developing countries. This is an important modification of phasing deduced from the East Asian experience. (The reasoning for this was given in detail in *DE*, chapter 6, section III.) To link it with phasing in terms of domestic productivity change, import expansion of manufactures is associated with subphase I of the primary phase. In subphase II, primary import substitution mainly occurs. Finally, secondary import substitution pertains mostly to the secondary phase.

In the conventional demarcation of trade patterns, manufactures are conventionally decomposed into "nondurables" and "durables." The authors would like to define the latter as producer durable equipment (PDE) due to the special significance of PDE as a carrier of the foreign technological knowledge required to upgrade the level of productivity in domestic manufacturing. With regard to the import pattern of manufactures, it is decomposed into two categories: "machinery and transportation equipment" and others as proxies in statistical treatment. Measurement of import substitution should focus on the ratio of imports to total demand for the commodities concerned. No systematic data are available to follow this orthodox procedure, and therefore the ratio of imports to the domestic production of the goods-producing sector, i.e., the sum of manufactures and nonmanufactures, is used in the present general framework, with the domestic output of sector S treated separately. It is hoped that this is sufficiently accurate for accessing import substitution trends in the broadest sense. Imports are treated as the "net" of exports; conceptually, this stems from recognition of "concurrent" import and export activities in the historical path of changes in trade structure in East Asian countries. For example, in Japan primary export substitution occurred in its later segment concurrently with the former segment of secondary import substitution, in the latter part of which an early start on secondary export substitution actually took place. The treatment of import as the net of exports integrates the results of the preceding discussion of exports. The calculated numerical values are listed in Table 7.12.

The data in Table 7.12 can be interpreted from various aspects, including resource balance. Here the focus is on aspects relevant to phasing. First, subphase I of the primary phase appears to be essentially characterized, as expected, by concurrent phenomena in traditional exports (nonmanufactures, column 5) and the initial expansion of nonmachinery manufactures (imports, column 4). This is mainly recognized in groups I and II, in particular subgroup F, II. Forces operate to create a greater imbalance M-X in this subphase, and it appears distinctly different between E and F (column 1). Second, subphase II of the primary phase is mainly characterized by the values for groups III and IV. A distinct decline in traditional exports and the initial start of manufacture import substitution are concurrently identified between groups II and III, where the demarcation between subphases I and II can be made, broadly consistent with the productivity approach. Finally, how should import behavior in the secondary phase be interpreted? One would expect this phase to be characterized by secondary import substitution. The figures in column 3 do not necessarily suggest that pattern, however. The import of machinery shows a slight trend of decline through II to IV. A sharp drop is only seen toward V. The authors are thus inclined to state that secondary import substitution is realized between IV and V, which is not necessarily contrary to phasing in terms of Di versus Ds.

Comments are required on two points: the technological requirement and the concept of E* proposed above. To achieve further advances in technology diffusion, latecomers require increased imports of PDE. Import substitution and this requirement occur together. Thus the figures in Table 7.12, column 3, are greater in E

Table 7.12
Imports Net of Export (M − X) in the Ratio to the Output of the Goods-producing Sector (G), 1980

(%)

Group	Merchandise Trade (1)	Manufactures (2)	Machinery (3)	Non-machinery (4)	Non-manufactures (5)	G Product/ GDP (6)
I	14.5	16.7	9.2	7.5	−2.3	64.1
III Average	16.3	39.8	18.7	21.7	−23.8	54.5
E	11.2	37.7	19.1	18.6	−26.1	57.0
F	21.4	41.8	17.0	24.8	−21.4	51.9
III Average	16.4	20.1	12.1	8.0	−4.7	52.9
E	15.7	23.0	12.1	10.9	−7.4	55.3
F	17.0	17.2	12.0	5.2	−2.0	50.5
IV Average	15.5	13.6	9.3	4.3	1.9	50.3
E	21.6	12.8	11.2	1.5	8.8	50.9
F	9.3	14.3	7.3	7.0	−5.1	49.5
V Average	−2.2	−0.8	0.7	−1.5	−1.4	46.7
E	−2.4	−0.9	0.6	−1.5	−1.6	58.0
F	−1.7	−0.8	0.6	−1.4	−1.1	35.5

Source: M − X/GDP in *DE*, *op. cit.*, Table 6.12 (originally, *World Development Report*, *op. cit.*, 1982, 1983, Indicator Tables 5, 8, 9, and 10).

Remarks: i) The ratio G product/GDP (column 6) is used to convert to this table.
ii) Negative figures mean exports > imports.
iii) Column 3 is a sum of columns 4 and 5.
iv) The sum of 2 and 5 does not necessarily equal 1 due to differences in data sources.

than in F through groups II–IV. The pattern of East Asia was elucidated previously using the concept of E*, that is, vigorous productivity growth. In this case, the magnitude of the ratio in column 3
would become greater than the group average. Actually, in the case
of Korea, the ratio begins to decline from the beginning of the
secondary phase. Such cases may be involved in the average figures,
in particular in E, IV. Secondary import substitution activity characterizes the secondary phase, but it is important to note that this
emerges with considerable variance between nations. As discussed
in chapter 4, a specific treatment of PDE instead of durable goods
has been proposed for import substitution in terms of import dependency (ratio to domestic investment). Such treatment enhances
the meaning of import substitution and should be examined further.
Countries of E* might make a shift to this activity during the 1980s.[8]

IV. Trend Acceleration and the Normal Path of Shifting Phases

By way of concluding remarks, we would like to focus attention on
what we call "trend acceleration (TA)" and the "normal" path of
development. TA is originally deduced from the historical records
of growth in Japan.[9] Here, TA is examined in terms of productivity
growth (indicated by D). It can be illustrated by the figures listed
in Table 7.3. The sum of sectoral indicators in Japan's case is:

(1)	(2)	(3)	(4)	(5)
1.6	2.4	2.7	3.4	11.7

The rate of macro productivity growth shows a long-term trend of

---

[8] The ratio of net import of machinery, comparable to the figures in column 3 of
Table 7.12 is −1.25 for Korea and 0.98 for Brazil in 1989 (estimated from *World Development Report*, 1991, relevant tables in World Development Indicators). It is suggested that Korea did make a shift to secondary export substitution and Brazil came
close to the turning point. Incidentally, the corresponding figure in the same year is
−21.6 for Japan and −3.7 for the average of industrialized countries. These are
largely comparable to the near-zero values of group V in column 3 in the table.

[9] Kazushi Ohkawa and Henry Rosovsky, *Japanese Economic Growth: Trend Acceleration in the Twentieth Century* (Stanford, CA: Stanford University Press, 1973), in
particular chapter 8, "Economics of Trend Acceleration."

an accelerating increase. This pattern is more distinctly seen in Di values in Table 7.12. These are affected by external factors, the greatest of which is World War II between periods 4 and 5. Conceptually TA is acceleration of the rate of productivity increase, which can be thought of as an endogenous process. Regarding the generalized framework of phasing proposed in this chapter, it is envisaged that through each step of shifting phases the rate of productivity growth will be increased.

With respect to contemporary developing countries, there are no long-term growth records from which to derive direct evidence for the possibility of TA. Nevertheless, it is hypothesized that these countries have the potential to realize TA and that distortions from this path occur due to disrupting factors. In compilations of cross-sectional data, subgroup E is assumed to have a greater advantage in realizing this potential as compared to subgroup F. TA is not a unique feature of E* countries, however. Sectorwise, the industrial sector plays a leading role in creating TA, whereas the service sector does not operate positively and often tends to operate negatively in TA. Table 7.13 confirms these hypotheses.

The group average of macro productivity in Table 7.13 shows the TA pattern, excluding group V. Subgroup patterns appear to be the same for E and F, respectively, although the magnitude of the productivity growth rate differs distinctly by subgrouping. However, a closer examination reveals that for F no pattern of TA is seen, as clarified below. Second, the pattern of services (Ds) appears different, and no trend acceleration occurs in group averages. By subgroup, E exhibits trend deceleration (TD), whereas F appears to have a mixed pattern. Following the procedure of demarcating primary and secondary phases, if Ds and Di are compared directly, there is a sharp contrast in group E: the TA of Di versus the TD of Ds, although in group F no such contrast is witnessed. These patterns taken together suggest that the elements contributing to TA are involved in developing paths in general and that in group E countries these operate more strongly than in group F countries. The criterion $Di - Ds$ implies the difference in the potential to achieve TA, and the negative role played by the service sector in this respect is noted.

The concept of the normal path of development is deduced empirically rather than through theoretical requirements. The historical performance of group E realized in 1960–1980 essentially represents the "normal" path, although it may be distorted to some extent by such external factors as the international environment. Not only the

Table 7.13
Productivity Growth Pattern of Developing Economies, 1960–1980

(%)

	Aggregate			Goods-producing Sector (Dg)			Industrial Sector (Di)			Service Sector (Ds)		
	Group Average	E	F	Group Average	E	F	Group Average	E	F	Group Average	E	F
I	0.4			0.2			0.5			2.0		
II	2.8	3.6	1.1	0.8	1.4	0.2	1.1	1.3	0.8	2.1	2.2	1.9
III	3.3	4.1	2.5	1.8	2.3	1.3	1.2	1.3	1.1	1.4	1.7	1.2
IV	3.7	4.9	2.9	2.2	2.9	1.4	1.4	1.9	1.0	1.6	1.7	1.6
V	3.1	4.0	1.8	2.1	2.2	1.2	1.5	2.0	1.0	1.0	1.3	0.8

Source: This volume, Table 5.18 and *DE*, *op. cit.*, Table 4.10.
Remarks: i) The original figures are rounded.
ii) Da is not listed to save space, but is Dg – Di.

1970s but also the first half of the 1980s should be noted in this regard, although those periods are excluded from Table 7.13. This argument does not depend on group averages and implies that subgroup F countries are beyond the present scope because no path of shifting phases is envisaged. In the normal path the possibility of achieving TA can be expected through the performance of E.

TA results from sustained operation of cumulative forces. Merely additive forces do not create the acceleration process. In this sense, TA is one possible pattern of productivity growth in historical perspective. The cumulative forces include various factors in the process of development through market mechanism operation. Any internal or external factor that discourages this operation distorts the realization of the normal path. The importance of such crucial factors as social capability (SC) components has been emphasized in this volume.[10] Since the combined process of absorption of advanced foreign technological knowledge and domestic technology diffusion is the major contributor to productivity growth, TA can be sustained by upgrading the level and components of SC until the technology gap between developed and developing nations essentially disappears.[11]

[10] See *DE, op, cit.,* chapter 1, in particular the notion of the "interaction mechanism" for upgrading the level and components of SC.

[11] The direct investment of capital from developed countries to developing countries has been increasing in recent years. It tends to strengthen the TA possibility through direct technology diffusion, realizing faster rates of industrialization in the developing path. The present analysis cannot deal with this important aspect.

Index